Backpack

Backpacking and Walking in Italy

Stefano Ardito

BRADT PUBLICATIONS, UK
HUNTER PUBLISHING, USA

First published in 1987 by Bradt Publications,
41 Nortoft Ave, Chalfont St Peter, Bucks SL9 0LA, England.
Distributed in the USA by Hunter Publishing Inc.,
300 Rariton Center Parkway, CN94, Edison, NJ 08818.

British Library Cataloguing in Publication Data

Ardito, Stefano
Backpacking and walking in Italy.
1. Walking—Italy—Guide-books 2. Italy
—Description and travel—1975- —
Guide-books
I. Title
914.5′04928 DG416

ISBN 0-946983-14-3

Line drawings by Clare King.
Maps by Hans van Well.
Cover photo of Portofino by Stefano Ardito.

Typeset by Acorn Bookwork, Salisbury, Wiltshire.
Printed and bound in Great Britain by
A. Wheaton and Company Ltd, Exeter, Devon.

About the Author

Born in Rome, 1954, Stefano Ardito has always been based in the 'eternal city'. A father from Piemonte, and a mother from Naples helped him in appreciating the country's many faces. Many years of mountaineering, a useless degree in Economics and some travelling around the world preceded his decision to try to earn a living from writing and photography.

Now he works as a freelance journalist and photographer for such Italian magazines as *Airone*, and for *Repubblica* newspaper, to both of which he contributes regularly. He has published about a dozen guidebooks about Italian mountains and trails, published by Zanichelli, De Agostini and Iter, plus *Magico Appennino* (Athesia), a photograph book, and *Montagne di parole* (with Gianni Battimelli published by CDA), an anthology of Italian mountaineers.

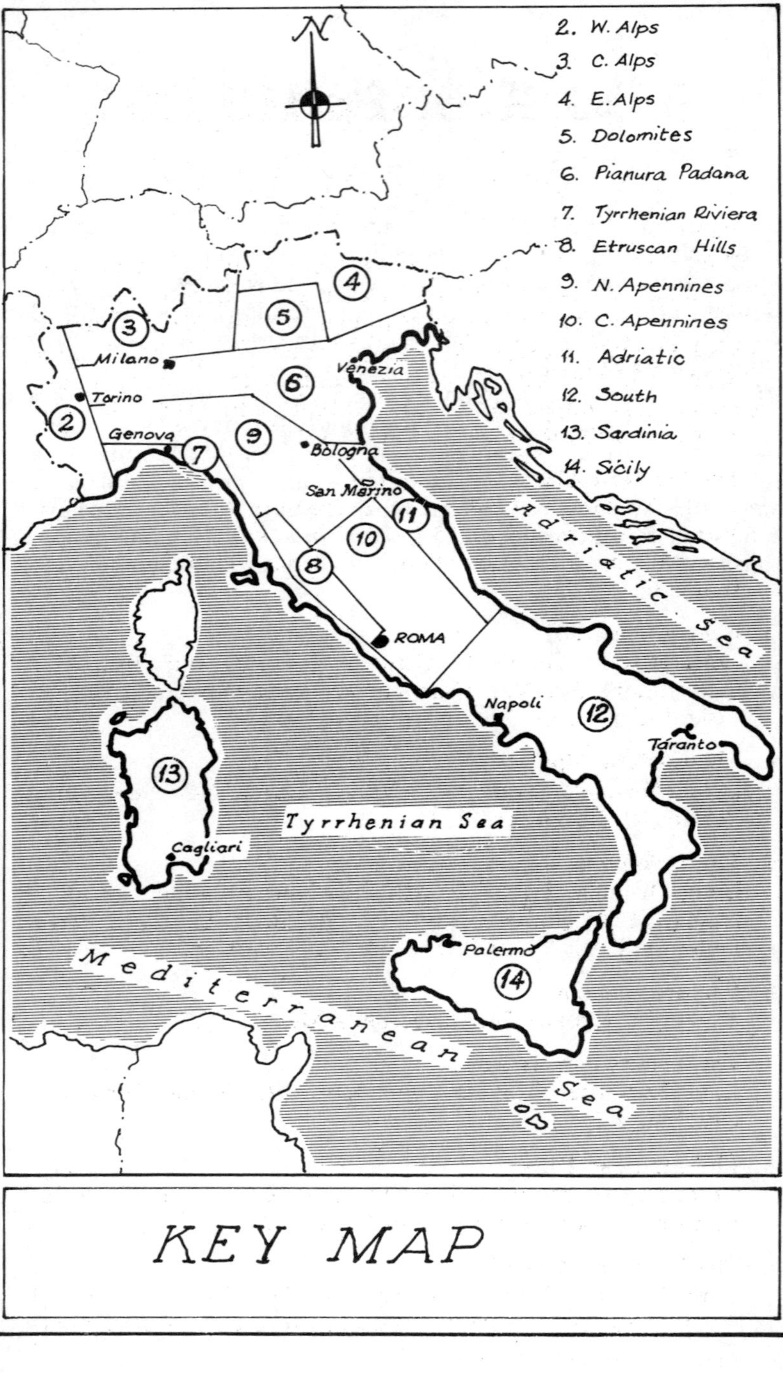
N
2. W. Alps
3. C. Alps
4. E. Alps
5. Dolomites
6. Pianura Padana
7. Tyrrhenian Riviera
8. Etruscan Hills
9. N. Apennines
10. C. Apennines
11. Adriatic
12. South
13. Sardinia
14. Sicily
Milano
Venezia
Torino
Genova
Bologna
San Marino
ROMA
Napoli
Taranto
Cagliari
Palermo
Adriatic Sea
Tyrrhenian Sea
Mediterranean Sea
2
3
4
5
6
7
8
9
10
11
12
13
14

KEY MAP

Contents

Introduction

Italy is a land of many surprises. It is a country where foreigners often see only a fraction as they rush through Rome, Venice and Florence; some probe deeper into Tuscany and Umbria and others stop for a while on a beach or at a ski resort. There are still many facets of this country completely unknown to the majority of foreign visitors.

But, as witnessed in many other European countries, the rapid industrial growth in the last several years is at odds with the environmentalist. This book introduces you to a land far away from the hustle and bustle of crowded cities. A country that offers the dramatic shapes of the Dolomites' limestone towers and spires; the rolling beauty of the 'Etruscan' hills and scenes evoking the Florentine painters. The variations do not stop there. Go south and discover the real Mediterranean wilderness, sometimes reminiscent of Anatolia, even central Asia. Hike along little known tracks near Etna and don't miss the Gran Sasso to the north. Sardinia, to some people, summons up a sophisticated image of the Aga Khan's beach resorts, but you can discover the desolate and magnificent hills of limestone just a few miles away from the sound of motor boats and intrusive music.

And Sicily is not just Mafia and Murder. It is also a detached fragment of the Apennines and has volcanic mountains, picturesque bays and headlands, numerous small islands and the famous flora of the Madonie mountains.

Italy needs more National Parks, but people are becoming increasingly aware that if bears and wolves, chamois and deer, vultures and eagles are going to survive, land must be made available for these creatures to live unmolested alongside the amazing diversity of plants, trees and flowers that cover Italy's hills and valleys.

But looking at nature should not mean excluding the history of man. Walking through the countryside is a splendid way of discovering 'masterpieces' quite different from the well-known urban wonders that tourists, as well as Italians, normally see. Etruscan cemeteries carved into volcanic rock. Byzantine churches hidden in the depths of wild limestone canyons, old trade routes crossing the Alps, hermitages and abbeys perched on top of the wildest ridges of the Apennines. Bronze age fortifications in Sardinia, traces of ancient populations everywhere; Salassi, Piceni, Sanniti, which most guidebooks hardly ever mention.

Quite obviously, this book has to compromise. It has information for dedicated backpackers who would like to spend a full holiday hiking in the Alps or in the south. The biggest part of the book contains a selection of 1- or 2-day walks, accessible to everybody, covering all parts of the country. How to spend a few days off the beaten track and where to go on your weekends. Most of these can be reached without a car.

What walking, hiking and mountaineering are all about is participating in the preservation of the outstanding beauty of Italy's nature and wildlife. This doesn't mean turning your holiday into a Save the Wolves campaign, nor are you even required to join one of the environmentalist groups, unless you actively wish to do so. But by avoiding the crowded beaches, the bustling traffic in the towns and even by dodging those huge steel edifices which seem so necessary to modern ski resorts, you are promoting and influencing the local administrations towards the right kind of tourism. Walking and exploring many of the protected areas suggested in this book is in itself an act of protection.

From here on, you will find information, suggestions and hints. All you have to bring with you is a pair of feet, curiosity, your eyes to have a good look around and you'll end up finding more than the few things that I have been able to cram into this book. Everything else will come by itself. To everyone, welcome to Italy!

Chapter 1

The Basics

Italy has an incredible variety of trails. This is partly because of the physical differences in the country: the country stretches from central Europe to the southern Mediterranean, with corresponding differences in climate. In the Alps you hike near to glaciers, where temperatures are well below freezing point even on summer nights. In the south, many hikes are hard in summer (and some are impossible) because of the heat. You will not find Arizona, nor Alaska; but be prepared for extremes, and plan the route before leaving.

A second difference comes from the uneven distribution of the hiking population. The most popular areas in the Alps have a perfect network of well marked paths, comfortable huts, and are described by a whole series of guidebooks and maps. In the Dolomites during the peak of summer, crowds on the trails can often cause problems. Some less-frequented areas in the Alps and most massifs in the northern and central Apennines are on a lower level; huts are scarce, marked trails and guidebooks exist only here and there and are quite often out of date. In the south, on the islands (and sometimes also in the lowlands of northern and central Italy) you are on your own. Fellow hikers are rare, and guidebooks and huts do not exist at all. In the lower areas old abandoned paths are often overgrown, whilst hiking in the mountains of Sardinia, Sicily and Calabria can be a real wilderness adventure.

ITALIAN HIKERS

Yes, they are a strange population. The key to understanding them can be found in their membership of CAI, Italy's huge Alpine Club and their 'mountaineer' consciousness. Even if most hikers do not have a real knowledge of mountaineering techniques, they feel as though they belong to the same world as the most famous climbers. They climb easy mountains at weekends, sometimes use crampons or ice axes on a glacier, or a rope and a helmet on a *via ferrata*. Lowland hiking, as it is normally practised in Britain or in the United States, is a very recent discovery for most Italian hikers.

Because of their belonging to a strong association, many Italian hikers tend to travel around the country's trails in large groups at weekends, a fact that has to be remembered if you're planning to use huts or just hike in the most popular areas. In the last few years, lowland hiking has grown and the hiking population has changed. I had the chance of a Siena–Tyrrhenian Sea trail in a story published in *Airone* magazine in 1983. Since then the trail has become incredibly popular, with a hiking figure approaching that of the most famous Alpine trails. Many hikers, on this kind of trail, are not CAI members nor do they have a 'mountaineering' approach to their hiking.

As far as the foreign hiker is concerned, there are often a variety of interesting people along the trail. On most Alpine trails, there is no difficulty in finding English-speaking fellow hikers, and getting reliable directions in your language. Things become more serious if you have to check your route in a guidebook. And reserving a bed in a faraway hut by telephone can be a serious problem. The glossary on page 19 is meant to help in situations where ordinary dictionaries do not cover.

LONG DISTANCE TRAILS

Long distance trails are a recent addition to the old network of 'local' trails criss-crossing Italian mountains and hills. The first areas to develop long distance trails were the ones nearest to the German and French influence. The Dolomites' *Alte vie* were started from the mid 1960s onwards, while Piedmont's *GTA* was begun about 10 years later. The Dolomites' *Alte vie* tends to follow a north–south direction, connecting the German speaking Val Pusteria to the Piave river and on to the Veneto foothills.

Other trails tend to follow the main chain ridge, following the ridge itself on easy ground, and skirting it with long ups-and-downs along the lateral valleys in the Alps, where the main border ridge is normally rocky or glaciated. More detailed information is given about long distance trails in different chapters of this book. There is not enough space here to describe most of them in detail; a notable exception is made for the oldest and best known of the Italian long trails, the Dolomites' *Alta via numero 1*.

In the last few years, long distance trails have really boomed. New trails have been marked, unmarked trails have been suggested by magazines and guidebooks. The idea is finally taking shape of a *very* long trail (it would be about 4,000 km) following the entire length of Italy's Alps and Apennines, from the Yugoslav border at Tarvisio to the Messina straits dividing mainland Italy from Sicily.

The westernmost part of the trail already exists; Piedmont's *Grande Traversata delle Alpi*, Liguria's *Alta via dei Monti liguri* and Tuscany's *Grande Escursione Appenninica* already connect Monte Rosa with the hills of Umbria. This is already a 100 day walk! In the northeast, a long trail could be prepared quickly: *Via dei Monti lariani*, *Alta via della Valmalenco* and *Sentiero Roma* already traverse the Alps of Lombardia, while *Traversata carnica* follows the border ridge east of the Dolomites, in Friuli's *Alpi carniche*. The real problems are in the southern part of the country; a few years from now, the trail will continue in the central Apennines, from Umbria to Lazio and Abruzzo. South of here it will take much more time.

Long distance trail enthusiasts find in Italy two very different kinds of challenges. Alpine trails are well marked, offer regularly spaced huts or cheap hotels, and can be hiked without tents and similar paraphernalia. Problems can arise from crowded huts (mostly in the Dolomites), and from strenuous going over high passes (in the western Alps). On established trails, there are no navigational problems. In the peak of summer reservations have to be made to ensure there is a bed to sleep in at the end of the day.

In the southern part of the country (i.e. from Tuscany onwards) and in the islands, long distance trails are backpacking adventures. Trails are not marked (or are only partly so), huts and hotels are well spaced, and sometimes it is necessary to carry food for 2 or 3 days, because of the lack of accessible restaurants or shops.

ITALIAN WILDLIFE

From the Alps to Sicily's southern coast, a huge variety of habitat exists in the country. Urban areas, roads and hunting have heavily spoiled what was one of Europe's nature realms. Still, variety exists.

In the Alps, *chamois* are found almost everywhere, while almost all parks and nature reserves have a population of *deer*, *roe deer* and *fallow deer*. *Marmots* are quite abundant everywhere in the high pastures, while *eagles* still fly in all of Italy's Alpine skies.

Ibexes were preserved only in Gran Paradiso national park, an old royal hunting reserve which was given to the nation in 1922: small groups of them have been reintroduced from Argentera to Stelvio parks. The *lynx* population had completely disappeared: a few animals are now entering the Italian eastern Alps from Yugoslavia. Trentino's Dolomites still host an extremely small (up to a dozen!) population of *bears*.

A better situation, as far as carnivores are concerned, is found in the Apennines. Abruzzo's *bears* are a larger population (around 100), mainly based in the area's national park. Twice as many *wolves* still roam the whole of the Apennine chain. *Chamois* of a special breed exist in the Abruzzo mountains, too, together with a small population of *deer*. *Moufflon*, a strong bighorn mountain sheep, still live in both the Sardinian and Sicilian wilderness.

Along Italy's coasts, marshes have been quickly reduced: only in 1966, when the Italian WWF was established, a tendency to save marshes and coastal lakes as ideal bird habitats started. Dozens of different species of *ducks* will be found in all the country's oases and reserves. Together with them, *egrets*, *herons*, *sandpipers*, *grebes* can be found, together with *cormorant* and *flamingos*. A similar amount of wild birds can be found in the Po plain's rice fields and marshes as in the same river's delba, one of Europe's most sensational areas for birdwatchers.

Forests are mostly *fir* (and *pines*) in the Alps, mostly *beeches* in the Apennines. They host a fairly common population of *foxes* and *badgers*, *wildcats* and *squirrels*: *otters* have almost been destroyed by water pollution, and are confined to a couple of rivers in the southern part of the country.

As far as the naturalist is concerned, Sardinia is easily the most amazing part of the country. Huge groups of *flamingos* feed in the marshes around Cagliari and Oristano, while *griffon vultures* are still fairly common in the hills of Barbagia. Sardinian *deer* are of a very special breed, while a few *seals* are still alive in the islands' waters. Gesturi's *horses* are the last truly wild population in the continent.

NATIONAL PARKS AND NATURE RESERVES

Throughout her history, Italy has never had many National Parks and there is an extremely low proportion of protected areas. Nowadays parks and reserves are increasing in number, in size and in 'quality' too; protection is better and research programmes get more funds. This is a complicated pattern, however; the number of National Parks is the same (five), State Nature Reserves and Regional Parks do increase every year (but each region operates in a different way). WWF and other associations increase the number of their own wildlife refuges every year.

It is difficult, then, to know the exact number of Italy's parks and reserves. A few of them have autonomous administrations, the others are directed by a series of different departments. For information, the best thing is to make direct contact with the officers on the spot.

NATIONAL PARKS

Parco nazionale dello Stelvio is the nation's biggest, in the central Alps between Lombardia and Trentino. It has mountains up to 3,900 m, deer, chamois and eagles. The headquarters are in Bormio. Telephone: (0342) 901582.

Parco nazionale del Gran Paradiso is the oldest one, and probably the best known amongst foreigners because of the large chamois and ibex populations. The headquarters are in Turin. Telephone: (011) 871187.

Parco nazionale d'Abruzzo lies east of Rome, and is the home of bears, wolves and Apennine chamois. The headquarters are in Pescasseroli. Telephone: (0863) 91315.

Parco nazionale del Circeo lies on the coast, midway between Rome and Naples. It has beautiful coastal scenery, interesting for bird-watchers from autumn to spring. The headquarters are in Sabaudia. Telephone: (0773) 57251.

Parco nazionale della Calabria is the youngest and the smallest, and it is divided into three separate areas. The headquarters are in Cosenza. Telephone: (0984) 26544.

STATE NATURE RESERVES

There are almost 150 of these, varying in size from pocket-size forests and lakes to big areas similar to the important National Parks. General information can be had at the Ministero dell'Agricultura e Foreste, Direzione per le Riserve naturali, Roma. Telephone: (06) 4655. The most important reserves (or groups of reserves) are the following:

Riserve delle Foreste casentinesi: huge forests in eastern Tuscany, including some interesting Franciscan monasteries. Telephone: (0575) 58763.

Riserve della Maiella includes impressive canyons on the Apennines' second highest summit. Telephone: (0872) 980970 or (085) 92285.

Riserve delle Dolomiti bellunesi includes the southernmost (and most 'mediterranean') part of the Dolomites, overlooking the Piave river valley. Telephone: (0437) 24830.

Riserva di Tarvisio includes magnificent fir forests growing in the northeastern corner of the country, on the border with Austria and Yugoslavia. Telephone: (0428) 2039.

Riserve del Gargano is located in the peninsula of the same name, in Puglia. *Foresta Umbra* is one of southern Italy's most interesting reserves. Telephone: (0884) 91101.

REGIONAL PARKS

Their number is very difficult to check: new parks are formed every few months, regulations vary incredibly. Some regions have dozens of parks (best one is Piedmont), some have none (Sardinia, Campania, Molise and Valle d'Aosta).

Piedmont parks are now 32, and 20 more are on their way. The biggest one is *Argentera* (0171/ 97397); other important ones include *Valle Pesio* (0171/ 734021), *Alta Valsesia* (0163/ 51555), *Alpe Veglia* (0324/ 72572) and *Garzaia di Valenza* (0131/ 953611).

Lombardy parks are not many, with the biggest mountain ones still blocked by bureaucracy. *Parco del Ticino* (telephone: 02/ 9794401) is the biggest lowland park of Italy; *Parco delle Groane* (02/ 9942329) is very near to Milan.

Trentino has two big parks. *Paneveggio-Pale di San Martino* includes magnificent forests and beautiful Dolomite scenery (telephone: 0462/ 51934), whilst *Adamello-Brenta* includes both glaciers and limestone spires (0461/ 982117).

Bolzano province, the autonomous German-speaking part of the country, has an extensive network of parks: *Fanes-Sennes-Braies*, *Puez-Odle*, *Sextener Dolomiten*, *Texel*, *Sciliar*. For all of them, telephone: (0471) 994311.

Tuscany has done very little, on the other hand. The most important park is *Parco della Maremma*, a wild area on the coast south of Grosseto (0564/ 407098).

Lazio started well, but little has been accomplished lately. *Riserva del Lago di Vico*, north of Rome, is the best existing one (0761/ 647444).

Sicily has also achieved little. Her autonomous Forestry Administration operates a large area on *Etna*, with magnificent pine forests amongst the lava fields. Telephone: (095) 690040-921124.

WWF SANCTUARIES

There are about 30 of these areas. Some come from private donations and others have been bought by the Association. Most of them are on the coast: *Bolgheri*, *Burano*, *Orbetello* and *Massaciuecoli* are in Tuscany; *Palo*, *Ninfa* and *Vulci* in Lazio; *Argenta* in Emilia; *Frattarolo* and *le Cesine* in Puglia, while Sardinia's last surviving deer live in the *Monte Arcosu* sanctuary. For detailed information, ask Italian WWF's national office (06) 852492-854892.

ENVIRONMENTALIST ASSOCIATIONS

Environmentalist concern is quite new in Italy. Nevertheless, the associations and groups are now amongst the most active ones in the world. Here is some information about the ones which do operate nationwide, and you can contact the national bureaux of each one to ask for addresses of local groups. Many of these also organize outings and nature tours; but please remember that the main job of these associations is not that of a travel agent!

World Wildlife Fund (*WWF*) was established in Italy in 1966, and has managed to establish a network of about 25 wildlife sanctuaries, and to save such endangered species as the Apennine wolf, Abruzzo bear and Sardinian deer. Headquarters are in Via Salaria 290a, Roma. Telephone: (06) 852492-854892.

Italia Nostra started as a group operating mainly on 'urban' themes and problems. Their first and most important battle was to save Venice. Now they are also active in outdoor conservation issues. The main office is in Rome. Via Nicola Porpora 22. Telephone: (06) 852333-856765.

Lega per l'Ambiente is the youngest and nowadays the most active association of all. They are extremely active on pollution, anti-nuclear and similar campaigns, but have started dealing with wildlife conservation too. Headquarters in Rome, Via Francesco Carrara 24. Telephone: (06) 35791.

Lega Italiana per la Protezione degli Uccelli (*LIPU*) is the birdwatchers' association, and a very active one on many wildlife conservation issues. They operate a couple of wildlife sanctuaries and a bird hospital. The headquarters is in Parma.

Club Alpino Italiano (*CAI*) is not an environmentalist association, but it hosts very active groups on the subject. This unusual association is dealt with below.

CLUB ALPINO ITALIANO

If your hiking is not limited to paths near to big cities or to coastal and hill itineraries, you will soon find your way to the *Club Alpino Italiano*, a big association (current membership is about 200,000) which is a key figure in many important aspects of mountaineering and hiking in the country.

Founded in 1863, the *Club Alpino Italiano* is not an élite association between climbers, as Britain's Alpine Club is. The extent of its membership makes the Club Alpino Italiano (everybody refers to it as 'CAI', and so shall we from now on) a very singular organization, and one where almost everything and everybody can be found. Amongst CAI members, there are pure rock climbers, serious, all-round mountaineers, hikers, simple mountain lovers who seldom venture out of town, hunters and militant environmentalists. Obviously, the character of the Club's over 450 *sezioni* varies accordingly.

Heavily subsidized by the State, CAI provides a series of public services, such as mountain (and cave) rescue, avalanche forecasts, and courses and examinations for professional guides. These 'national' services are provided by independent branches of the Club. Individual *sezioni* are responsible for well over 500 mountain huts and *bivacchi*, for marking thousands of miles of paths, for the building and maintenance of fixed ropes, cables, ladders and complete *vie ferrate*. Every town in Italy has a branch of the Club; in the Alpine regions, you can find a *sezione* even in very small villages.

If you're planning a fair amount of hiking into the Alps, you should seriously consider joining the Club. Members have a sharp 50 per cent reduction on overnight fees in the huts and a 10 to 20 per cent reduction on food. The 30,000 to 50,000 lire annual fee (it varies according to *sezione*) can repay itself very quickly. As a member, you receive the six annual issues of the CAI official magazine (*Rivista*) and, if they have one, the bulletin of your own *sezione*. Most important of all, an automatic insurance covers mountain rescue expenses everywhere in the Alps and the Apennines. If you consider how high a helicopter bill can be (and you need one even for a broken ankle in a faraway place), this is an important benefit. If you're visiting more than one Alpine country, remember that the same advantages come with any club's card, and that the CAI's card applies everywhere in the Alps and in most mountains of Europe. Last but not least, you are entitled to join organized hikes, mountaineering courses at every level and, if you are judged competent by the organizers, even organized climbing and ski-mountaineering tours at weekends.

There is, however, one major problem. In theory, CAI is still organized as a private association; you have to be presented by two members (but almost everywhere you will find members willing to sign your request), and enrolment can take up to three or four weeks, which is obviously too long for the average visitor. As a rule, while big city branches take their time, mountain centres welcome members (and admission fees) from faraway places. The Alpine *sezione* of CAI have many Roman members. Far more, in fact, than in their own *sezione* in the capital.

One last hint. Some big cities have more than one branch of the Club: some of them are old independent associations, who have merged into CAI but still like to have their own traditions. Such is the case with Turino's UGET, Milan's SEM, Genoa's ULE and so on. In the province of Trento, which includes many famous Dolomite groups, there is SAT (*Società degli Alpinisti Trentini*), which is again a member of CAI as a whole. In bilingual South Tirol, in the province of Bolzano, you will find both the Italian-speaking CAI and German-speaking AVS (*Alpenverein Süd Tirols*). Here are the addresses of some branches: if you're searching for a CAI office somewhere else, have a look in the telephone directory, ask the nearest Tourist Bureau, or telephone the national centre of the Club: this is in Milan, Via Ugo Foscolo 3. Telephone: 02/ 864380.

Ancona: via Cialdini, 29 a
Aosta: piazza Chanoux, 8
Ascoli Piceno: corso Mazzini, 81
Belluno: via Ricci, 1
Bergamo: via Ghislanzoni, 15
Bologna: via Indipendenza, 2
Bolzano: piazza delle Erbe, 46
Bormio: via De Simoni, 42
Brescia: piazza Vescovato, 3
Cagliari: via Principe Amedeo, 25
Como: via Volta, 56
Cortina d'Ampezzo: largo Poste, 2
Cuneo: via Allione, 1
Firenze: via del Proconsolo, 10
Genova: piazza Luccoli 2/5
Genova (ULE section): vico Parmigiani 1/3
L'Aquila: via XX Settembre, 99
Lecco: via Roma, 51
Lucca: cortile Carrara, 18
Milano: via Silvio Pellico, 6
Napoli: Castel dell'Ovo
Padova: galleria S. Biagio, 5
Palermo: via Agrigento, 30
Perugia: via della Gabbia, 9
Reggio Emilia: corso Garibaldi, 14
Roma: via di Ripetta, 142

Sondrio: via Trieste, 27
Torino: via Barbaroux, 1
Torino (UGET section): galleria Subalpina, 30
Trento (SAT): via Manci, 57
Trieste: via S. Pellico, 1
Venezia: S. Marco, 1672
Verona: Stradone S. Mattei, 8

ORGANIZED TOURS

The prominence of CAI has always curtailed the need for independent organizations and associations concerned with hiking and backpacking tours. Apart from professional guides (see below), there is only one big agency and many small local organizations, usually co-operative ones, and in most cases connected to a hostel, a hut or a camping site. The most important one is *Trekking International* (Corso Sempione 60, Milan, 02/ 3189161-3189421) which organizes mainly treks and climbs amongst the world's main mountain areas. They have some programmes concerning Italy which are expensive but very well organized. The following addresses are much cheaper (even if not as cheap as a CAI collective tour), and not always very efficient. None the less, they are friendly and helpful.

Gruppo Trekking Firenze, piazza S. Gervasio 12, (055) 585320-446017
Cooperativa lu Viol, Sampeyre (Cuneo), (0175) 96517
Cooperativa lou Baus, Entracque (Cuneo), (0171) 978458
Cooperativa la Melacotogna, c/o Pro Loco, Sabaudia (Latina) (0733/55046)
Cooperativa Re Medello, via Cavour 25, Bagno di Romagna (Forlì) (0543) 911337
Associazione la Montagna, via M. Colonna 44, Roma, (06) 351549
Ulisse Club, Via Manara 7, Nonantola (Modena) (059) 549319
Cooperativa Tecnomonti, via Tuillo 48, Terni (0744) 57876
Cooperativa la Lumaca, Modena (0536) 883277
Cooperativa la Ginestra, Reggio Emilia (0522) 21890
Sardegna da Scoprire, via Dante 29, Nuoro (0879) 30400
Amici della Val Codera, viale Tibaldi 56, Milano (02) 8324576
Trekking Italy, via Donizetti 1, Milano (02) 70260

PROFESSIONAL GUIDES

There are hundreds of professional mountain guides in Italy and all of them receive the same severe training. After a three-part course (rock, ice and ski-mountaineering) they get an *Aspirante Guida* title. After two years in the job, and three further courses, they are awarded the full title of *Guida alpina*. An *Aspirante*, however, is already a full professional, even if he cannot be alone with clients on some serious expedition without the supervision of a full guide.

The traditional pattern has changed; many of the modern guides come from big cities, and have a more 'urban' approach to the sport. Because of the number of applicants every year, selection is becoming more and more difficult. On the buyer's side, this is a further guarantee. However, beware of the Etna and Stromboli guides: they are little more than tourist guides, but an old law equates them (in theory) to all other professionals.

Guides are good but expensive. If you want a guide to look after a hiking party, or to lead a ski-mountaineering tour, share the expense. For an authentic climb, a guide will not be able to lead more than two (and in some cases, one) at a time, and expenses will rise. Prices for easy to moderate climbs are fixed, others must be negotiated privately. The minimum price (fixed by law) is around 150,000 lire per day, plus all the expenses (food, transport, etc.).

It is very easy to find guides in mountain villages and resorts (big centres have their own *Ufficio Guide*). Here are some addresses elsewhere, both of organizations and freelance professionals:

le Settimane di Giorgio Peretti, via dello Stadio 23, Cortina d'Ampezzo (Bellunoa), (0436) 61594
Maestri d'alpinismo, via M. Colonna 44, Roma, (06) 351549
Giuseppe Miotti, via Caimi 16, Sondrio (0342) 640873
Giampiero Di Federico, via F. Salomone 15; Chieti (0871) 32563
Stefano De Benedetti, Genova (010) 318922
Giancarlo Grassi, via Fucine inf. 5, Condove (Torino) (011) 9644163
Cooperativa Guide alpine Torino, Torino (011) 927817
Alberto Paleari, corso Sempione 129, Gravellona Toce (Novara) (0323) 848095
Montagna Viva, Dogana di Chiavenna (Sondrio), (0343) 34619
Scuola della Montagna, Scaramuccia-Orvieto scalo (Terni) (0763) 25054
Guide alpine di Lecco (034) 590140
Marco Preti, Brescia (030) 361751
Leo Breitenberger, Merano (Bolzano) (0471) 34663
Alberto Giolitti, via Montenavale 8, Ivrea (Torino) (0125) 44158
Montagna Insieme, corso IV Novembre 25, Nuovi Orizzonti Cuneo (0171) 56739
Scuola di montagna Alpi Apuane, via 7 Luglio 40, Carrara (0585) 76637
Nuovi orizzorn, via Del Ponte 2, Schio (Vicenza) (0445) 28216

VIE FERRATE, EASY SNOW CLIMBS . . .

. . . are not included in this book, but are nevertheless fairly important for Italian 'hikers'. The fact is, that hiking and backpacking in Italy has traditionally been a mountain affair, and hikers have always been, even if at a very low technical level, mountaineers.

In the Western Alps, many normal routes are easy, or very easy walks on snow: you have to rope up because of crevasses, you must have crampons and an axe, but many tours have no, or few technical difficulties of any kind. The easiest summits are Gran Paradiso and Breithorn, whilst Punta Gnifetti (Signalkuppe on Swiss maps) on Monte Rosa is also easy. Mont Blanc has its easiest climbs on the French side, whilst Pizzo Bernina, in the Central Alps of Lombardy, belongs to the same class.

More or less the same applies to winter ascents of many smaller peaks, both in the lowest fringe of the Alps, and in the Apennines. As a consequence, many Italian hikers know how to operate in these conditions. If you do not, try these ascents, which are not difficult, only tiring; but you would be better to ask the assistance of a professional guide (see above).

Vie ferrate are a different affair. They are ancient rock climbs, which have been equipped with ladders, ropes and cables: they are easy, strenuous, and exposed (in many cases, *very* exposed). Again, some people will tell you that 'even their grannies climb ferrate'. This is not true, and, from an experienced climber's point of view, many of the people crowding the Dolomites' *ferrate* are potential suicides. To climb a *ferrata* properly, you must be used to heights and to space beneath you. Take the proper equipment (helmet, harness, rope and carabiners). It is most important to have a perfect knowledge of belaying techniques: a rope held by somebody who does not know the job is an invitation to collective suicide. If you're not sure of yourself, the usual suggestion applies; turn to an easy path, or hire a guide.

THE WINTER SCENE: WHICH KIND OF SKIING?

As winter comes, snow starts to fall heavily over the Alps and the whole of northern Italy. At weekends, many hikers turn to skiing, but, again, there are many varieties of the game.

'Normal' skiing, downhill on a beaten track, is the most popular and the furthest away from the natural environment. The crowds on the popular runs at weekends make them similar to summer beaches.

Ski-mountaineering is a serious and tiring job: it involves an ascent on foot, after which you can enjoy a beautiful descent through wild scenery. It is tiring and requires a knowledge of mountaineering techniques and of snow conditions and dangers. Many of CAI's *sezioni* organize ski-mountaineering courses and tours and so do the professional guides.

Cross-country skiers are divided into two definite types. The 'fast', competitive skier who does not wander off the beaten track, and is equipped with 5 cm skis and lightweight clothing unsuitable for anything but a fast race, and skiers who leave the tracks, wear 7.5 cm skis allowing them not to sink too much in the powdery snow, and carry everything they need for survival with them into the hills: extra clothing, food, water bottle, map and compass and so on. This last game is the nearest one to summer hiking, and is not difficult even for very moderate skiers. Because you travel on flat or not very steep ground, it can be tried by novices if they have enough experience of the hills. Snowshoeing is not popular in Italy.

THE CLIMATE: WHEN AND WHERE TO GO?

From the Alps' highest summit to the southern coast of Sicily, there is obviously a huge range of climate and temperatures. Seasonal weather must also be taken into account. Here are some very general directions about when and where to go.

Summer months are obviously the time of the year when the most foreign tourists arrive. July to September is the best period to hike in the Alps, September being the best month because of clear skies and good views. In August, because of the heat from the nearby plains there are frequent thunderstorms, both in the Western Alps and in the Dolomites. There can also be overcrowding problems; peak season normally lasts from 20 July to 20 August. June and early July often have snow problems on some passes and high trails: some of these can become severe and dangerous, others just require a better pair of shoes.

Travelling south, keeping on the mountains, things change only a little. Although hotter than in the Alps, the Apennines' trails, from Liguria to Calabria (and Sicily's mountain trails) can be hiked all summer long. The good season is longer. (June and September can be included whilst October offers glorious yellow and red forest scenery.) The most highly recommended periods do not include the warmest weeks of summer.

Things change for lowland trails and hikes. Everywhere in the country, these can be walked year round, apart from some occasional snowfall. Even during the severest part of winter, there is no durable snow under 1,000 metres. Spring is by far the best time of the year to walk on 'Etruscan' hills north of Rome, in Sardinian wilderness or along most coastal trails. Autumn is good too, although mud is a possible problem on some paths after heavy rain. Coastal trails, from Portofino to Uccellina and from Circeo to Conero, are interesting in all seasons; they have no snow in winter and their normally rocky ground does not accumulate much mud and the sea breezes make them agreeable (if hot) even in the peak of summer.

EQUIPMENT

Again, the difference between mountain paths and lowland trails is important. On the mountains, you will need a pair of lightweight boots which are better than jogging shoes because of the protection they offer round your ankles. These have to be full heavy boots if you want to venture on snow or on easy rock scrambles. The Alps in summer can be extremely hot and extremely cold on the same day: dress accordingly and never start on a trail with only your shorts or your woollen high altitude trousers.

In the lowlands, a pair of jogging shoes will be enough in most situations. Boots (or gum-boots) can be good in muddy areas and during most seasons, although you can dress almost as you want. One important detail, though: many low altitude trails can be seriously engulfed in vegetation, such as nettles and thorns. Even in August, walk in shorts but always bring a pair of long trousers and a long-sleeved shirt.

What to bring in the way of pullovers and anoraks, should be obvious to everybody; my suggestion is that a lightweight anorak (or umbrella), a pair of sunglasses and a water bottle should always be carried in one's rucksack. Everywhere on limestone mountains, on the coast and on many hills, water can be a serious problem; don't forget a water bottle which should be a large one especially in summer.

Food and provisions should vary according to the area and the length of your trip. Alpine *rifugi*, if open and supervised by a warden, will normally serve all kinds of meals; remember that in the Dolomites the *rifugi* are usually very close to each other, whilst in the Western Alps they are normally well spaced. But for most Apennine and lowland hikes bring everything you need with you.

A lightweight tent is normally needed only on long distance walks in the southern part of the country (i.e. south of Tuscany), as in many long Alpine walks, it is an unnecessary extra weight; there are plenty of huts, the ground is very often rocky and parks and many other areas forbid camping and only allow high-altitude bivouac. A sleeping bag can be nicer to sleep in than a hut's blankets anyway, whilst a lightweight foam mattress is a good idea for emergency situations in crowded huts in summer. To save money take a stove; huts are generally cheap to sleep in although meals are expensive. However, only some huts allow you to cook your own food inside the building.

Although unnecessary on a well-marked Alpine trail, a compass is an excellent companion for hikes in remote places. We will deal with maps later on.

HOTELS, YOUTH HOSTELS, CAMPGROUNDS

Italy has obviously one of the world's largest networks of hotels and pensions. This book will not try to give you information about top class establishments like Venice's *Danieli* or Rome's *Grand Hotel*. In the big cities, if you are a real addict, you can also find US-like *Sheratons* and *Hiltons*. Other guidebooks can give useful information about cheap hotels and pensions in and around the main tourist areas.

Out of the big cities, hotels become rarer, and in many cases much cheaper. Not every small town has one, however: small, old-time hotels tend to close down, to the advantage of bigger (and more expensive) motels along the main roads. A couple of hints can be useful.

If you want to save money, a good idea is to try and look for a room in a private house (a *camera* all around the country, or a *zimmer* in German-speaking South Tyrol). *Aziende di Soggiorno*, the tourist information bureaux, can assist in finding one, as can the *Pro loco* associations in the smaller towns. Another good rule (and pretty obvious) is to try to avoid the biggest skiing resorts. In the lesser-known areas of the Alps, and in the Apennines, their hotels can be 300 per cent more expensive than nearby towns' pensions.

Youth hostels are rare and usually quite ugly: their official organization, *AIG*, has about 20 of them, almost only in the big cities. Private hostels are found somewhere else, and can be quite nice: Abruzzo national park, for instance, has a few: in the Alps their role is usually played by private, roadside *rifugi*.

Campgrounds are also abundant, both near the big cities and in the main tourist areas. During summer's peak season they can be terribly crowded: it will be very difficult to find a tent-site in a seaside campground in August, while in the mountains you will stand a better chance: do not expect a relaxing and quiet atmosphere, anyway!

Out of this period, camping around is a good idea: just remember to check campgrounds' opening periods, often restricted from June to September. In the mountains, some campgrounds stay open in winter too, and offer skiers with a cheap option: do not try to camp there in a tent!

Free camping can be practised here and there, and becomes a frequent option in the Apennines and in the main islands' hills. Just remember that this is strictly forbidden in all national and regional parks, and in many tourist areas: nobody will harm you for bivouacking on a high mountain ridge, but attempts to camp illegally in the Dolomites will invariably end up with a fine.

In the parks, mountain *rifugi* play the role that US parks reserve for campsites. Only Abruzzo national park has a network of *aree di campeggio*, campgrounds where it is possible to camp for a very small charge: you need to register at the nearest park bureau, and to remember that the site's resources will usually be confined to a meadow and a source of good water.

RIFUGI AND BIVACCHI

An extensive network of huts covers all of the Italian Alps. Exact figures are difficult to give but there are probably about a thousand, two-thirds of them belonging to CAI and the others to private owners. *Rifugi* started as mountain huts for hikers and climbers and can vary tremendously in size and in style. Some small hotels accessible by road call themselves *rifugi* but they operate as hotels.

The different standards at various *rifugi*s are normally a result of their distance from the nearest road or téléphérique (cable car). The huts in the Dolomites are normally near to each other), and are well kept and organized like small hotels; almost half of them are private, and all require sleeping reservations during crowded periods. In the central or western Alps *rifugi* are simpler, and more reminiscent of their original purpose. Check beforehand that they are open and fully staffed.

The normal opening period goes from early July to mid-September. Many open also for weekends in June, some (mostly in the Dolomites) are open also in early October. Out of these periods, many huts have small winter quarters open year-round. Some can be opened up for groups if the warden is asked well in advance. Some of the smaller ones have keys which you can pick up in the nearest village. You need to be a CAI member to do so.

Bivacchi are very small huts, with 6 to 9 bunks, a few blankets (a sleeping bag is recommended) and sometimes a simple stove. They are built in remote places, can sometimes be used without paying a fee, but can become extremely unpleasant if too crowded. Remember that most of them are meant for climbers approaching a mountain so for hikers to occupy one on a summer Saturday night is really unfair. They are always open.

MAPS

Do you need them? In the most frequented Alpine areas they will probably be more useful to put a name to every summit you see than to solve route finding problems. In the lowlands, or in southern Italy's mountains, they are one hundred per cent necessary. And here the problems arise.

Italian large-scale maps (1:25,000, 1:50,000 and 1:100,000) are made by the *Istituto Geografico Militare*. They are often old and are usually quite difficult to find. Every important town will have one or more bookshop selling a selection of them, but only for the best known surrounding areas. The complete series can be found at IGM's central bureau in Florence (Viale Strozzi 44, near Fortezza da Basso). Any specialized bookshop can order all the maps you need, but this is a complicated proceeding lasting normally a couple of weeks.

The situation is much better in the Alps. *Touring Club Italiano*, Italy's best map maker, has a limited series of very good large-scale maps (they specialize in road maps). *Kompass* covers all of the Dolomites and most of the Western and Eastern Alps, all in a 1:50,000 scale. South of this, they only have a few; Monti Sibillini, Capri and Costiera Amalfitana being the most useful ones. They are not very accurate (IGM's are much better), but clear enough in most situations.

Tabacco 1:25,000 and 1:50,000 maps are better than Kompass, but they are only for the Dolomites and Central Alps. *Istituto Geografico Centrale* (IGC), based in Turin, makes 1:50,000 maps of the Western

Alps and Liguria and they are even less accurate than Kompass. Local publishers, and some of CAI's sections, have maps of many more areas. In this book the relevant maps are always mentioned for the walks suggested.

BIBLIOGRAPHY

As you would expect, almost all of the existing bibliography about Italian hikes and trails is in Italian. English material is limited to a few travel reports, or to general information included in guidebooks written for the average tourist. If you really want to explore, probably your best bet is to try and learn a few words of Italian (guidebooks are almost always quite easy to understand, once you know the meaning of *destra* and *sinistra*), and then to carry a good book in English to read. For many of Italy's wilderness areas you can find magnificent reprints of old travel reports which can make your walk much more interesting. (Many are available in London at The Travel Bookshop, 13 Blenheim Terrace, or Stanfords Map Shop, Long Acre.)

There is a complete bibliography for the less frequented areas, and another for the hiker's main paradises such as the Dolomites and the Valle d'Aosta. Within Italy, almost any big city has a bookshop specializing in books about wilderness, mountaineering and trails. *Libreria Alpina* (via Coronedi-Berti 4, 4013 Bologna, (051) 345715) is the country's (and one of Europe's) best bookshop specializing in a postal service. If you are planning your hikes in advance it is a good idea to contact them before starting.

As Italian hikers are traditionally mountain oriented, information about new guidebooks and new trails can be obtained mostly through the mountaineering press. *Alp* and *Rivista della Montagna* are two available magazines; whilst CAI's *Rivista* is posted to members, but not sold to the general public. *Airone*, the country's best nature magazine and sometimes its competitor *Atlante* have stories about trails, both in the mountains and on lower ground.

Italian wildlife

Eric Duffey's *Natural Parks and Reserves of Western Europe* (Harrow House, 1982) is a good introduction to the country's wilderness areas for English-speakers. If you can read Italian, then *Parchi nazionali e Riserve naturali in Italia* (Touring Club Italiano, 1982) is an interesting and comprehensive anthology on the subject. Franco Tassi (director of the Abruzzo National Park) and Fulco Pratesi (Italian WWF's president) have written a series of illustrated guidebooks for Mondadori: *Guida alla Natura d'Italia* is a general introduction, while more volumes have been dedicated to separate regions in the country. Fulco Pratesi's *Oasi d'Italia* (Musumeci, 1986) describes in detail the 25 wildlife sanctuaries established and owned by the Italian WWF. Guidebooks and photograph books have been dedicated to all National Parks (except Calabria), and to many amongst State reserves and Regional parks. They are normally available on the spot.

Italian guidebooks for the hiker
Many of these are published every year. A comprehensive bibliography is very difficult to prepare as far as the Dolomites or the mountains of the Valle d'Aosta are concerned. On the other hand, very little exists for the southern half of the country, and for the islands. In each one of the walks, I have suggested the guidebooks to the area.

Good general information can be had on Lorenzo Bersezio and Piero Tirone's *Parchi delle Alpi* and *Parchi degli Appennini e delle Isole*, published (1985 and 1986) by De Agostini, in a series including also my *Andar per Sentieri* (1986), a selection of 75 day walks all around the country, and *I Grandi Sentieri* (1987), including 15 walks in the 7–10 days range.

For the western Alps, Piero Giglio and Palmira Osières *Valle d'Aosta: le grandi escursioni* (CDA, 1985) is good for general information. In Valle d'Aosta, many guidebooks exist: Franco Brevini's *Grand Paradiso* is published by Musumeci, while Alessandro Giorgetta's *Valdigne*, Piero Giglio and Carlo Dellarole's *Ayas Gressonney Valtournanche* and my own *Intorno al Monte Bianco* are published by Zanichelli.

In Piemonte, *Grande Traversata delle Alpi* (Priuli & Verlucca) describes the long walk crossing the region's mountains. If you're planning serious explorations in the Maritime and Cuneo Alps, you should consider Piera and Giorgio Boggia's guidebooks; there are about a dozen, and are published by L'Arciere. Around Monte Rosa, Piero Carlesi's *Alti sentieri intorno al Monte Rosa* (Tamari) is interesting and complete, together with Alberto Paleari's *L'Ossola a piedi* (Gubetta).

Slightly to the east, *Sentieri di Lombardia* is a good selection of itineraries in the region's mountains, published by CAI in 1985. Alessandro Gogna and Giuseppe Miotti *A piedi in Valtellina* (De Agostini, 1985) specializes in the Sondrio area, while *A piedi in Lombardia* (Iter, 1986) includes walks in the lowland part of the region (a second volume is planned). Two guides published by Tamari allow exploration in the mountains nearer to Milan; G. Mauri's *Escursioni nelle Grigne* and Angelo Gamba's *Itinerari escursionistici nelle Alpi Orobie*. Renato Floreancigh is the specialist for the area around lakes Garda and Iseo; his guidebooks are published by Ramperto.

In the Dolomites, one should not miss Luca Visentini's many books, dedicated to *Catinaccio*, *Marmolada*, *Latemar*, *Dolomiti di Sesto*, *Antelao Sorapiss Marmarole*; they are published by Athesia, and are also available in German. Sepp Schnurer books (*Vie ferrate sulle Dolomiti*, and *Quattordici vie alte sulle Dolomiti*) are published in Italy by Zanichelli. The publisher Tamari, based in Bologna, has a catalogue of about 35 books on the Dolomites, including the complete series of guidebooks to the area's well known *Alte vie* (by Piero Rossi, Mario Brovelli, Sigi Lechner and Toni Sanmarchi). Gino Buscaini's *le Dolomiti orientali: le 100 più belle escursioni e ascensioni* (Zanichelli) is mainly a book for the climber, but includes interesting walks and has beautiful photographs throughout.

To explore the Eastern Alps, most of the existing literature is in German. Ettore Tomasi's *Traversata Carnica* is one good exception, describing the 7 day walk from S. Candido (Innichen) to Tarvisio.

Much less is to be found for the peninsula's mountains. *Alta via dei Monti Liguri* (Unioncamere liguri, 1982) describes the 25 day trail along the Ligurian Alps and Apennines, while Alfonso Bietolini and Gianfranco Bracci's *Grande Escursione Appenninica* (Tamari, 1985) describes the long walk along the hills of Tuscany. More guidebooks exist about the Alpi Apuane, but they are mainly for mountaineering purposes.

In the central Apennines, the *Guida dei Monti Sibillini* by Alberico Alesi and Maurizio Calibani (CAI Ascoli Piceno, 1983) is excellent. I am mainly responsible for what exists south of that area, including the two volumes of *A piedi in Abruzzo* and the two of *A piedi nel Lazio* (all by Iter publishers).

Very little exists, up to now, describing the trails and the wilderness of Italy's real south. Donato Vece's *Alta via dei Monti Picentini* should be an example, describing a very interesting series of hikes in the mountains between Avellino and Salerno. Mario Tommaselli's *il Massiccio del Pollino* (BMG, 1984) is a good introduction to southern Italy's most spectacular mountain. Alessandro Gogna *Mezzogiorno di Pietra* (Zanichelli, 1982) though is meant mainly for climbers, has a huge amount of information for the hiker, including the whole southern part of the country, plus Sardinia and Sicily.

Travel books in English

A book describing walks in ancient Italy can be a very interesting companion when exploring the mountains and hills of the country. Here are some suggestions:

W. Brockedon *Illustrated Roadbook from London to Naples* (1835)
W. Brockedon *Journal of Excursions in the Alps: Graian, Cottian, Rhetian, Lepontian and Bernese* (1833)
R. H. Busk *The Valleys of Tyrol* (1874)
Norman Douglas *Siren Land*
Amelia B. Edwards *Untrodden Peaks and Unfrequented Valleys* (1872)
C. E. Engel *Mountaineering in the Alps*
J. D. Forbes *Travels through the Alps*
J. Gilbert and G. C. Churchill *The Dolomite Mountains* (1864)
S. W. King *The Italian Valleys of the Pennine Alps*
Leslie Stephen *The Playground of Europe, 1871*
Francis Trench *A Ride in Sicily* (1851)
F. F. Tuckett *Zigzagging amongst the Dolomites* (1871)
Edward Whymper *Peaks, Passes and Glaciers*
Edward Whymper *A Guide to Chamonix and the Mont Blanc Range* (republished by West Col, 1974)
Edward Whymper *Scrambles amongst the Alps*

Hiking and Climbing Guides

Martin Collins *High Level Walks in the Dolomites* (Cicerone Press).
Cecil Davies *Via Ferrata. Scrambles in the Dolomites* (Cicerone Press).
W. Reifsnyder *Adventuring in the Alps* (Sierra Club, USA).
Brian Spencer *Walking in the Alps* (Moorland).
Some of West Col's climbing guides cover the Italian alps.

GLOSSARY

road	strada
motorway, freeway	autostrada
dirt road	strada sterrata, carrareccia
railway	ferrovia
station	stazione
train	treno
bus	autobus (in town) pullman (out of town)
bus stop	fermata
timetable	orario
hitch-hiking	autostop
taxi	taxi
parking	parcheggio
cableway	funivia
chairlift	seggiovia
mule track	mulattiera
path, trail	sentiero
paint mark, blaze	segnaletica
cairn	ometto
ascent	salita
descent	discesa
level	in piano
easy	facile
difficult, hard	difficile
strenuous	faticoso
steep	ripido
right	destra
left	sinistra
near	vicino
far	lontano
slope	pendio
face	parete
ridge	cresta
summit	cima, vetta
col, pass	passo, colle, valico
névé	nevaio
snow	neve

glacier	ghiacciaio, vedretta
rock	roccia
plateau	altopiano
valley	valle
forest	bosco, foresta
village	paese
town	città
junction	bivio
hut	rifugio
bivouac hut	bivacco
campground	campeggio (organized)
	area di campeggio (unorganized)
bed	letto
bunk	cuccetta
blanket	coperta
sleeping bag	sacco a pelo
foam mattress	materassino
(hut) warden	custode, gestore
breakfast	colazione
lunch	pranzo
dinner	cena
stove	fornello
canteen, water bottle	borraccia
gas cylinder	bomboletta di gas
kettle	pentole
knife	coltello
fork	forchetta
spoon	cucchiaio
(club) member	socio
(club) card	tessera
tent	tenda
no camping	divieto di campeggio
mountain boots	scarponi
gum boots	stivali di gomma
jogging (tennis) shoes	scarpe da jogging (da tennis)
rucksack, pack	zaino
anorak, parka	giacca a vento
down jacket	duvet, giacca di piumino
gloves	guanti
sunglasses	occhiali da sole
woollen hat	berretto di lana
rope	corda
ice axe	piccozza
crampons	ramponi
carabiner	moschettone
fixed rope	corda fissa
ladder	scala

national park	parco nazionale
nature reserve	riserva naturale
park ranger	guardaparco
chamois	camoscio
deer	cervo
ibex	stambecco
bear	orso
wolf	lupo
fox	volpe
eagle	aquila
vulture	avvoltoio
hawk	falco
heron	airone
wild bear	cinghiale
wildcat	gatto selvatico
roe-deer	capriolo
fallow-deer	daino
flamingo	fenicottero
seal	foca
moufflon	muflone

Chapter 2

The Western Alps

The Alps are a long, compact barrier, separating Italy from the rest of Europe; west to east, they mark the border with France, Switzerland, Austria and Yugoslavia, and offer a wide variety of landscapes and climates. They are the continent's grandest mountains.

The highest peaks of the Alps are clustered around the northwestern corner of Italy. Mont Blanc, at 4,810 metres the highest in Europe, is on the French–Italian border. Monte Rosa, 4,633 m and Cervino (Matterhorn in German, 4,478 m) are on the frontier with Switzerland, surrounded by many more 4,000 m peaks. The most barren part of the chain stretches south from Mont Blanc, connecting the Aosta Valley with the French Riviera by a long series of mountains, valleys and high plateaux.

Trails are a-plenty, but the sport is not the same as in the Dolomites. There, the hikes are normally short or not-too-long, there are plenty of huts, and cablecars offer the hiker the chance to easily negotiate the hardest uphill walks. In the Western Alps you normally have to walk hard, climbing up important slopes by starting from faraway valley bases. Mountaineering in the Alps was born here and on many trails and valleys Europe's mountains look as they did before tourism was invented.

This applies mostly to Piedmont's Alps, which form the true western border of the country. North of that, the tiny Aosta Valley is one of the

'autonomous' regions with influential powers of its own. Officially the area is bilingual (Italian/French), but French is used everywhere, from public administration paperwork to roadsigns.

The region seems to have used its power by inflicting severe wounds on the mountains and landscape. Gran Paradiso National Park, Italy's oldest, has always been bitterly fought over by the Aosta local governments, and the region's achievements include Cervinia, probably the ugliest resort in the whole of the Alps, a true Third World cluster of tall apartment buildings right in the middle of what was once known as some of the best scenery in the Alps.

Piedmont, on the other side, has been the Italian region dedicated to establishing the most parks and protected areas; the mountain hiker will encounter wildlife and unspoilt landscapes in a dozen major reserves and parks. Valle Pesio and Argentera in the southern part of the chain, Val Troncea near to the Sestriere skiing area, Alta valle Sesia and Alpe Veglia in northern Ossola are the most important ones.

The big, isolated mountains make most hikes very pleasant. Marguareis, 2,650 m, is the highest summit near to the Mediterranean, and boasts a huge limestone wall. Argentera, 3,297 m, is in the centre of a very important park which was once an ancient royal game reserve. Monviso, 3,841 m, is the summit you can easily see from Turin (Torino), an impressive isolated pyramid surrounded by lakes. Gran Paradiso, 4,061 m, is on the border between Valle d'Aosta and Piedmont and has interesting wildlife and the easiest 4,000 m peak in the Alps. Monte Bianco, Cervino and Monte Rosa are the best known summits in the Alps. In their shadow, you can walk in the footsteps of Edward Whymper and other early explorers of the highest summits of Europe.

Where and when to go A series of international roads crosses the Western Alps, giving the motorized traveller a choice of approaches. South to north, these are the Colle di Tenda road (Cuneo to Nice), the Colle della Maddalena (or Col de Larche, Cuneo to Barcellonette and Gap), the Monginevro (Torino to Briançon), the Moncenisio (Torino to Modane). Piccolo San Bernardo is the ancient road between Aosta and Bourg Saint Maurice, while the Mont Blanc tunnel is the quick connection to Geneva and Paris. Finally, Gran San Bernardo connects Aosta to Switzerland, and Sempione (Simplon) links Milan with western Switzerland and northern France.

Turin, the first capital of the country, is a good starting point for many hikes, and the centre of a good road and motorway network. There is an airport and local communications to many valleys. The smaller towns of Cuneo and Aosta play the same role for southern Piedmont and for the Valle d'Aosta lateral valleys.

The altitude makes the best period quite short. During June and the beginning of July there is still a lot of snow on the trails (take an axe, crampons, and make sure you know how to use them). August is the most popular season, despite clouds rolling in from the sea. September is usually the best time of the year, whilst in a good year October can be better still, with yellow forests and clear skies. Mountain huts, however, normally close around mid-September, causing some problems for long expeditions.

THE LONG DISTANCE TRAILS

The example of long distance trails came from the east, and from the Dolomites but the idea soon spread to the Italian Western Alps. Today, the Western Alps' long distance trails are amongst Italy's finest and best organized.

Grande Traversata delle Alpi, normally referred to as *GTA*, was established in the mid-seventies following the examples of the Dolomites' *Alte vie* and the French *Grande Traversée des Alpes*. It starts from Carnino, near the Ligurian border, travels north across Argentera massif and the many valleys of the Cuneo province, then skirts the Monviso and continues as far as the foothills of Gran Paradiso. Skirting again the Aosta valley, it ends at Macugnaga, at the foot of Monte Rosa (and the Alps' most impressive face).

In its entirety, *GTA* is 55 days long; all the trail is marked with red and white paint. A good network of huts, cheap hotels and *posti tappa* make a tent unnecessary, so it is possible to travel light. Because the trail goes alongside the main chain, crossing all the lateral valleys, a lot of ups and downs have to be negotiated. *GTA* is easy but tiring. Snow on the highest passes stays until the beginning of July.

In many places, you can leave the Italian trail for the French *GTA*. In other areas loops and lower trails are included into the *GTA*'s 'system'. The *Monviso tour*, a very interesting 4 day hike, is amongst these. A network of buses allow you to join and leave the *GTA*'s main trail at the end of practically every day.

Also, the Aosta valley has developed a comprehensive network of long trails. *Alta via numero 1* is nicknamed the 'Giants' trail', as it skirts the biggest mountains of the Alps. It starts in Gressoney, winds in front of Monte Rosa, the Matterhorn, Grand Combin, and ends in Italy at Val Ferret, in front of the Mont Blanc massif. It takes 8 to 10 days. *Alta via numero 2* works its way along the southern part of the region, from Champorcher to Mont Blanc's Val Veny. A long stretch of the journey (from Cogne to Rêmes valley) passes through Gran Paradiso National Park, one of the country's largest and best known parks. You need about 7 days, and an axe is required all the summer round to cross Col de Planaval, on an easy glacier, between Valgrisenche and la Thuile.

Last but not least is *Tour du Mont Blanc*, the 11 day loop around Europe's highest summit. Two days of the trail are in Italy (the rest is shared between France and Switzerland), but they are frequently skipped by hikers who prefer a short cut by bus along Val Veny and Val Ferret. It is a pity, as these are magnificent parts of a marvellous trail.

ARGENTERA PARK: THE VALASCO AND VALSCURA TO FREMAMORTA HIKE

At the southwestern corner of Piedmont's Alps, the Argentera park was established by the regional government on the site of an old royal game reserve. Scenery is wild, mountains are steep and barren. Argentera's 3,297 m are the area's highest point, while nearby Gelas is the Alps' southernmost glacier. It is an area of beauty, of fairly strenuous trails, and one of the places where mountaineering developed earliest in the Alps: Corno Stella's routes are extremely popular amongst rock climbers.

From Valdieri, where the Park's headquarters are situated, the valley branches off. To the left is Entracque, a pleasant village and a good base for some wildlife-seeking tours around Genova or Federici *rifugi*. On the main valley, continue to Sant'Anna and then to Terme di Valdieri, and park there. The old wooden cottage near to today's luxury hotel was built a century ago for the *Bela Rosìn*, 'beautiful Rosie', the favourite female companion of King Vittorio Emanuelle II.

Memories of this hunter king are to be found on almost all trips; often you walk on paved mule trails, sometimes you reach old buildings built especially for the king's parties. At Valasco, an extremely beautiful grassy plateau, you can find a unique example of Vittorio Emanuele's *case di caccia*, resembling a small fortress like the fort of some John Wayne movie. An easy walk leads to the *casa di caccia*. A longer expedition includes the magnificent Valscura lakes, and the *rifugio* Questa close by, near to another interesting lake. It is a day's walk, but it can be split into two days, which gives more chances of meeting chamois and ibexes around sunset and dawn.

The area has many more interesting walks. From the Fremamorta lakes, you can watch magnificent sunsets on Argentera. The Remondino hut is the base for the easy scramble to Argentera's main summit. For the romantic walker, Gias del Lagarot offers a perfect view of the imposing Lourousa ice gully. Patrizia Rossi and Giuseppe Canavese's *Parco dell'Argentera* guidebook will help you in finding more walks. The map to use is IGC's 1:50,000 *Alpi Liguri e Marittime* sheet, which is accurate enough for the visitor.

How to get there From Cuneo, access is quick and easy to Valdieri and then Terme di Valdieri (1,358 m), where there is a carpark. Or take a Nuova Benese bus from Cuneo: for information phone (0171) 2929.

The trail Near to the *Terme* main building, follow a small dirt road leading to a group of buildings. Park immediately after these and start walking on an old military road, with clear shortcuts, as far as the entrance of the Valasco plateau. This is truly magnificent; you cross it to reach the *casa di caccia*, a small fortress at 1,762 m and 1½ hours from the start.

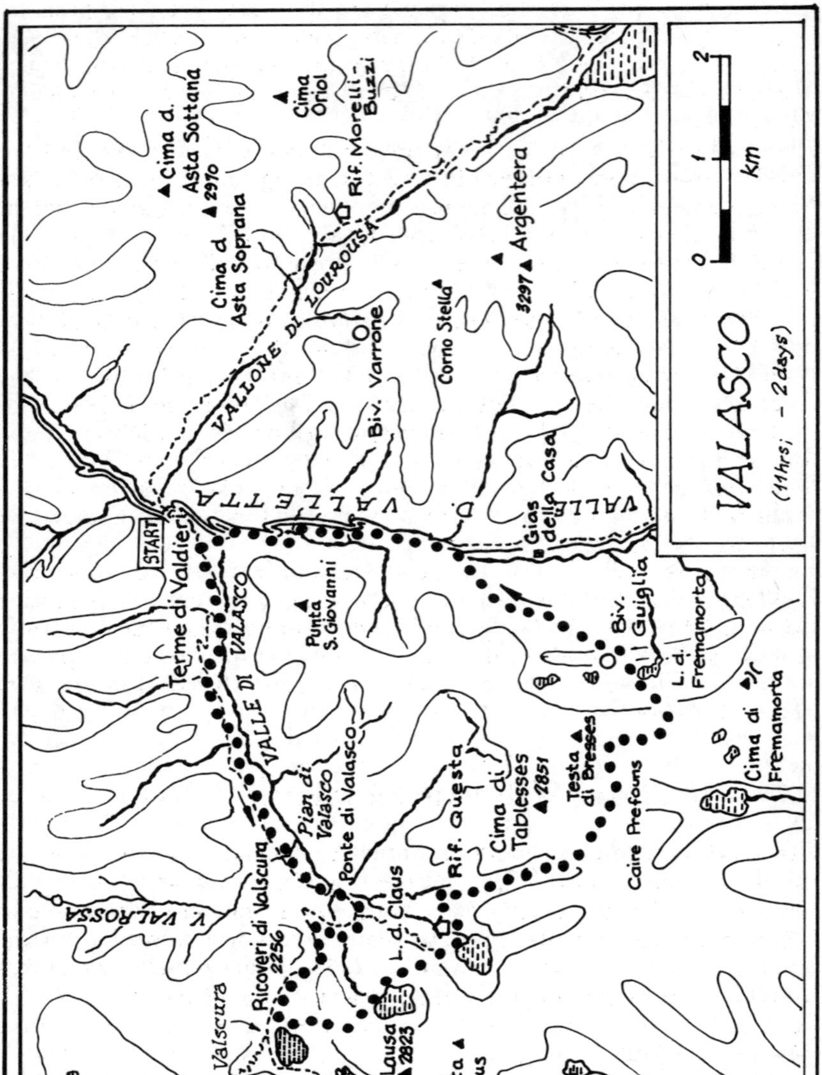
VALASCO
(11hrs; - 2days)
0
1
2
km
START
Terme di Valdieri
VALLE DI VALASCO
VALLETTA
VALLONE DI LOUROUSA
Cima d. Asta Sottana
2970
Cima d Asta Soprana
Cima Oriol
Rif. Morelli-Buzzi
Argentera
3297
Corno Stella
Biv. Varrone
Gias della Casa
Punta S. Giovanni
Biv. Guiglia
L. d. Fremamorta
Cima di Fremamorta
Testa di Bresses
Cima di Tablesses
2851
Rif. Questa
Caire Prefouns
Pian di Valasco
Ponte di Valasco
Ricoveri di Valscura
2256
V. VALROSSA
L. di Valscura
L. d. Claus
C. d. Lausa
2823
Testa d. Claus
2804
Cima di Tavels
T.ta Malinvern
2939
Tête Mercière

Then continue on the old road, leaving on the left side a direct path to *rifugio* Questa, and climbing again to the west. The road passes a small tunnel, continues along a narrow gully, and reaches the lower Lago di Valscura (2,274 m, 1¼ hours from Valasco). This part boasts the best preserved of the king's ancient trails, and offers spectacular views across the lake.

On your right leave the GTA trail to upper Valscura lake and the border, and follow another old trail traversing left. You cross a first ridge, descent to Lago del Claus, then continue to *rifugio* Questa, at 2,388 m and less than 1 hour from lower Valscura lake. Lago delle Portette is nearby. To descend back to Valasco, follow the direct and quicker trail; you will need 2 hours to reach Terme di Valdieri.

It is more interesting to sleep in the *rifugio*, and next morning follow the trail descending to the east, and to the narrow Vallone del Prefouns, which leads steeply to Passo del Prefouns, at 2,620 m on the French border. Descend into France, climb left on scree to Testa Sud di Bresses (2,820 m, 2½ hours from Questa), on the border again and one of the park's best viewpoints. An easy descent leads to Colle di Bresses, and then left again to Fremamorta lakes, where *bivacco* Guiglia lies at 2,421 m. All this area offers magnificent views of Argentera's main chain.

From the lower lake, an excellent and recently restored trail descends into the Vallone della Valletta which is reached at Gias delle Mosche's 1591 m. The last part of the descent has beautiful views onto Corno Stella's smooth southwest face. On the road, the last part of which is surfaced, you reach your starting point (3 to 4 hours from Testa di Bresses).

THE MONVISO LAKES' HIKE

At 3,841 m, Monviso is not one of the Alps highest summits, nor one of the very best known ones. But it is high, beautiful, and isolated. Its pyramid can be seen clearly from Turin, and from almost the whole of Piedmont on clear winter days. Its shape is very well known to hikers, climbers and skiers. At its summit, in 1863, Quintino Sella, a member of the new-born Italian parliament, conceived the idea of founding 'an association similar to the English Alpine Club'. Italy's CAI was born a few months later.

Approach to Monviso can be made from several different directions. From France, it is an easy hike from the end of the road to the Baillif hut, dominated by the mountain's pyramid (which lies entirely in Italian territory). From the south, a long and gently sloping valley climbs from Val Varaita to *rifugio* Gagliardone. From the north, the best route of all starts from Pian del Re, which is the source of the River Po, and zigzags south, passing a series of magnificent lakes dominated by the main summit and Visolotto's twin pyramids. At the end of the walk, *rifugio* Quintino Sella is the starting place for the ascent to the summit (an easy but *very* long scramble on moderate rock) and a convenient resting place for hikers.

Scenery is harsh and rugged, the trail climbs near to huge boulders, the lakes reflect rock spires and ice gullies. It is a harsh atmosphere, but this is the Western Alps' true spirit and image; Monviso's foothills are one of the very best places to experience it. If you have more time, walk the whole of the 4 day *Monviso tour*. On day one you reach Quintino Sella; on day two you cross Passo di San Chiaffredo, reaching Vallone di Vallanta and climbing again to *rifugio* Gagliardone and *rifugio* Vallanta; this is the most strenuous day.

On day three you cross Passo di Vallanta and descend to the Baillif hut: this is an easy day and you could continue to complete the loop in three days. The last stage is another climb to Colle delle Traversette's 2,950 m; nearby Buco di Viso is probably the first tunnel ever dug in the Alps. A steep trail descends back to Pian del Re.

How to get there From Saluzzo, follow the Po valley up to Crissolo, and then continue on a very small and winding road to Pian del Re, at 2,020 m, where there is a cheap hotel open all summer long. Board an ATI bus in Saluzzo (there are direct buses from Turin or Cuneo) that

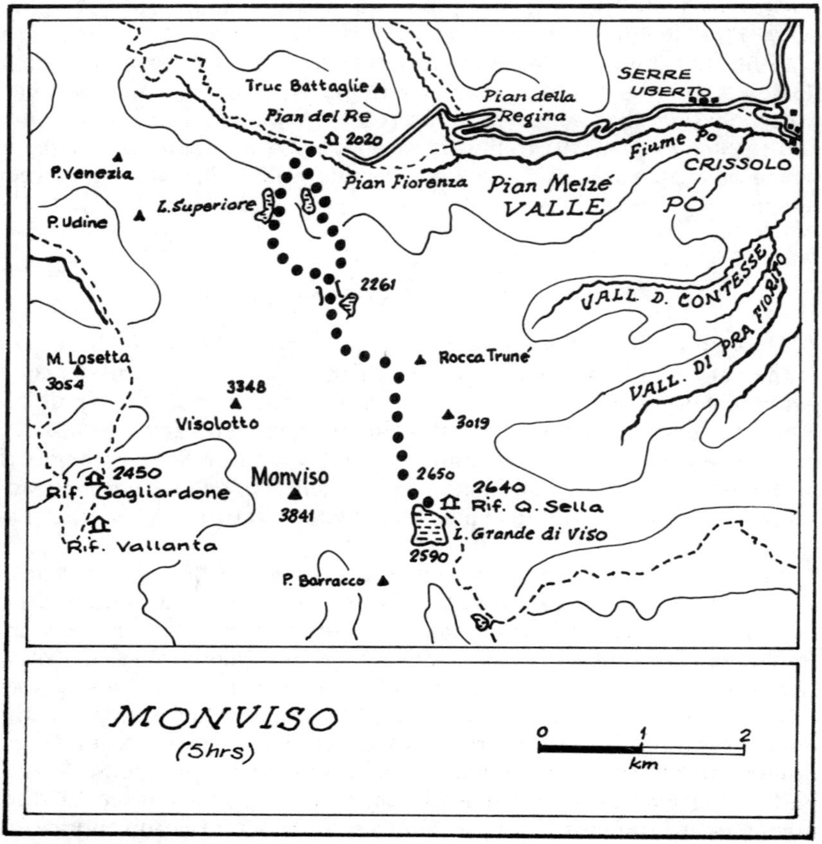

will drop you off in Crissolo at 1,318 m. To Pian del Re you will need about 2½ hours on foot, although it is quite easy to hitch-hike. At Pian Melzé, 1,700 m, there is another cheap place to stay.

The trail From the roadhead at Pian del Re, cross the grass plain and start climbing on a large, zigzagging trail. A short ascent leads to Lago Fiorenza, the first of a long series of lakes, facing a perfect view on Monviso. The trail climbs again, traverses for a while, then passes high above Lago Chiaretto, to reach a huge boulder field, dominated directly by Monviso. The imposing snow and ice gully is the start to the mountain's north face Coolidge route, one of the best known in the Alps.

The trail veers left, climbs again with good views, then enters an impressive, level moraine valley again dominated by Monviso's east face. At the end, you cross Colle di Viso, and traverse a little to the left to *rifugio* Quintino Sella (2,640 m, 2½ hours from Pian del Re). If you sleep in the hut, you should consider climbing towards Viso Mozzo in the early morning, to have a better view; Viso Mozzo is 3,019 m and the ascent requires 2 hours for the round trip, but it involves no technical difficulties.

On the way back, you can include the most spectacular lake of all. Descend the same way to Lago Chiaretto, and turn left at the junction to the next trail, heading for *rifugio* Giacoletti. The trail crosses a grassy saddle, then forks again, in front of another lake. Leave the main trail, descend to the lake, pass by the right of it and descend a little more to Lago Superiore, the largest in the area. From the northeastern corner of the lake, another good trail descends, crossing a rocky gully, then zigzags on grass and moraine slopes to Pian del Re. Allow 2½ hours for a return trip this way.

GRAN PARADISO: THE CHAMOIS' LAUSON TRAIL

Gran Paradiso is probably the best known amongst Italy's National Parks. It started more than a century ago, serving as a game reserve for the royal family: in Sarre, near Aosta, one beautiful castle is still dubiously decorated with thousands of ibex horns on the walls. In 1922 it became a National Park, the country's first.

The park lies across the regional border between Piedmont and Valle d'Aosta and includes on the Aostan (northern) side the easiest climb in all the Alps up a 4,000 m peak. From Valsavaranche, thousands of mountaineers ascend every year to the summit of Gran Paradiso, 4,061 m. The western part of the park has greener scenery (Rhêmes valley is particularly pleasant), while the southern part presents impressive views over rocky terrain.

The Lauson hike, from Cogne's Valnontey to the Vittorio Sella hut, is one of Italy's best known, and should not be missed. Around the hut, animals are easy to see in all seasons, and an overnight stop in

Vittorio Sella is recommended in order to have a closer look at the wildlife at sunset and dawn. There are problems, however. As the area is extremely crowded during summer weekends, and in early August, I really do suggest choosing another of the nearby trails.

There are many to choose from. Valnontey's main trail is an excellent and very easy walk through a thick forest dominated by

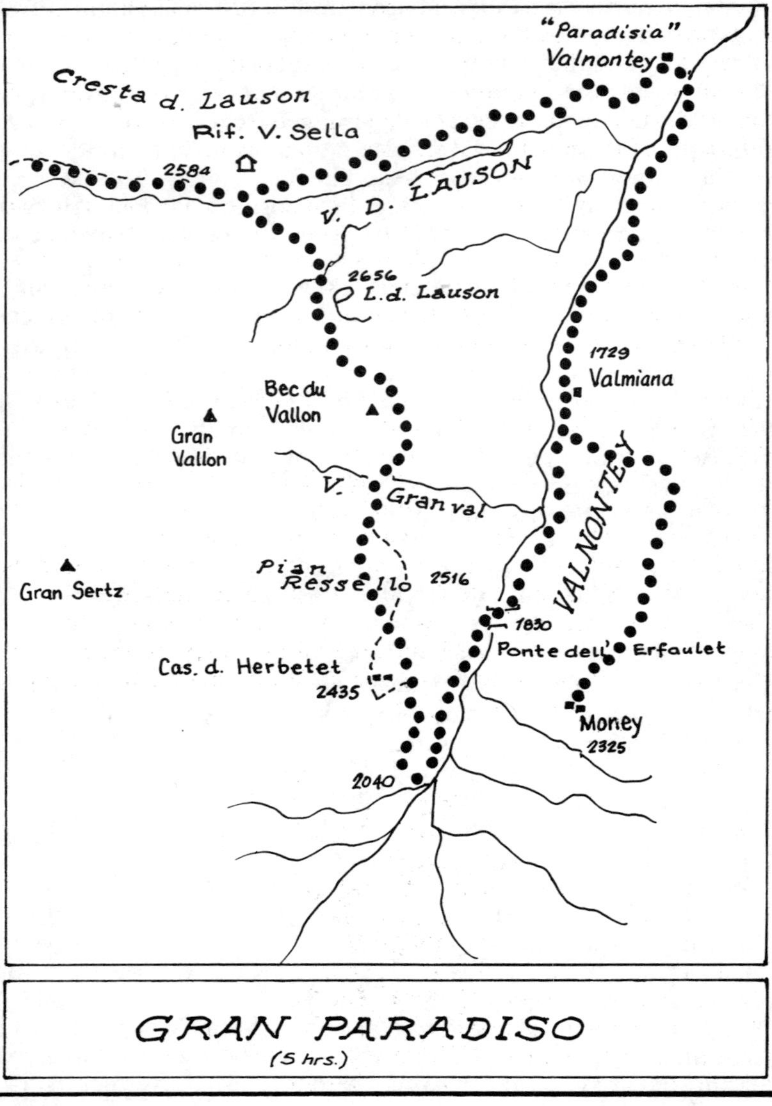

GRAN PARADISO
(5 hrs.)

impressive glaciers. From nearby Lillaz Valeille, the area is much wilder, with barren mountains and absolute solitude. From Valnontey itself, one of my favourite walks in the area is the one to Money. Pass the houses at Valmiana to a trail junction, turn left onto a steep trail, that traverses a magnificent plateau, one of the finest view points of the Alps, and maybe the best of all on Gran Paradiso. Here wildlife can be easily seen. The Park's regulations forbid you to camp but while Money *bivacco* was not built for wildlife watchers it is a shelter for climbers ascending the peak of Gran San Pietro and is perched 500 metres higher up on the mountains.

Like many other walks, the Lauson trail is best walked out of the main tourist season. In the Alps, in September and early October the skies are clear and there are good views, but for the wildlife enthusiast May and June can be better still. There is a lot of snow around but ibexes and chamois descend very low into the valleys, and you can admire a lot of them within a very short walk from Valnontey.

How to get there Cogne is one of Valle d'Aosta main tourist attractions, and it is very easy to reach. Drive west of Aosta (i.e. do not reach Aosta if you come from Mont Blanc's tunnel) and turn south onto a side road leading there. Valnontey is 4 km south of the main village. There are buses from Aosta to Cogne: from there to Valnontey walk for an hour, or hitch-hike as a lot of cars pass by.

The trail From Valnontey's parking areas 1,666 m, cross the bridge, and then turn left following directions to the Vittorio Sella hut. Pass near a botanical garden, enter the pine forest, and begin climbing within it, with a series of long zigzags. The trail leads out of the forest, and starts a diagonal ascent, with interesting views of the glaciated peaks (Punte Patri, Gran San Pietro, Roccia Viva) onto Valnontey's far side. More zigzags lead to the grassy plateau where the *rifugio* is, at 2,584 m and 2 to 2½ hours' walk from the start.

There are two good places where you are particularly likely to encounter animals. One is in the upper Lauson valley; to reach it just go on walking for about half an hour, up to another grassy plateau

Alpine anemone

where a lot of ibexes are normally found at sunset. For the other, cross the stream near the *rifugio*, and follow another large trail to the small Lauson lake, again an area much frequented by wildlife. If you are confident enough to walk on an easy but sometimes very exposed trail, continue along this trail to the Herbetet Ranger huts, and then descend to Valnontey floor on another zigzagging trail. From the upper Lauson basin, a perfectly easy (but really long) trail climbs to Colle della Rossa's 3,190 m, and descends amongst extremely wild scenery to Cogne.

MONT DE LA SAXE: OVERLOOKING MONT BLANC

High and mighty, the Mont Blanc massif dominates the far end of the Valle d'Aosta where the scenery is completely different from the northern (French) side. On the Chamonix side, the huge glaciers of the chain flow downhill towards the villages and the main road. Here, on the Italian side, the Giant is a huge rock wall, menacing the valley below with small suspended glaciers. Apart from Mont Blanc itself (on the left), the best summits to look at are Dente del Gigante (a striking rocky tooth perched on the ridge), and Grandes Jorasses, a mountain with the most impressive peak of all.

Courmayeur, however is not a very attractive place to stay. It is very expensive, very smart, more like a fashionable beachside resort than a mountain village. It was built in the traditional, safe way that mountain people built their villages: rocky Mont Chetif shelters the village it is impossible to see and Mont Blanc itself from the village. To live cheaply you must move to a campsite, either in Val Ferret (turn right when you go uphill) or in Val Veny (turn left). To have a look at Mont Blanc walk a bit uphill.

This is my favourite trail, but obviously there are many, many more. You can read my own *Intorno al Monte Bianco* (Zanichelli, 1985), or other guidebooks in French and have a look at the maps: the best one is *Le massif du Mont Blanc*, 1:25,000, by France's IGN. Gobbi's sport shop in Courmayeur stocks it. Looking for a trail, always remember a rule; paths going towards Mont Blanc (i.e. to a hut, to a glacier) are steep, and the views, though striking, are seldom panoramic. Climbing the easy, grassy mountains on the opposite side of both valleys, leads to excellent views.

How to get there Easy. Courmayeur is on the main road to Mont Blanc tunnel and France. By public transport there are quick *Autostradale* buses from Turin and Milan, or a slow train to Aosta and Pré St. Didier, and then a bus from there. If you are scared by prices, be careful not to be stranded in Courmeyeur for the night!

The trail From the church square in Courmayeur, start uphill on the road to Villair village. Cross it (beautiful views of Mont Blanc on your

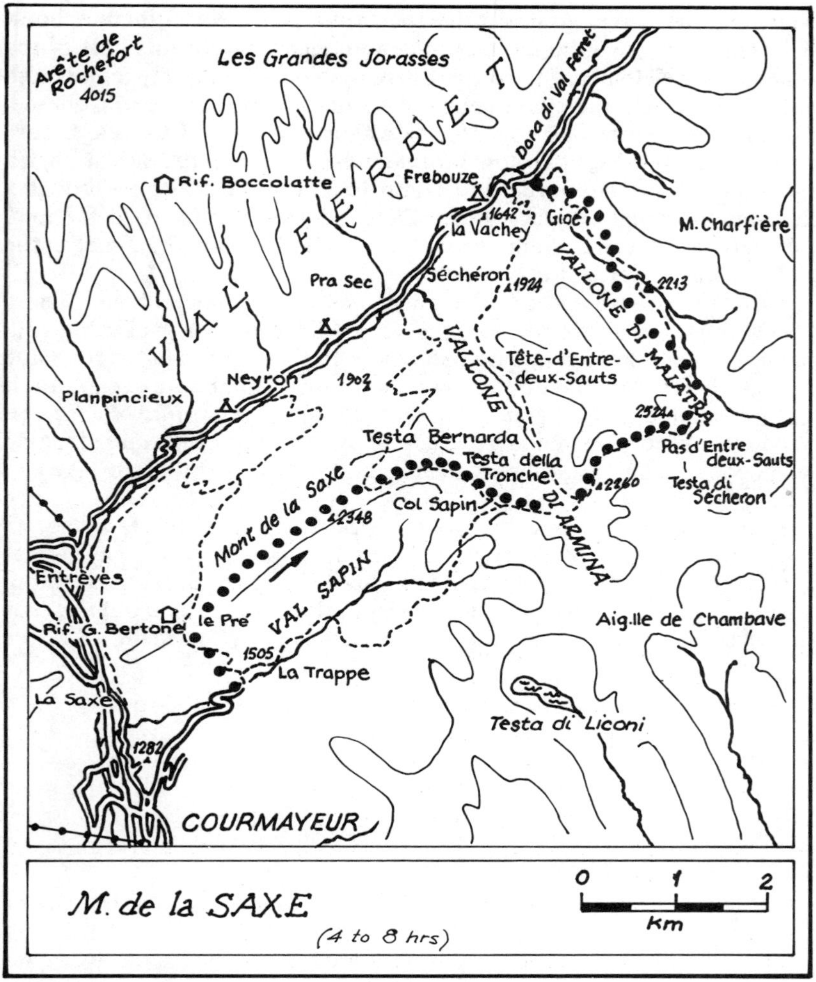

M. de la SAXE
(4 to 8 hrs)

left), and continue on a dirt road through the valley above: cross the river by a bridge, and then climb a couple of switchbacks. Follow the path on the left. Leave the road, climb through the pleasant forest, leaving it at about 1,700 m, traversing left and then climbing again. At the end you reach a beautiful grassy plateau, near a group of shepherds' huts. The biggest one has been transformed into *rifugio* Giorgio Bertone, owned by the famous mountain guide, Renzino Cosson.

At 1,980 m, the uphill walk has taken about 2½ hours, and this is a wonderful place to stop for the night. You can get here even starting quite late from Courmayeur. The dawn on the east-facing Brenva slopes of Mont Blanc is a sight not to be missed!

After dawn and breakfast, start again on a path going uphill, reaching the large, grassy ridge of Mont de la Saxe in one hour. Edward Whymper, the famous mountaineer, wrote of this part of the hike as 'one of the best . . . everywhere', and you can easily understand why. On the left, the chain peaks of Mont Blanc continue to Colle del Gigante, to Dente del Gigante, to Mighty Grandes Jorasses, before rising again into Mont Dolent and Aigiulle de Leschaux. Skirt right on the rocky Testa Bernarda and climb to grassy Testa de la Tronche, 2,584 m your highest place today. Descend a short ridge to Col. Sapin, turn left, and escend briefly through the Vallone di Armina, near to the Secheron shepherds' huts.

Cross the stream and climb again to Pas-d'Entre-Deux Sauts. There everything goes downhill. On reaching Malatrà cwm, walk downhill passing several hamlets, and finally keep to the right as far as the Gioè huts. In front, Aiguille de Leschaux and Mont Dolent are seen at their best. A small dirt road zigzags down the hill, into beautiful Val Ferret. When you reach the main road, just follow it keeping left, and reaching la Vachey, 1,642 m where you can board a bus (or hitch-hike) to Courmayeur.

From *rifugio* Bertone, allow 2 hours to Testa della Tronche, 1½ hours to Pas-d'Entre-Deux-Sauts, and 2 hours to la Vachey. Quite surprisingly, this hike is the real first day of the famous Tour du Mont Blanc. But today's hikers are in a hurry and they tend to avoid this part of the trail, just boarding a bus to la Vachey. Pity for them!

Chapter 3
Central Alps

East of Monte Rosa, the Alps veer eastwards, marking Italy's border with Switzerland and Austria. An impressive system of summits, glaciers and valleys forms this part of the chain, stretching for more than 200 km as the crow flies. A large triangle of Swiss territory – Canton Ticino – descends well into what is geographically Italian territory. East of it are the highest summits of this part of the chain, Bernina being the tallest of all, and the easternmost peak in the Alps to reach 4,000 m above sea level.

Many of the best known massifs are on the border line between Italian Valtellina and Switzerland; apart from Bernina they include Disgrazia, 3,678 m, and the lower but striking granite peaks of Bregaglia, Badile, Cengalo, and Pizzi del Ferro. To the east lie the Ortles and Covedale massifs. Stelvio includes Italy's largest National Park. To the south, Adamello is another impressive granite mountain, flanked by a huge, flat glacier.

But the Central Alps are not only a land of mighty summits and extended glaciers; south of the main chain are Prealpi, a lower chain, directly overlooking Lombardy's lakes and clearly seen from Milan. Monti Lariani is on the Swiss border west of Lake Como, Grigna is a limestone massif well known amongst climbers but also affording excellent walks to the hiker. Orobie are a complete system of wild and isolated peaks, separating Valtellina from Lombardy's lowlands.

Lake Como

In character, this chapter's walks do not differ much from their western counterparts. In the high mountains they tend to be long (often very long on Bernina and Bregaglia), without the crowds which can be found on many Valle d'Aosta trails. Usually shorter walks can be found on Prealpi. Many trails overlooking Lake Como are pleasant and anything but strenuous: almost all of them offer magnificent views of the lake and the nearby mountains, and conditions are good even when higher mountains are still clad in snow.

Stelvio National Park is a magnificent area, the richest in wildlife in all the country. Here, amongst large glaciers and deep pine forests, it is possible to encounter Italy's largest population of deer, chamois and ibexes, much wilder than their Gran Paradiso cousins, and stare at an eagle's imposing flight. Together with nearby Swiss Engadina National Park, Stelvio forms one of the largest and most interesting protected areas of all Europe.

I mentioned the problem of crowds. From many points of view, Italian mountaineering was actually born in Lombardy. The region still hosts half of CAI's all-Italy membership, the largest amount of huts, the widest possibilities (this is a record shared with the Dolomites) for those who seek long distance trails and expeditions. A June or September weekend spent walking on Grigna's trails is more like a Saturday night stroll in central Rome than a wilderness experience. Many other trails offer solitude, though: the choice is yours, and all trails can be reached in a weekend from Milan.

THE LONG DISTANCE TRAILS

The Central Alps have a huge variety of long distance trails; some are hard mountain expeditions, others are easy walks at middle heights, suitable for late spring or autumn instead of summer.

In the west, first of all, Piedmont's *Grande Tràversata delle Alpi* reaches Macugnaga, at the foot of Monte Rosa's eastern face. We have already dealt with this trail; it is being extended to reach Lago Maggiore in the next few years. North of this, *Alta via dell'Ossola* is a complete traverse of the valleys between Monte Rosa itself and Switzerland. It starts in Varzo (Val Divedro) to end in Val Formazza, and it requires a week of hard going, with daily stretches of up to eight hours.

Switzerland's Canton Ticino divides Ossola from the Lake Como region; on the hills west of this are three interesting trails. *Via dei Monti Lariani* is both the most popular and the only really 'long' one. It starts in Cernobbio, a few miles north of Como, and follows all the border ridge to Sorico, a week away, at the junction between Valtellina and Chiavenna valley. In Breglia, at the end of Via dei Monti Lariani's third day, two more trails start. Both are shorter; *Sentiero delle Quattro Valli* is a 3 day trail heading west to Lugano; *Alta via del Lario* is a more difficult, 3 to 4 day walk following exactly the border ridge, with some difficult and steep sections. Via dei Monti Lariani maintains a low altitude (1,000 to 1,500 m), and can be hiked at its best in mid-season.

Between Pizzo Badile and Disgrazia is *Sentiero Roma*, the very first long distance trail to be established in the country. It is a 6 day walk, circling Val Masino's upper part, involving some steepish snow gullies and some rock scrambling. For experienced hikers only, this is a tough but exhilarating trip.

Immediately east of Val Masino is Val Malenco: here is *Alta via della Val Malenco*, another interesting and quite popular trail. It makes a 360° tour of the valley, starting in Torre S. Maria and ending in Chiesa, and can normally be walked in 8 days. As many roads and escape trails are touched on the way, it can be walked in separate 1 or 2 day stretches, to form a sort of 'commuter's long trail'. If joined (in between are the beautiful *Val Codera* and easy *Preda Rossa* passes) *Via dei Monti Lariani*, *Sebiero Roma* and *Alta via della Val Malenco* form a 3 week trail including more than half of Lombardy's mountains.

South of these, on the Prealpi and in Bergamo province, is *Sentiero delle Orobie*. An interesting 6 day walk, this starts in Valcanale and ends in Lizzola, passing a series of pleasant huts and many magnificent lakes. Presolana, Orobie's most impressive – if not highest – summit can be clearly seen on the last day.

East again, in the heavily glaciated massifs marking the Central Alps' eastern border, are two more interesting trails. *Alta via camuna* (Camuni where the ancient inhabitants who left a lot of graffiti in Val Camonica's granite) makes a 4 day loop at Stelvio Park's southern end; it starts in Ponte di Legno and ends in Vezza d'Oglio. *Alta via dell'Adamello* is a 5 day walk on the western side of the massif; it starts from Breno or Bagolino, reaching north Garibaldi hut and Ponte di Legno.

RIFUGIO MENAGGIO AND GRONA

Very close to Milan, Lake Como is one of the best known of Italy's lakes. It offers good waterside resorts and interesting cuisine and pleasant trips by motorboat, small ferries or hydrofoils. It is surrounded by a series of interesting limestone mountains, some of which are extremely popular and much visited.

East of the lake, directly overlooking Lecco, is Grigna massif: its highest summit (Grignone, 2,400 m), is crowned by a big *rifugio*, whilst smaller Grignetta (2,187 m) is surrounded by a series of beautiful limestone towers. These are one of Italy's best known rock climbing areas, as they offer excellent opportunities for the hiker who can deal with easy rock scrambling and fixed ropes and ladders. Piani Resinelli is the starting point for many walks; the area can become unbelievably crowded on summer weekends.

Much quieter and very attractive, the mountains on the lake's western shore offer a beautiful selection of walks. Their main ridge marks, over a long distance, the border with Switzerland. On the ridges and in the valleys, forts and military roads can be found almost everywhere; these were hastily built around 1915, when the Italian army feared a German invasion through Switzerland. Today, many of the old buildings have been turned into mountain huts.

Rifugio Menaggio is a magnificent viewpoint, ideal for a 2 hour walk; nearby Grona offer trails of all levels. The area gets a lot of sun, and it is clear of snow for most of the year.

How to get there To reach the trail's starting point, you must first reach Menaggio, on the lake's western shore, and at the beginning of the road leading to Lugano, Switzerland through the Valsolda. From Milan drive through Como. Or take a train to Como, then a ferry across the lake. A winding road leads to Breglia; buses do exist, but hitch-hiking is the best bet. From Breglia, a smaller road leads to Monti di Breglia, where you must park immediately before the road ends. On foot, allow 45 minutes for this stretch.

The marked trail climbs left of the road, touches a small house, and then turns left reaching a junction. Both trails lead to the hut in about the same time, and a good idea is to use one of them for the ascent and the other on the way down. The upper (right, when going up) trail offers better views, the lower (left) trail has more shade and a steep bit at the end. You reach *rifugio* Menaggio in about 1¼ hours from the start. The *rifugio* is at 1,400 m and has magnificent views.

If this is not enough there is a choice of trails. A steep trail climbs right of Grona's pinnacles to Forcoletta col: from here you can walk left to Grona summit (1,729 m, 1 hour from the hut, the last part involving some easy scrambling), or right, on a large and easy grass

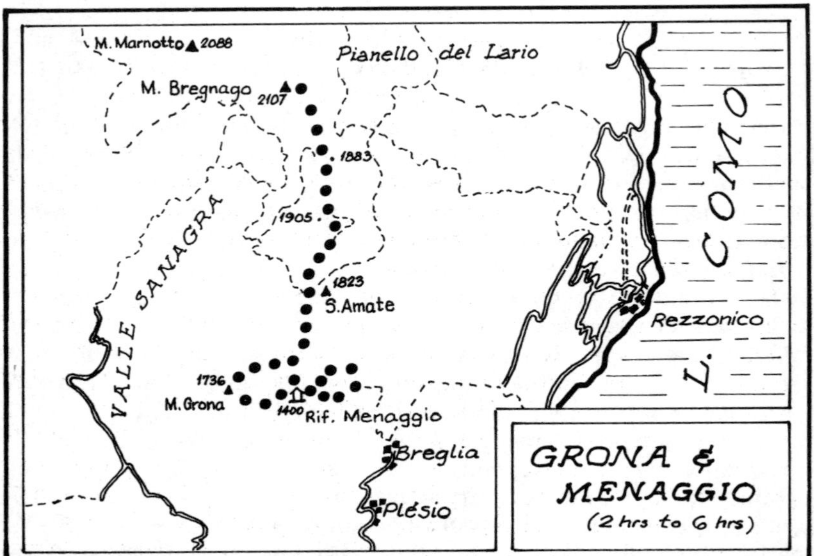

ridge to Sant'Amate chapel and to the long Costone del Bregagno ridge. Monte Bregagno's summit, 2,107 m, is a long way (2½ hours) from the hut, and has the best viewpoint in the area.

East of the *rifugio*, a few minutes' walk leads to a small col offering another interesting view towards Lake Lugano and the nearby Swiss border. From here, an easy but steep and sometimes exposed trail leads to Grona's summit, but this is reserved only for sure-footed hikers. Even more direct, a '*via ferrata*' climbs directly to the summit. From the *rifugio* menaggio to the road, allow 45 minutes, either way.

AMAZING VAL CODERA

Rocky Val Codera is truly an amazing place to walk around. First of all, because of the scenery. Here is the westernmost tip of the granite chains of Bregaglia, continuing eastwards into Pizzo Badile, Cengalo, and many beautiful peaks. Towards Lake Como and the small Lake Mezzola, imposing spurs and giant slabs are the background to steep valleys and tiny hamlets.

The second point of interest is the human character of the area. Because of the very steep granite slabs barring the entrance from the lakeshore, Val Codera has become one of the very last valleys in all the Alps to be inhabited all year round, even though it has no road. To reach Codera, the main village, on a sunny terrace at 835 m, and further up Saline and Bresciadega, everybody has to walk.

At the end of the level part of the valley, *rifugio* Brasca offers an ideal spot to rest, even for more than one day. It is built near Coeder hamlet, overlooking beautiful pastures dominated by the impressive rocky face of la Sfinge – the 'Sphynx'. At its summit, 1,300 m, you can park your car and start walking. To get to *rifugio* Brasca, you need about 4 hours.

In an area of rough mountain scrambles and difficult climbs, Codera is a soft option for the hiker. It is a beautiful mid-season walk, and September and October are probably the best times of all. In winter, the sunny position of Codera village makes it normally approachable without having to hike on snow. In summer, remember not to walk the first part of the trail, Mezzolpiano to Codera, during the hottest hours of the day.

The best map is Kompass n. 92 *Chiavenna-Val Bregaglia*. Donato Erba's *Intorno al Pizzo Badile* (Zanichelli, 1982) is the best guidebook to other hikes in the area.

How to get there Easy. In a car, drive from Milan to Lecco, then on the east shore of Lago di Como, and on *statale* 36 to Novate Mezzola, on the road to Chiavenna and to Spluga and Maloja passes. By train, get off at Novate Mezzola station, a few minutes away from the beginning of the path.

The trail From Novate, proceed to Mezzolpiano, a tiny hamlet at the start of the trail: you will find a sign before entering Novate, on your

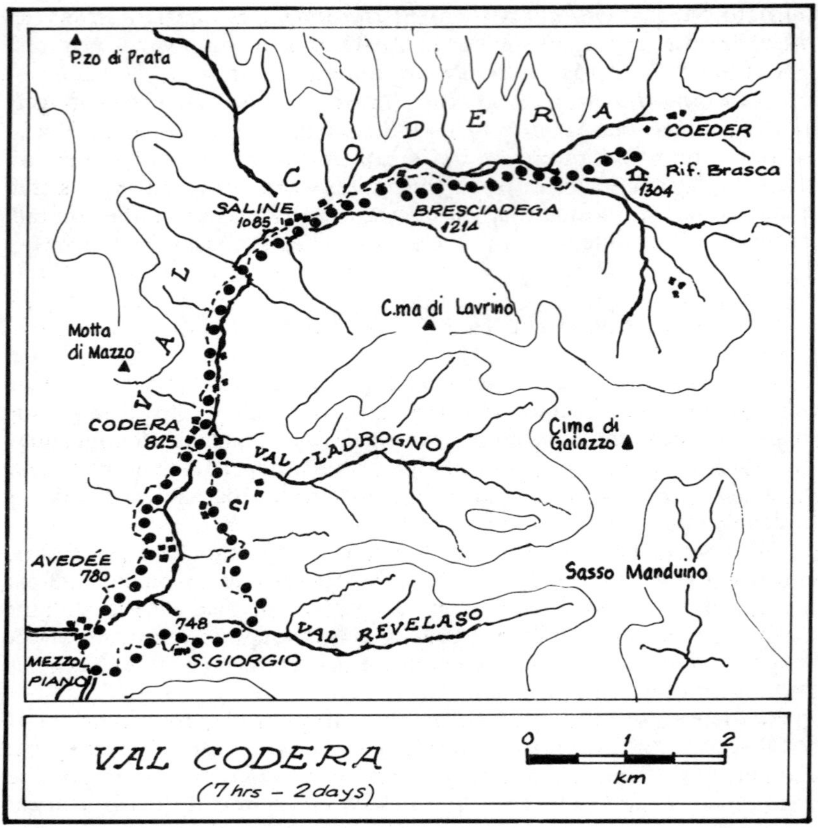

VAL CODERA
(7 hrs – 2 days)

right coming from Lecco. At Mezzolpiano, you'll find a parking place, a water fountain and the beginning of a steep path, zigzagging on steep granite slabs.

The first hour or so is the hottest and most tiring part of all; you start on a continuous staircase, reach an old quarry, then skirt right across a huge slab, after which you do a short climb to the hamlet of Avedée: at 780 m this is the first group of houses in the valley. The path becomes level, passes underneath a waterfall, then climbs again to Codera, the main village of the valley. You are at 825 m and 2 hours from the starting point of the trail. Luxuries of the place include a public telephone, a couple of very basic and friendly pensions and restaurants and an interesting, small museum, which you can visit if you manage to find its warden.

From Codera, the path continues along open ravines, near a small dam and up to Saline village, at 1,085 m. Then it turns right, crosses the river, and enters a completely different part of the valley, through a beautiful, dark pine forest, that leads to Bresciadega (1,214 m, 1½ hours from Codera). This is another nice hamlet, inhabited only in summer: there is a designated campsite nearby, and water is good. A further half hour brings you to *rifugio* Brasca at the end of the level part of the valley. On the right, when coming up, you'll see a couple of beautiful waterfalls, and the smooth, impressive north face of la Sfinge.

Further explorations from *rifugio* Brasca lead you to *bivacco* Vaninetti and Pizzo di Trubinasca in the north, and an incredible view of Pizzo Badile's north face. It is an easy, but very long walk with some easy scrambling towards the end. Allow for 8 to 10 hours, for the return trip. Towards the south, you can walk to *bivacco* Valli, and to the base of the north wall of la Sfinge (3 hours including return). From the *bivacco*, a difficult path, involving some steep and exposed scrambling brings you to Passo Ligoncio and to *rifugio* Omio on the Val Masino side.

On the way down, follow the same path to Codera (1½ hours). Then veer left, descending to a path which crosses the river by an ancient stone bridge, then cross a smaller stream by a similar bridge, and climb up steeply to Cì hamlet. After climbing for a few minutes you reach the *tracciolino*, a big level path following the water pipeline coming down from the dam above. You turn right, and follow *tracciolino* across a steep valley. When you reach the entrance to a second, bigger valley, you leave the level track for the ancient path that descends steeply, crosses a stream, and then climbs again to San Giorgio, another village in a beautiful position (748 m, 2 hours from Codera). You must not miss the *avello celtico*, an ancient tomb cut into granite, on the slopes just above the village.

Another impressive but perfectly easy path zigzags down the rocky spur supporting the village, and plunges down towards the valley. At the end, when you reach level ground, turn right near a fountain and cross the next bridge. Mezzolpiano is only a few metres along a paved road, right where the walk started (1¼ hours from San Giorgio).

VAL MALENCO HIKES

'A 200-km long museum.' This is the slogan that has been used, for almost 20 years now, to describe Val Malenco, one of Central Alps' most interesting valleys, immediately north of Sondrio, Valtellina's main centre. A genuine museum was opened here in 1970; it can be seen in Chiesa's old church, and is one of the most interesting of its kind. It contains old tools, furniture, and complete collections of minerals from the valley.

What is unique to Val Malenco, though, is the fact that the museum has extended out of the village. Around the valley, a series of 'museum trails' allow visits to old hamlets, quarries and places of interest. This has been developed by the museum support group since 1975. *Alta via della Val Malenco* is one of Italy's earliest (and still, most interesting) long distance trails.

East of the valley is Pizzo Bernina, the Alps' easternmost (4,000 m) peak. West of it is Monte Disgrazia, a 3,700 m, heavily glaciated, impressive mountain. North, a rather featureless ridge marks the border with Switzerland. Val Malenco's *Alta via* is an 8 day loop around the valley's basin, touching all the most interesting spots and huts. Chiesa is the valley's biggest centre, quite low in altitude and thus pretty hot in summer. Chiareggio, a smaller village, is the most pleasant place for a stay in the hot season: there are a few hotels and a lot of places to camp.

Nemo Canetta and Giancarlo Corbellini's *Valmalenco*, published by Tamari, is the guidebook for the valleys. Kompass n. 91 *Bernina-Sondrio* map is the best of the area.

How to get there A 16-km road connects Sondrio to Chiesa and then forks to reach Chiareggio to the west and Campo Moro dam to the east. By public transport Val Malenco is easy to reach: you must travel by train from Milan to Sondrio, and then board a bus to Chiesa and upwards. There are buses to Chiareggio, but not to Campo Moro.

Porro hut trail This is a short, perfectly easy and highly recommended walk, in very pleasant surroundings. Start from Chiareggio, by descending to the river, cross it by a bridge, and continue on a slowly ascending dirt road, entering Ventina Valley. The last bit is a steeper path and leads to *rifugio* Porro (about 1 hour from start). *Rifugio* Ventina is a few minutes ahead and it too is at the entrance of a magnificent grassy plateau, dominated by Pizzo Cassandra's north face. You can have a longer walk by descending a few minutes from the hut and then turning right to Lake Pirola, a large basin commanding a beautiful view towards Disgrazia. Hiking to the lake takes 1½ hours return. The descent to Chiareggio is about 40 minutes.

Bernina glaciers trail This is a much wilder and more tiring enterprise, reaching one of the Alps' most famous huts with an excellent panorama over a magnificent series of summits. Heavy snow boots are required, but an ice-axe is only necessary for crossing Bocchetta di Caspoggio.

From Chiesa a quite steep road leads to Lanzada, Franscia and Campo Moro. Hitch-hiking at weekends and in summer is easy. A few hundred metres beyond Campo Moro's small hotel, a dirt road descends left to the dam (you can cross this by car), to end on the far side. The first part of the trail is steep: it climbs diagonally left, and requires about 30 minutes to walk round a rocky ridge and continue along gentler slopes amongst beautiful fir trees.

Another strenuous part of the trail, a series of long zigzags, leads to *rifugio* Carate Brianza, at 2,636 m. A few metres upwards, and you reach (2 hours from the start) Bocchetta delle Forbici, a small col from which Pizzo Bernina and its glaciers appear for the first time. A magnificent sight the trail at the bottom of a rocky ridge (snow throughout the summer), descends to Vedretta di Caspoggio's moraine, and then climbs to *rifugio* Marinelli, at 2,813 m and one more hour from Carate.

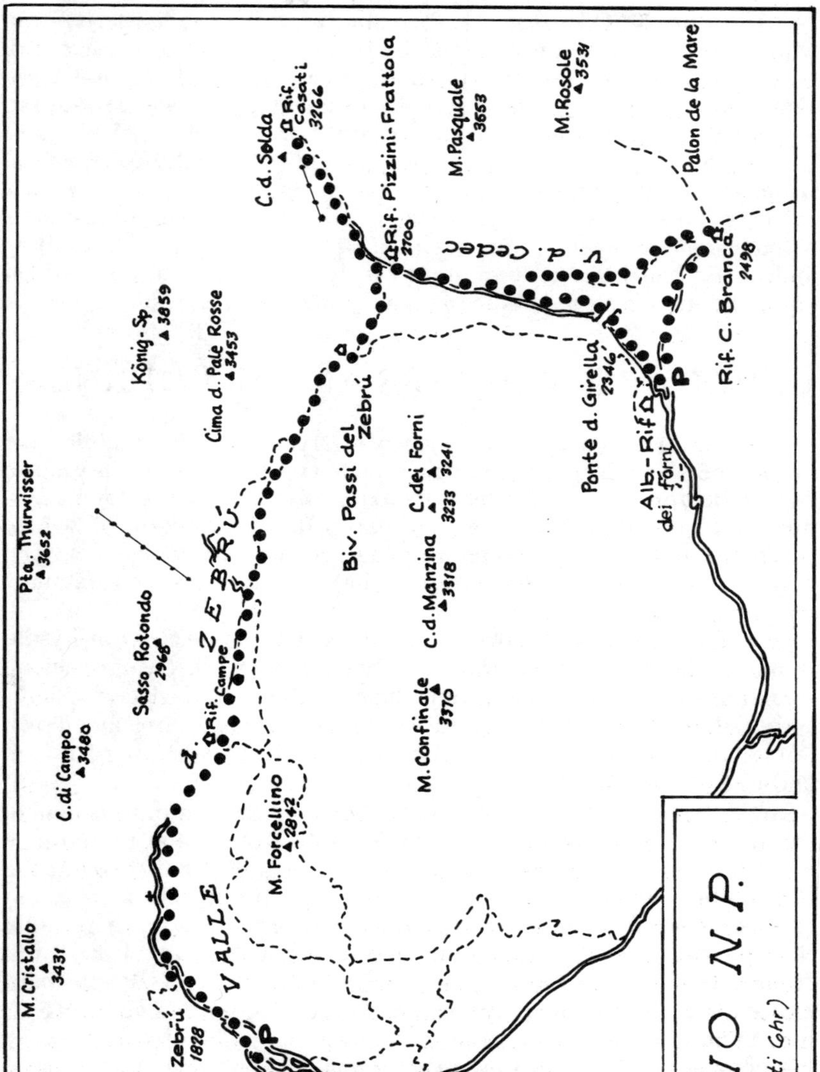
STELVIO N.P.
(Branca 2hr; Casati 6hr)
Cresta di Beit 3075
VALFURVA
S.Antonio
Rif. Zebru 1828
M.Cristallo 3431
VALLE
C.di Campo 3480
M. Forcellino 2842
Rif. Campo
ZEBRU
Sasso Rotondo 2968
Pta. Thurwisser 3652
M. Confinale 3370
C.d.Manzina 3318
C.dei Forni 3233 3241
Biv. Passi del Zebru
Cima d. Pale Rosse 3453
König-Sp. 3859
C.d. Solda
Rif. Casati 3266
Rif. Pizzini-Frattola 2700
M.Pasquale 3653
M.Rosole 3531
Palon de la Mare
V. d. Cedec
Ponte d. Girella 2346
Alb.-Rif. dei Forni
Rif. C. Branca 2498

The hike's length suggests an overnight stop in the *rifugio*. A perfectly easy viewpoint can be reached following the trail (often snowy) continuing up from the hut, and reaching the western Passo Marinelli, at the entrance of the huge and magnificent Vedretta di Scerscen. It requires little more than one hour, return. If you have a minimum knowledge of snow and glacier techniques, traverse south to eastern Passo Marinelli and continue south on Vedretta di Fellaria to descend to *rifugio* Bignami. Another descent leads to Alpe Gera lake, from which a dirt road descends to Campo Moro.

The popular 'trail' towards Marco e Rosa hut and Pizzo Bernina is actually a mountaineer's route; it involves easy but steep rock climbing and a thin ice ridge to the top. It can be tried by everyone, if well equipped, by hiring a guide: you can do that in Chiesa.

CEVEDALE GLACIERS AND WILDERNESS

Stelvio National Park is the country's largest, and it straddles the border between Milan's Lombardy and Trentino. Its north-eastern corner belongs to the German-speaking province of Bolzano. Culminating with Ortles' 3,921 m, the park offers a selection of Alpine landscape and wildlife. Hiking through it, you can easily meet deer and chamois, ibexes and eagles. Dense pine and fir forests cover many valleys.

Above the tree line, Stelvio's mountains lack Monte Rosa or Monte Bianco's steep and rocky grandeur, but offer awe-inspiring glaciers, sometimes reaching Himalayan dimensions. Forni glacier, easily accessible from S. Caterina Valfurva, is Italy's largest, surrounded by a horseshoe ridge stretching from Cevedale's 3,769 m to Vioz's 3,645 m and to S. Matteo's 3,678 m.

Right at the entrance of the valley, Forni hotel is an old-fashioned, very pleasant place to stay for a while. Both Branca and Pizzini huts are well kept and agreeable, and offer beautiful views over the surrounding summits. Because of the high altitude, the area is not recommended for seeing wildlife. Excellent opportunities of spotting chamois and deer can be had on a longer expedition requiring 2 full days: you reahc Branca hut, sleep at Pizzini, then cross Passo dello Zebrù to desscend through the long and magnificent Valle dello Zebrù, surrounded by deep forests.

Kompass n. 72 *Ortles-Cevedale* map is the best one for the area. Heavy boots are required to reach Casati hut and Passo dello Zebrù, but unnecessary for walking to either Branca or Pizzini. Cevedale itself is a very easy snow climb, popular and recommended. Guides can be hired at Bormio, S. Caterina or directly at the Forni hotel.

How to get there Bormio and S. Caterina are reached from Sondrio (and Milan) through Valtellina, or from Merano through the Stelvio pass. At 2,758 m, this is one of the Alps' highest roads open to car traffic. Passo di Gavia road from Ponte di Legno is a spectacular but difficult dirt road. A small road climbs from S. Caterina to I Forni. By bus, you can reach Bormio and S. Caterina from Sondrio or Tirano, where the railway ends. For the last stretch, you can hire a taxi or have the usual choice between walking (1½ hours) or hitching a ride.

The Forni trail to rifugio Branca This is the easiest of all, offering wonderful views over the glacier. It can easily be combined with the next walk. From the hotel car park take the descending dirt road, with beautiful views over the glaciers. Descend near to a small lake, cross the Cedec valley stream, and then climb on a moraine to *rifugio* Branca, which is reached in about 1 hour. Continue on the moraine for about ½ an hour for closer views of the ice fall. Descent to I Forni requires about 45 minutes. Alternatively, you can descend for only a few minutes and then turn right onto a marked trail, traversing beautiful pastures to reach Cedec valley, about 20 minutes lower than Pizzini hut. From Branca to Pizzini, you must allow 1½ hours.

The Cedec trail to rifugi Pizzini and Casati If you prefer the shorter, direct approach to these, leave Forni hotel on the upper road, climbing steeply for a while and then traversing almost level into Cedec valley, with beautiful views on the right towards Forni glacier. The route to the hut is straightforward, the *rifugio* is at 2,700 m and 1½ hours from Forni: it is the starting point to Gran Zebrù, a magnificent 3,859 m peak.

A smaller track traverses east on the moraines, reaching the start of the téléphérique used to ferry loads to Casati hut. A small path zigzags under the téléphérique (it is often an easy trail on snow) to reach Casati hut, at 3,266 m and a further 1½ hours from Pizzini. The view is magnificent. On a rock nearby is a series of cannons reminding the visitor that the ancient border between Italy and Austria saw fierce fighting in the 1914–18 war.

From Casati, experienced and well equipped hikers (rope, crampons, axe) can make an ascent to Cevedale summit in about 2 hours. The descent from Casati to Pizzini requires 1 hour, and the same is needed to descend back to Forni. To cross into Valle dello Zebrù; allow 1 hour from Pizzini to Passo del Zebrù and 3 to 4 for the descent to Pecenaccio bridge, where the road ends. A descent on foot to S. Antonio, midway between Bormio and S. Caterina, requires about 1 more hour.

Chapter 4

The Eastern Alps

Yes, the Dolomites are there! But they are not alone: instead, they are right in the middle of a complex system of mountains and glaciers, stretching from the Swiss border of Engadina to the Yugoslav frontier at Tarvisio. Adige river flows east from Resia pass and then south across Bolzano, Trento and Verona, forming one of the area's main geographical features. Further to the east, more rivers (Tagliamento, Piave, Brenta) flow in the same direction, with their valleys providing the most important links across the Alpine chain.

To the north, a long and impressive line of glaciated mountains mark the border with Austria. They stretch for about 120 km from Resia pass to Ries massif: right in the middle is the famous Brenner pass, for centuries the main crossing point between Italy and the German speaking world to the north. As everybody probably knows, the area immediately south of the border is politically Italian but German speaking: both the glaciated mountains on the border and the Dolomites' northern valleys are more frequented by German and Austrian hikers and mountaineers than Italians. Innsbruck and Munich are nearer than Milan, while even Vienna is not far away.

German is the area's first language, though Italian is spoken by everybody. As a result, mountains and valleys have bilingual names – keeping both in mind will help you to get correct information about your whereabouts. West to east, the area's main summits are Palla Bianca/*Weisskugel* (3,738 m), Similaun's Cime Nere/*Hintere*

in the Breonie

Schwarze (3,624 m), then Altissima/*Hohe Wilde* (3,480 m), dominating the interesting Tessa Natural Park.

At Pan di Zucchero/*Zuckerhütl* (3,505 m) the chain turns east again, quickly descending to Brenner's 1,375 m. East of this, Gran Pilastro/*Hochpfeiler* (3,510 m) is imposing again, and then the chain turns north east again; at 2,911 m, Vetta d'Italia/*Glockenkarnkofel* is the country's northernmost point. The Vedrette di Ries/*Rieserferner* massif is the link with the Italian Pusteria valley, marking the Dolomites' northern limit.

East of the Dolomites proper, summits and valleys still have a 'dolomitic' flavour and landscape. Alpi Carniche extend from the Piave river valley to the Yugoslav border at Tarvisio, forming the northern part of Friuli region. It is an interesting area, seldom visited by foreigners and little known to Italian hikers themselves; in some valleys German dialects are still spoken. The main summits are Peralba (2,693 m), and Coglians (2,780 m) in the rocky western sector, Avostanis (2,194 m), Poludnig (1,999 m) and Oisternig (2,052 m) in the lower and heavily forested eastern section. South of Tarvisio, Alpi Giulie are the Italian Alps' easternmost massif: they offer attractive scenery with white limestone peaks dominating huge forests, and directly overlook the Yugoslav border. Their main summits are Jôf di Montasio (2,753 m), Jôf Fuart (2,666 m), Canin (2,587 m) and impressive Mangart (2,666 m), whose northern face is one of the Alps' hardest to climb. The Giulie and the Tarvisio district feel different to the rest of Italy. This is the country's finger extending into Central Europe: the climate, traditions and landscape remind us of that.

THE LONG DISTANCE TRAILS

The so called 'European trails', crossing the continent from north to south, are almost non-existent in Italy. *E2* passes west of Italy, across the French Alps from Geneva to Nice, *E6* descends from Hamburg to Rjeka on the Adriatic sea crossing Germany, Austria and Yugoslavia. *E7*, descending through Switzerland, exists only in theory: in practice it crosses the Lombardy plain on wide motoring roads, making the Como to Genova stretch of absolutely no interest to the hiker.

E5 travels from Bodensee (on the Swiss-German border) to Verona, and is the only one of any real interest. It is also the Eastern Alps' most important long distance trail, leaving the Dolomites' *Alte vie* aside for the moment. It enters Italy at Passo del Rombo, descends to Val Passiria, climbs again to the wide plateaux north of Bolzano, and descends to the capital of the South Tyrol. Then it travels east of Adige valley, crossing the foothills of Catinaccio, on through the Trento valleys to Valsugana, along Pasubio massif and the Lessini hills to Verona.

East of the Dolomites, two important trails follow the Alpi Carniche's main ridge. *Karnischer Hohenweg* travels on the northern (Austrian) side of the border, while *Traversata Carnica* passes south of it, connecting, on the Italian side, Sesto (*Sexten*) to Pontebba and Tarvisio in about 10 days. The two are really 'twin' trails; it is possible to leave one for the other in many places.

INTO VALLE AURINA

Italy's northernmost point boasts the chauvinistic name of Vetta d'Italia, or 'Italy's Peak'. Its rocky but unremarkable 2,911 m summit is not the most interesting one in the beautiful curve of mountains crowing the green and pleasant Valle Aurina. For the native, German-language inhabitants, Vetta d'Italia is *Glockenkar Kofel*, whilst the valley's name is Ahrntal.

The area can easily be reached, both from the Dolomites or from a trip to the Brenner border; the final drive north from Brunico (*Bruneck*) is a very pleasant one, with Gran Pilastro's glaciers overlooking a green valley whose main centre is Campo Tures (*Sand im Taufers*). Valle Aurina itself is the central and northernmost one of the three in which the main one branches off. Westward bound Valle dei Mulini (*Mühlwalder Tal*) leads to Lappago (*Lappach*) and to Gran Pilastro (*Hochpfeiler*) glaciers, whilst the eastern Valle di Riva (*Raintal*) leads to the small Riva di Tures (*Rain im Taufers*) village, and to the Ries massif glaciers. Both flanking valleys have interesting, if harder, walks to offer.

Valle Aurina itself has a nice series of small villages and green lush meadows, well provided with pleasant hotels and pensions. The trail leading to the hut is easy and feasible and very popular with most of the valley's holiday makers. The hike, as a result, is a crowded and popular one, offering a series of small private huts if you need a stop on your way.

How to get there By car, exit from the Brenner motorway at Bressanone, drive to Brunico, and then north to Campo Tures and Valle Aurina itself; Lutago (*Luttach*), S. Martino (*St. Martin*), S. Giovanni (*St. Johann*) and Cadipietra (*Steinhaus*) are the valley's main villages. The road ends after Casere (*Kasern*) at Fonte alla Roccia (1,666 m). If you travel by bus, you can find one to drive you from Brunico to all Valle Aurina' villages. Brunico itself has good rail links to Bolzano, Verona and Rome.

The trail From Fonte della Roccia, the beautiful and clear trail climbs gently along the riverside, passing alternately woods and meadows and reaching Malga della Svolta at 1,842 m. A steeper section leads to Malga Lana (*Lahner Alm*), 1986 m: this is a magnificent old house, commanding an interesting view over the valley's summits.

The path continues crossing a grassy plateau, then starts climbing with a series of regular zigzags. *Rifugio* Brigata Tridentina (*Birnlücken hutte*, 2,440 m) is reached after crossing an interesting small valley. From Fonte alla Roccia allow 2½ hours. A steep 45 minute walk leads to the border ridge, which can be reached at Forcella del Picco, 2,667 m.

From the hut, a longer and very interesting possibility (sleeping in the hut is recommended but not necessary) is to walk west on *Alta via della Vetta d'Italia* (*Lausitzer Weg*) trail for about 1 hour to a junction. On the right, another trail leads to Vetta d'Italia's summit (2,912 m, 1½ hours from the hut), where there is an old ruined hut. On the way back you can reach the 'Alta via' and follow it again to the west, where it meets *rifugio* Vetta d'Italia (2,568 m). A steeper trail descends directly to Fonte alla Roccia; allow 2½ to 3 hours for this descent, 1¾ for a direct descent from Brigata Tridentina to Fonte alla Roccia.

TO PIAVE'S SOURCES AND PERALBA

The River Piave is one of Italy's most important and best known. It marks the Dolomites' eastern border, and flows through the fertile Venetian plains. In the national rhetoric, it became the 'sacred river' because of the strategic role it played, as a defence barrier, during the most difficult (for Italy) part of the First World War. Monuments and war memorials are scattered all along the river.

This atmosphere becomes lighter as the river's source is approached. Sappada valley is a beautiful, lush green cirque, with old wooden mansions reminiscent of both Pusteria and the Austrian Alps. White and beautiful, Peralba, Siera and Rinaldo massifs add the ideal background for many possible walks and expeditions. The atmosphere is more casual and relaxed than in the nearby Dolomites. From Calvi hut – perched in an impressive spot amongst vertical limestone faces – and from Peralba summit, magnificent views can be had of both the Dolomites and Austrian Alps.

Peralba summit itself offers a score of interesting possibilities to the rock climber; the hiker has a choice between the very easy normal route, a simple *via ferrata*, and some scrambling on the southwest ridge. The surrounding summits (Chiadenis, Avanza) have more interesting possibilities for the adventurous hiker. Passo Sesis, a mere half hour from the hut, is a magnificent viewpoint which is reached by following a large mule trail. Everywhere, there are buildings and other war relics. A map is unnecessary but the best one for the area is *Tabacco*'s n. 1, obtainable both at Piave's source and at Calvi.

How to get there Sappada is on the Veneto–Friuli border, and can be approached by road either from Belluno (through Pieve di Cadore) or from Udine, via Tolmezzo. A beautiful road comes from Sesto (*Sexten*) through Monte Croce Comelico pass. From Sappada, one must drive 4 km east to the Cima Sappada pass and turn onto a very steep and very beautiful small road (crowded at weekends) climbing to Sorgenti del Piave. By bus, an easier approach is from the Belluno side. You can also start from Calalzo where the railway ends. From Sappada, try hitch-hiking: the 8 km from Cima Sappada is a long road!

The trail The road winds up the mountain, through a narrow valley, to reach a series of beautiful grassy plateaux and Piave's source. There is a restaurant, and a small monument dedicated to the river's source. A dirt road, not very pleasant to walk on but in beautiful surroundings, climbs towards the *rifugio*. You can avoid the first part of it by taking a small path climbing from the left, starting near the restaurant's car park. In the upper part you have to stick to the road, that passes a quarry and reaches the hut in about 1 hour (2,160 m). The *rifugio* is dominated by the impressive west face of Chiadenis.

A broad trail climbs on scree slopes to Colle Sesis, at 2,312 m, less than ½ an hour from the hut. This is an excellent viewpoint on the Carniche summits farther east, and across the Austrian Gail river valley, on the far side of which Lienzer Dolomiten can be seen. On the left the trail leaves the *via ferrata* start (easy of its kind), climbs through a scree gully to a junction (here it meets up with the Austria trail leading to the summit), and continues zigzagging along the summit ridge. In the last part, war buildings and trenches can still be seen; allow 1½ hours from *rifugio* Calvi.

Descent is quick and easy. If you want to sleep in the hut, you can include in your conquests both Chiadenis (easy but exposed, with some scrambling; 2½ hours return) and Avanza (perfectly easy but longer, 4 hours round trip).

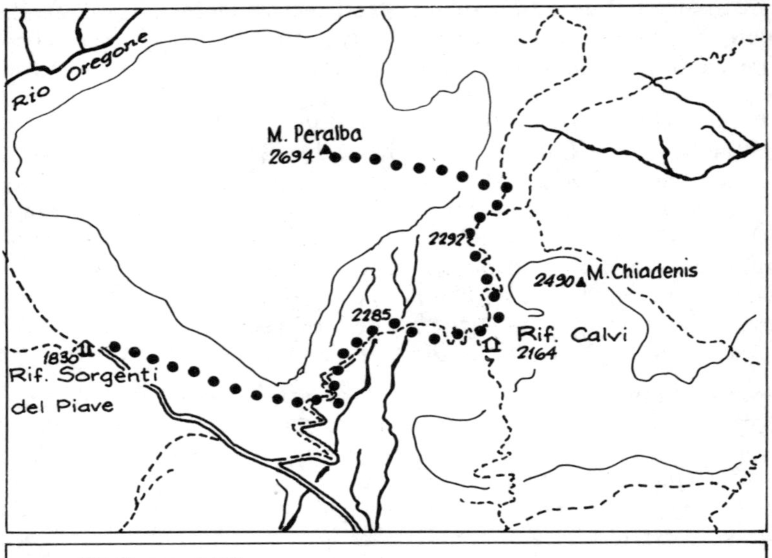

PIAVE - PERALBA
(4 to 6 hrs)

THE FUSINE TRAIL

At Italy's northeastern corner, Tarvisio is a border town; here Italy meets both Yugoslavia and Austria amongst deep pine forests, south of which loom the limestone spires of Alpi Giulie. This is obviously an interesting, if not much used, gateway to the country: visitors will find a quiet atmosphere, reminiscent of Central Europe. Around Tarvisio, as in all the valley leading to it, interesting trails and hikes are abundant. For the geographer's sake, it can be noted that Tarvisio and Fusine are already on the 'far side' of the Alps: their waters flow into Gail river, and thence to the Danube and the Black Sea.

Green in summer, the Tarvisio area is a favourite destination for cross-country skiers; together with nearby Austria's Villach and Yugoslavia's Kranjska Gora, Tarvisio has been proposed as a location for an 'international' version of the 1992 winter Olympics. The proposal has been rejected now, but could obviously be put forward again.

East of Tarvisio, the twin Fusine lakes are a pleasant location for short walks and a rest. Longer suggestions include easy rock ascents towards Ponza Grande and Ponza di Mezzo, and the trail described here; an extremely pleasant and spectacular tour of the Fusine forest, including magnificent views towards the rocky north faces of Mangart and Piccolo Mangart. These are cold, spectacular, and 500 m. Here some of the eastern Alps' most difficult rock routes have been established from the 1950s on. In this area there are no easy border crossings: remember that, while the Austrian border is open to anyone with a regular passport, the Yugoslav border can be crossed only at authorized points: violations by mountaineers and hikers alike are met with official disapproval. Crossing the official border at the established

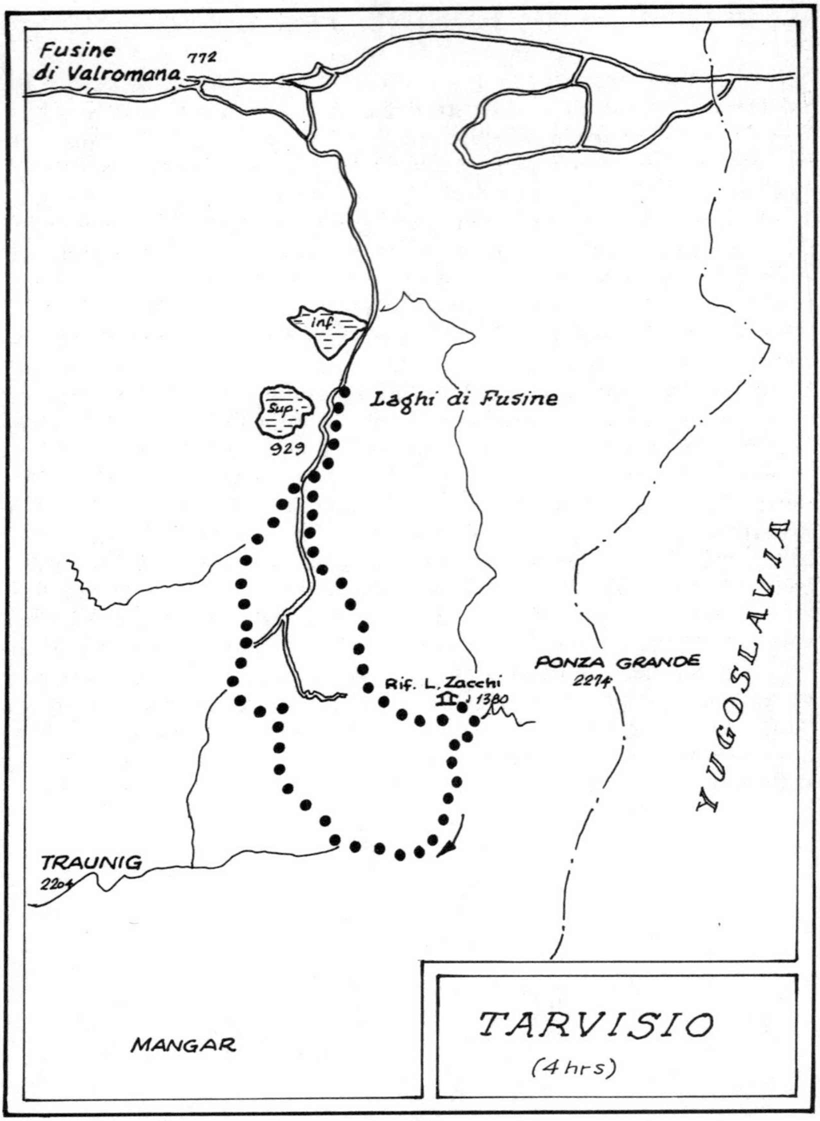

Fusine and Predil checkpoints will allow the walker a series of very beautiful walks into Yugoslavia's Triglav National Park. *Tabacco*'s n. 8 map is the best one of this area.

How to get there A new, modern highway connects Tarvisio with Udine and Venice, and continues to Villach and Vienna. An important international railway travels the same route; Tarvisio is an easy place to reach if you are travelling by public transport. The Fusine lakes are

9 km from Tarvisio on the road to the Yugoslav border: there is no scheduled public transport here.

The trail Coming up from Tarvisio, the road by-passes the lower Fusine lake, ending just east of the upper basin, at 930 m. After a short walk on the lake shore, impressive views can be had of the Mangart and Piccolo Mangart faces.

You continue on a dirt road, entering a magnificent forest of fir trees, following the marked trail to *rifugio* Zacchi. At the first junction keep left, and then turn right at the second one: the path zigzags amongst tall beeches to the hut (1,380 m), a pleasant wooden building which is reached in about 1¼ hours. From the hut's entrance there is a good view towards Mangart.

You start again walking along a descending dirt road, and turn left at the junction with path no. 513: this crosses an ancient moraine, and enters the scree slopes dominated by the faces of Piccolo Mangart and Strugova. The atmosphere is cold and impressive. Later on, you keep right at a further junction (the left hand trail climbs to *bivacco* Nogara) and enter the forest again. The trees are firs again, then beeches: the trail continues descending, quite steeply in places, reaching the hike's starting point by the lakes. From Zacchi, allow 2 hours. If you are not horribly tired, press on and complete a spectacular tour of the upper lake: it takes a further 30 minutes.

Chapter 5
The Dolomites

Dramatic limestone spires, green lush meadows, old wooden houses, crowded huts and trails; this is the popular image of the Dolomites, both Italy's and the Alps' best known mountain range. In the peak of summer, this is probably true, but it is always possible, even then, to find less popular places and valleys. In June, early July, September and October, even the more heavily trodden paths become pleasant again. The views are great all the year round.

The Dolomites are not a political region; in fact they have always been a meeting point for different peoples and cultures. In the north, the Dolomites are on the edge of the German world: politically they belong to the province of Bolzano, Italy's South Tyrol, and in a much smaller part to Austria's Lienz district. In the south, they belong to the provinces of Trento and Belluno and have an Italian culture. Right in the middle, around Sella massif, live the Ladini, a small ethnic group speaking their own language, and having their own traditions and culture.

The geographical division of the area is in four parts. In the west are the *Dolomiti di Brenta*, separated by the Adige river from the chain's main part. The *Western Dolomites* lie between Adige and Isarco in the west, along a line following Val Badia in the north and the Cordevole river valley from Passo di Campolongo to Agordo and Belluno. The *Eastern Dolomites* include the area between this line and the Piave

river. *Dolomiti d'oltre Piave* are the little known chains east of Piave, and are shared between the regions of Veneto and Friuli.

Because of the peculiar limestone structure of the region, the Dolomites are formed by a series of isolated massifs, making a complicated pattern of valleys and ridges. To complicate the geography more, many mountains in the northwestern part of the area have both German and Italian names. Access is easy because the main motorway links Verona to the Austrian border at Brenner. In the eastern part, another motorway links Venice to Vittorio Veneto and good roads continue to Cortina and Auronzo.

Dolomiti di Brenta, the westernmost group, form an isolated massif on the border of the limestone region. It culminates in Cima Tosa (3,173 m) and its best known summit is the elegant Campanile Basso, much appreciated by climbers. Other mountains (Bondone, Paganella) west of Adige are of little importance.

East of Bolzano, are many of the best massifs. Sciliar (2,564 m) overlooking the capital of the South Tyrol, Sassolungo (*Langkofel*, 3,179 m), and the wild Odle-Putia chain in the north, between Funes (*Villnöss*) valley and Badia. Sass Rigais, Odle's highest, is 3,025 m, and Funes valley is well-known as Reinhold Messner's birthplace. A little to the south east is the Sella massif, culminating at 3,151 m in Piz Boe. Around it runs the famous road crossing the Sella, Pordoi, Gardena and Campolongo passes.

Between Bolzano and Val di Fassa lies Catinaccio (*Rosengarten*), culminating at 3,002 m. South of it is Latemar, overlooking the beautiful Lake Carezza. More to the south is the Lagorai massif, a red granite presence in the world of limestone. East of it, Pale di San Martino have their highest summit at Cimon della Pala (3,185 m) and again afford an incredible selection of spires and dramatic faces. North of these, Marmolada has the highest summit of all at 3,342 m, and boasts on its northern slopes the only real glacier of the area.

The Eastern Dolomites begin with Fanes and Conturines overlooking Val Badia and continue to the east with imposing Tofane directly overlooking famous Cortina d'Ampezzo. A little to the east, Croda Rossa (*Hohe Gaisl*, 3,146 m) is one of the least visited groups of all. On the far side of Val di Landro, Tre Cime di Lavaredo (*Drei Zinnen*, 2,999 m) are completely the opposite; their northern view is probably the best-known postcard of all the Dolomites and the paths are unbearably crowded in the peak summer season.

The same does not apply to the mountains immediately to the east and south: Croda dei Toni (*Zwölferkofel*, 3,094 m) Popera (*Hochbrunner*, 3,046 m) and smaller Cadini di Misurina. South of Tofane, the chain forms the smaller Cinque Torri group, elegant Croda da Lago, and the mighty Pelmo (3,168 m) and majestic Civetta (3,220 m), whose north face first climbed by Solleder and Lettenbauer in 1925 is the biggest in all the Dolomites. South of Civetta, a long complicated chain separates the Dolomites' main body from the Veneto plains: these are the *Dolomiti bellunesi* and include the Tamer, Pramper, Schiara and Vette Feltrine groups.

East of Cortina and Valle d'Ampezzo are more isolated massifs of great beauty: Cristallo (3,221 m), Sorapìss (3,205 m), Antelao (3,263 m) and Marmarole (2,961 m). On the far side of the Piave river valley, a long complicated chain is formed by a series of little known massifs: from Sappada to the plains, these are Tudaio, Cridola, Spalti and Monfalconi, imposing Duranno (2,652 m), Messer and Cavallo. In the Spalti chain is Campanile di Val Montanaia, a striking tower which has been described as 'a damned soul's petrified scream'.

Selected itineraries are difficult to suggest in the Dolomites. Interesting trails are everywhere, many of them are outstanding and six main *Alte vie*, north to south long-distance trails, cross the area between Pusteria and the Piave valley. Almost all the paths are clearly marked and heavily used in the peak season; there is little doubt that the Dolomites are a hiker's paradise!

For the hiker approaching the area, the best solution depends on the crowds. Out of the main tourist season (i.e. up to mid-July, and from the last weekend in August onwards) you can hike pleasantly everywhere. Between these dates, after a few crowded hikes, you'll probably want to escape to some quieter area. Most crowded massifs are Brenta, Catinaccio, Sella, Pale di San Martino, Lavaredo and Civetta. Others are safer, and Dolomiti bellunesi and Dolomiti d'oltre Piave can be isolated and wild even in mid-August.

Rifugi are everywhere in the area, and there are many private establishments near to CAI huts. Again, crowds can be a problem and groups are strongly advised to reserve their beds well in advance during the peak season. After the spring snow has melted, hiking is perfectly easy on normal trails, which can also be very exposed in some parts. Remember that some of these can be *vie ferrate* (see Chapter 1 for details) and that dangerous steep snowfields can stay all summer long even on heavily-used trails.

We will shortly describe the best known *alta via* and some shorter expeditions. You can find more information in dozens of guidebooks, both in German or Italian; many more trails can be followed just with the Kompass or Tabacco 1:50,000 maps, that again can be found almost everywhere. Tourist bureaus can also be of help. The main ones are in Bolzano (piazza Walther 22, telephone 0471/ 992111), Trento (corso 3 Novembre 134, telephone 0461/ 980000), Belluno (via R. Psaro 21, telephone 0437/ 22043), but every valley and village has its own. Belluno's tourist office (EPT) has brochures in many languages (including English) describing *Alte vies nos 1* and *2*.

LONG DISTANCE TRAILS

ALTA VIA NUMERO 1

Alta via numero 1 is truly 'number one' amongst Italy's long distance trails. It was one of the very first to be established (around 1965). It is still the best known and one of the most heavily used. Like the other five *alte vie*, it crosses the whole of the Dolomites region north to south; from Lake Braies to Belluno it takes ten days to two full weeks.

If you have less time than that, the *alta via* can be divided into three parts. Part one goes across Fanes, Lagazuoi and Tofane massifs to the edge of the Cortina valley. Part two crosses smaller mountains to the impressive Pelmo and Civetta massifs and to Agordo. Part three continues across the little known Dolomiti bellunesi, to the wild Schiara massif and Belluno.

The trail is marked (a blue triangle with a '1' inserted in it), and is almost always found close to other 'local' red and white marks. Huts are everywhere in the first two parts, so your days can be as long or as short as you like. In the last third, however, they become rarer, and here you are obliged to keep to a fixed schedule. Variations are just too many to be listed in detail. The main path is easy; along the track you can find *vie ferrate* and easy rock scrambles.

Groups of up to four people can try and hike the *alta via* without hut reservations. For this it is advisable to start early in the morning in order to arrive at the next hut as soon as possible. A sleeping bag and a foam mattress are a good idea to make your night in an overcrowded hut less uncomfortable. If you're a large group, either book well in advance, or hike elsewhere; remember that many huts will not accept just a phone call, but will ask for some money in advance to keep your reservation.

The trail is well marked: Kompass or Tabacco 1:50,000 maps are quite adequate to hike with. The complete guidebook is Piero Rossi's *Alta via delle Dolomiti n. 1* (Tamari, last edition 1985).

How to get there You can ride a bus or a train to Monguelfo (*Welsberg*) or Villabassa (*Niederdorf*), and then a bus or a taxi to Lake Braies (*Pragser Wildsee*), 1,495 m, at the *alta via*'s starting point. If you're driving a car, you have the choice of dropping it either in Braies or in Belluno. By public transport, the Belluno–Cortina–Braies trip (130 km) will take almost one full day.

The trail Once in Braies, there you are! Normal timetables allow for a late start so normally *day one* brings you to *rifugio* Biella (3½ hours), leaving time for a hike up nearby Croda del Becco (*Grosser Seekofl*, 2,810 m, 2 hours return).

On *day two* you quickly reach *rifugio* Sennes (2,126 m), then *rifugio* Pederü (1,548 m) and the long, wild valley leading to *rifugio* Fanes, at 2,100 m and 4½ hours from *rifugio* Biella. Nearby is another smaller *rifugio* la Varella (2,040 m).

Day three starts crossing the Jü de Limo pass (here you find Ladini names) then skirt around Alpe di Fanes Grande, and keep right to Forcella da l'Ega (or Passo Tadega, 2,153 m). Keep climbing steeply to Forcella del Lago, and then plunge down a steep scree slope to Lake Lagazuoi (2,185 m) and a well deserved rest. Up again, you reach *rifugio* Monte Lagazuoi, 2,571 m in 5 hours from Fanes.

On *day four*, cross Forcella Travennanzes, then Forcella Bois,

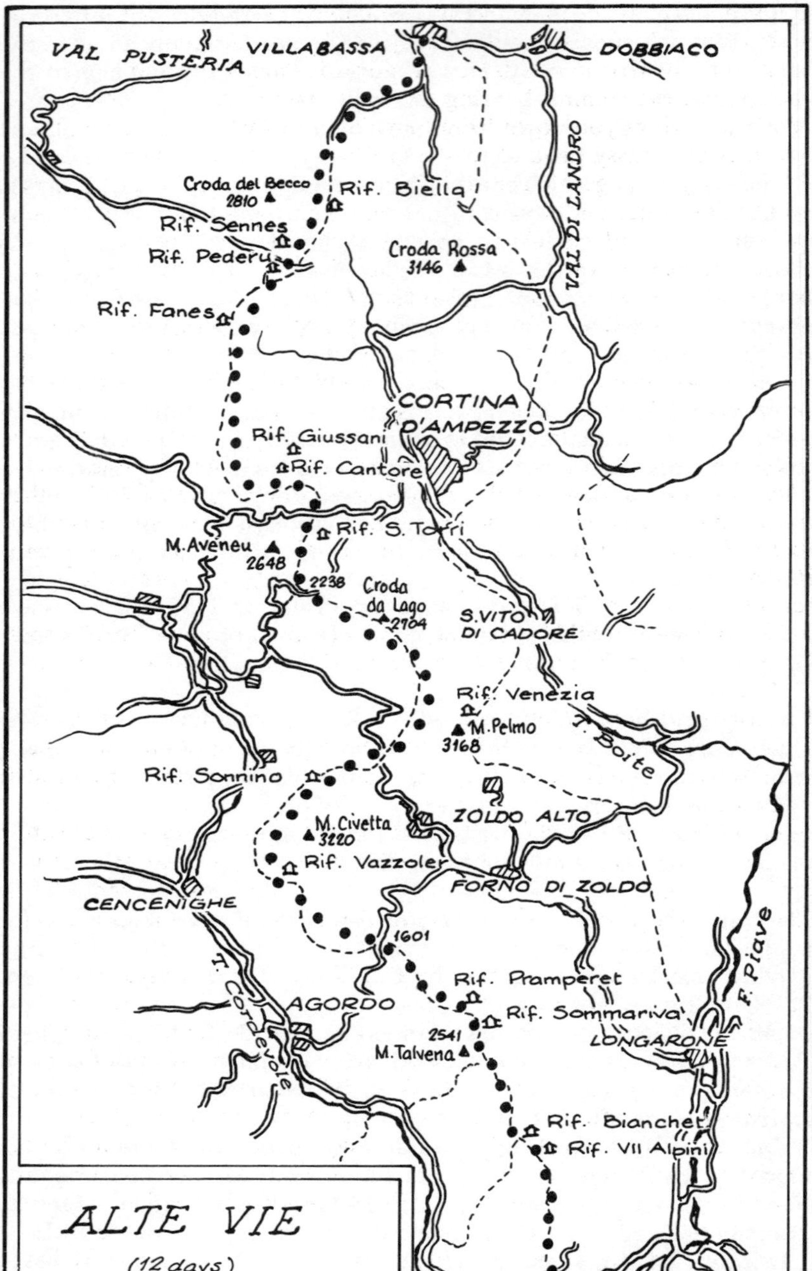
VAL PUSTERIA
VILLABASSA
DOBBIACO
Croda del Becco
2810
Rif. Biella
Rif. Sennes
Rif. Pederu
Croda Rossa
3146
VAL DI LANDRO
Rif. Fanes
CORTINA
D'AMPEZZO
Rif. Giussani
Rif. Cantore
Rif. S. Torri
M. Aveneu
2648
2238
Croda
da Lago
2704
S. VITO
DI CADORE
Rif. Venezia
M. Pelmo
3168
T. Boite
Rif. Sonnino
M. Civetta
3220
ZOLDO ALTO
Rif. Vazzoler
FORNO DI ZOLDO
CENCENIGHE
F. Piave
1601
Rif. Pramperet
T. Cordevole
AGORDO
Rif. Sommariva
2541
M. Talvena
LONGARONE
Rif. Bianchet
Rif. VII Alpini
BELLUNO
ALTE VIE
(12 days)

reaching the foot of Tofane. Nearby Castelletto, a smaller summit, was an Austrian stronghold destroyed with underground mines by Italian troops in 1916. After that, you have a choice of destinations: you can climb Tofana di Roces and then sleep at Giussani or Cantore huts, or speed on to the Cortina–Falzarego road and *rifugio* Nuvolau (2,575 m, 5 hours), on the summit bearing the same name.

Day five brings you down from Nuvolau to a steep rocky gully, then continues on grassy ground to Passo Giau (2,236 m) where there is another *rifugio*. A gentle ascent brings you to Forcella Giau (2,373 m) and a series of ups and downs to Forcella Ambrizzòla (2,277 m). Then you continue to *rifugio* Città di Fiume (4 hours, 1,917 m).

Majestic Pelmo is the start of *day six*. Follow the 'Triòl dei Cavai' ('the Horses' path' in the local dialect). Go down near to Forcella Staulanza (1,800 m), then cross a high plateau to *rifugio* Venezia (1,947 m, 2½ hours). If you want to push on, you need not reach this *rifugio*: from the col before it you can follow the path directly down to Palafavera (1,514 m, 1½ hours), where there is accommodation. Up again, you end a long day at *rifugio* Sonino (2,190 m, 2½ hours). Sunset on the big wall of Civetta is maybe the best sight along the whole trek.

Day seven is easy and level, and has to be walked quietly. Follow the base of the 'biggest face of the Dolomites' to small lake Coldai, and to *rifugio* Tissi (2,280 m, 2 hours). Then pass Col Rean, and descend to *rifugio* Vazzoler (1,725 m, 2 hours) in front of Torre Venezia, Busazza, and Torre Trieste.

Day eight is another short one (you can easily save a day here); cross Forcella del Camp to *rifugio* Carestiato (1,839 m, 3½ hours) at the foot of Moiazza.

Then, on *day nine*, enter the least known part of your route. Descend to Passo Duran, climb to Forcella Moschesin (1,940 m) and then descend slightly to *rifugio* Sommariva al Pramperet (18,57 m). This is a 5 hour day.

On *day ten*, continue along Pramper massif, discovering Van di Città cwm, and then the imposing Schiara massif. A descent leads to a shepherds' hut converted into a bivouac (3 hours from Sommariva), turn right at a junction and descend to *rifugio* Biancha (1,250 m, 2½ hours from the bivouac).

On *day eleven*, follow an easy but very exposed *via ferrata*: climb to the foot of Gusela del Vescovà and a nearby *bivacco* Dalla Bernardina (3 hours), and then descend *via ferrata* Zacchi to *rifugio* VII Alpini (3 hours). Here there are many choices; you can climb to the summit of Schiara (on clear days you can see Venice!), and then descend *ferrata* Zacchi, or jump the descent to *rifugio* Bianchet and cross directly to the Schiara massif which takes a long day, where there is one more *bivacco* (del Marmol). If you don't want any scrambles at all, you can walk from *rifugio* Bianchet to the Belluno–Agordo road and take a bus to town.

If you're sticking to the trail, on *day twelve* walk down to Belluno from *rifugio* VII Alpini. In two hours you reach Case Bortòt, where you can phone for a taxi. In one further hour, you reach Bolzano

Bellunese, where you can board a bus to town (a mere 45 minutes away).

MORE ALTE VIE*: NUMERO 2 TO NUMERO 6*

After the first one's success at the end of the 1960s, *alte vie* began to spread around the Dolomites. Number one is still by far the most popular; it has been calculated that it receives almost the same amount of hikers as all the others. All of them travel north to south, Val Pusteria to Piave. Not all are perfectly marked and some parts offer such difficulties as rock scrambling and *vie ferrate*. All have detailed guidebooks: those to *Alte vie nos 2, 4, 5* and *6* have been published by Tamari, while no. 3 guidebook is published by Ghedina.

Alta via no. 2 is the westernmost of all and goes from Bressanone (Brixena) to Feltre in the Veneto lowlands. It crosses Odle, Puez, Sella, Marmolada (where a short glacier must be negotiated), Pale di San Martino and Vette Feltrine, and takes two weeks. It is also known as *Alta via delle Leggende*, the Legends' Trail.

A little to the east, *Alta via no. 3* has the nickname of *Alta via dei Camosci*, the Chamois' Trail. It starts in Villabassa (*Niederdorf*), and travels south through Croda Rossa, around Cortina to Sorapìss, then to Bosconero, ending in Longarone. Some parts of the trail are steep and exposed and signposting and marking need to be improved at the time of writing. It takes ten days.

East again, *Alta via no. 4* and *no. 5* have an important common feature, and are dedicated respectively to Paul Grohmann (a famous Austrian climber of the late nineteenth century) and to the famous painter Tiziano (Titian), who was born in Pieve di Cadore, where both trails end. *No. 4* starts in San Candido (*Inmichen*), crosses the famous Tre Cime massif, then Cadini di Misurina by a short *via ferrata*, and then travels south across Sorapìss and Antelao massifs, with long difficult stretches on exposed trails.

A little to the east, *Alta via no. 5* starts in Sesto (*Sexten*), zigzags across Croda dei Toni (*Zwölferkofel*) and Popera (*Hochbrunner Scheid*) massifs, then crosses Val d'Ansies to the beautiful Marmarole chain. At *rifugio* San Marco, between Soraìss and Anteloa, it reaches *no. 4*. Both require ten days.

Easternmost of all, *Alta via no. 6* is *Alta via dei Silenzi*, the Silent Trail. It starts near Sappada, at the Piave's source and then travels east of it, across a series of beautiful and little known massifs marking the border between Veneto and Friuli regions. These are Tudaio, Cridola, Spalti-Monfalconi, Duranno and Cavallo. The last stretch crosses Cansiglio plateau, to end in Vittorio Veneto. It takes two weeks.

THE BRENTA TOUR

West of the deep-cut Adige valley, the Dolomiti di Brenta are a world apart from the rest of the Dolomites. In front of them lies the glaciated plateaux of Adamello and Presanella, and Ortles and Cevedale massifs can also be seen. Brenta's perfect rock formation makes the area a paradise for the climber and the group also boasts the famous *Via delle Bocchette*, an easy, but extremely exposed *via ferrata* crossing a series of tiny incut ledges.

At 3,137 m Cima Tosa is the highest summit of all, and forms, with nearby Crosson, a huge wall of grey rock. To the north, Cima Brenta (3,150 m) is the group's second highest, with a small glacier descending towards *rigugio* Tuckett. Further to the north, is a beautiful, less dramatic but very interesting chain, and east of it a deep valley where the famous Lake Tovel likes. This is by far the least travelled part of Brenta, and offers quiet trails even during the peak of summer.

Between Tosa and Cima Brenta are the best known summits: Campanile Basso is a perfect, square-shaped tower 400 m high (summit's height is 2,877 m) and nearby Campanile Alto (2,937 m) is slightly less imposing. To the south, the deep valley descending to the shores of Lake Molveno is dominated by 1000 m Croz dell'Altissimo southwestern wall.

The best access to the group is from Madonna di Campiglio, a modern ski resort west of the area. From there, you have a wide choice of trails, with the possibility of alternating Brenta's limestone atmosphere with Adamello granite valleys: Val di Genova is the best known and most beautiful of these. In the peak of summer, crowds can be a real problem; the tour described here, in the central part of the massif, should not be hiked during July and August weekends. If you must hike then reserve your bed in advance, or reach the huts very early in the day!

How to get there To Madonna di Campiglio, there are direct buses from Trento (and in summer from Milan as well). Grostè cablecar starts right from the village.

The trail The cablecar will take you up to 2,437 m, on the massif main ridge, a wonderful viewpoint overlooking the deep valley descending to Lake Tovel. To the east, you will see most of the Dolomites. To the west, there are the Adamello glaciers and many more summits. Stelvio National Park can also be seen. A little lower, near to the cablecar, is *rifugio* Graffer, which can be used for overnight sleeping. The normal path descends to the south across a stony plateau.

You turn around a series of complicated spurs and reach *rifugio* Tuckett and nearby *rifugio* Sella, dominated by the small and impressive Punte di Campiglio. From here take the path veering left (another direct one descends to Madonna di Campiglio), and then turning left to Sella del Fridolin (not marked on maps), after which you descend to the main path to *rifugio* Brentei. This is at 2,120 m, and is a main turning point of the area. Views on Cima Tosa and Crozzon big walls are incredible, the hut staff is friendly, and this is probably the best place to spend a night. From Grostè, you will need 3 to 4 hours.

From Brentei, you continue along the main valley, passing under-

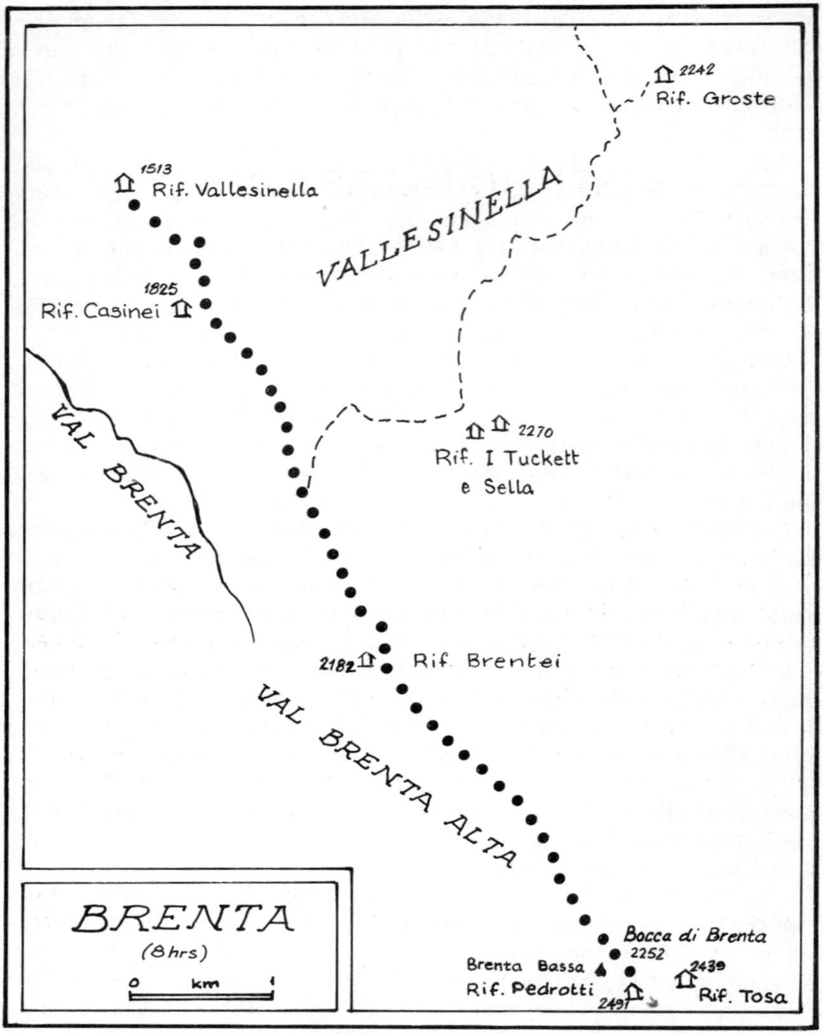

neath Campanile Basso, and then climbing up a series of snow slopes to Bocca di Brenta, at 2,552 m. Immediately after the col are *rifugio* Tosa and *rifugio* Pedrotti, situated on a series of broad scree terraces and commanding an exceptional view towards the east and the south.

If you have a car in Madonna di Campiglio, retrace your steps to Brentei (3 hours round trip to Tosa and Pedrotti), and then follow the main path down the valley, to *rifugio* Casinei and Vallesinella, which is reached by a dirt road from Madonna di Campiglio.

If you are travelling by bus, your best option is to descend to *rifugio* Selvata, *rifugio* Croz dell'Altissimo, Valle delle Seghe and Molveno.

The descend is steep and long (Molveno is at 864 m), but extremely beautiful. Croz dell'Altissimo dominates the valley, and Lake Molveno, at the end, is a pleasant surprise. About 3½ hours is needed for a leisurely descent. After which, there are frequent buses to Trento.

SENTIERO DELLE ODLE

Right on the northwestern corner of the Dolomites, near to the Isarco river valley and to the Bolzano–Brennero *autostrada*, Val di Funes (the German name is *Villnöss*) is one of the most interesting in the whole chain. South of it, towards the sky, the Odle chain is a wild series of steep limestone teeth. Lower down, the valley has magnificent forests, included in an important Park established in 1979 by Bolzano' provincial government.

Lower still, the villages – St. Peter, St. Magdalena – are two of the very best examples of the old Tyrol villages, with wooden houses, churches with pointed spires, and a leisurely atmosphere where you can relax for a day or a month. Germans and Austrians make up the vast majority of hikers visiting the place.

Val di Funes has jumped to international fame because of her famous son, Reinhold Messner, who has started his astonishing climbing career on the Odle's faces. In his articles and books, Reinhold has talked a lot about 'his' valley and 'his' summits. Really, they do deserve a visit. Sentiero delle Odle (*Adolf Munkel weg* for German hikers) is one of the best level paths in the whole Dolomites. It can be walked in one day, or included in a two day tour with an overnight stop at *rifugio* Genova. Near this passes *Alta via no. 2*, whilst the Herrensteige trails on the north side of the valley offer more opportunities to those who want to stay more than one day.

How to get there By car, from Chiusa-Klausen exit of the Bolzano–Brennero motorway, you follow the valley's road to St. Peter, St. Magdalena and to the roadhead at Zanseralm, at the entrance of the Park. By bus, you can start from Bolzano. From St. Peter and St. Magdalena, where there are hotels and pensions, a local bus continues to Zanseralm in the morning.

The trail From the car park (1,680 m), you pass near Sass Rigais hotel, and start climbing on a grassy path on the left of a stream, reaching a dirt road near to a junction. You turn right and immediately after a bridge, turn left to the start of Sentiero delle Odle, a long level traverse between the forest and the steep scree slopes leading to the foot of the Odle. The going is flat and the scenery just fantastic. (If, instead of turning right before Sentiero delle Odle you turn left, you can reach Malga Gampen and then *rifugio* Genova in 1 hour.)

The path is perfectly easy to find and to follow, and goes westward in a series of ups and downs, giving perfect views of Furchetta, Sass Rigais, Odla di Valcussa, Piccola and Grande Fermeda. On the right,

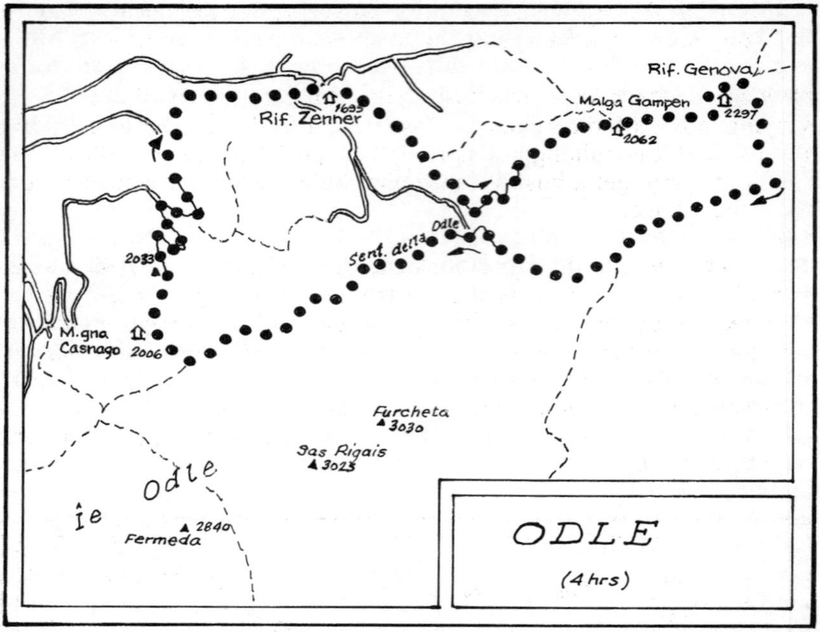

two short variations can bring you to Malga Glatsch and Malga Casnago, where it is possible to stop and eat at simple restaurants. After a last ascent, the path reaches Malga Brogles, on a beautiful plateau, and at the end of 'Sentiero delle Odle' proper. You're at 2,045 m: hiking time is 2½ hours from Zanseralm, a little more than 4 hours including the ascent to *rifugio* Genova and return.

From Brogles, you retrace your steps and then turn left onto another path in the forest, descending directly to the valley floor. You continue along a dirt road and then turn right onto another road leading to Zanseralm, your starting point. This descent requires 2 hours.

VIEL DAL PAN

Between the rocky Sella group and the majestic Marmolada's ice dome, this is another of the Dolomites' best known and more heavily used trails. Known by German language hikers as *Bindelweg*, after the German Alpine Club's president who organized its restoration in the first years of the century, the path was originally a corn smugglers' way between Venice and the Tyrol. *Viel dal pan* means 'trail of bread' in the Venetian dialect.

Viel dal Pan is a perfectly easy path, level at the beginning and then descending to the Fedaia lake shores, in front of the great Marmolada glaciers. It is included in *Alta via no. 2* and the original tour is much reduced by the new Passo Pordoi cablecar, which curtails it to a half-day outing, with some of the most beautiful in the Alps.

How to get there Canazei lies at the top of Valle di Fassa, at the starting point of the roads to Passo Sella and Val Gardena, Passo Pordoi and Livinallongo, Passo Fedaia and Cordevole valley. The easiest place to get a bus to Canazei is Trento. Pordoi's cablecar starts from the village.

The trail Once out of the cablecar, at 2,382 m on Col dei Rossi summit you start towards the northeast, on the path reaching the original Viel dal Pan that starts at Passo Pordoi itself. On the main trail turn right and start a long, beautiful traverse on steep grassy slopes, where the trail is always very wide and safe.

Going on, you get nearer and nearer to the Gran Vernel rocky pyramid and to Marmolada glacier, reaching a small *rifugio* Viel del

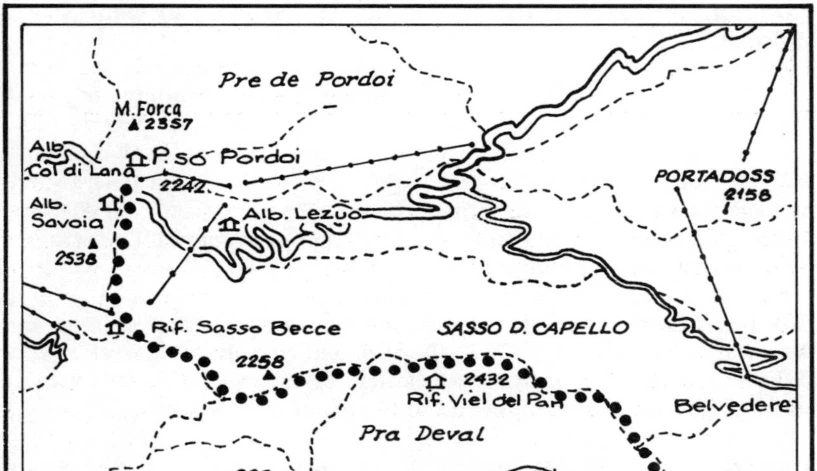

VIEL DEL PAN
(3 to 4 hrs)

Pan, a magnificent place to stop for a rest and a look at the scenery. From the hut's 2,432 m, continue along your level traverse for a while, then slant right and descend along a grassy valley to the lakeshore of Fedaia, near *rifugio* Castiglioni. The walk itself does not require more than 3½ hours. From *rifugio* Castiglioni, the best chance is to hitch a ride to Canazei. You can also walk the old path down the valley (3 hours from Castiglioni to Canazei), or sleep here and continue your explorations next day, towards the Marmolada glacier.

ACROSS VAL CIVETTA

Val Civetta is not a valley, as the name seems to suggest, and not even an amphitheatre, or a cwm. It is a terrace, perched on the side of the 'wall of the walls', as the north face of Civetta has been called by more than one author – series of meadows with large stony slopes, dominated by a huge wall culminating in Punta Civetta, 3,320 m. By opening with a severe climb on the face, Solleder and Lettenbauer accomplished what is normally seen as 'the first grade six climb' in the Dolomites.

Seen from the hiker's point of view, the mighty walls of Civetta are one of the best sights anywhere in the Alps. To be thoroughly enjoyed, they should be seen at sunset from *rifugio* Sonino, near the tiny Lake Coldai that mirrors the face's changes in colours from brown to dark red. Sleeping at the *rifugio* (where *Alta via no. 1* passes) is a good intermediate stop on the complete tour across Val Civetta. At the very bottom Lake Alleghe is a fresh, cool and nice starting point, where it is good to rest for a day or more.

How to get there Alleghe is on the main road connecting Belluno and Agordo to the Fedaia, Giau, Pordoi and Falzarego passes. From Belluno, buses are frequent and the trip takes less than one hour. By car, Alleghe is situated right in the centre of the Dolomites.

The trail From Alleghe, at 983 m, you have to walk to the houses of Fontanive, and then up a well marked trail, to Lander plateau, through a series of pastures and meadows, and then to Forcella di Alleghe a large grassy col at 1,820 m and 2½ hours from town. Leave another path descending on the opposite side towards Pecol and climb a steep path on the right, reaching *rifugio* Sonino, at 2,135 m and 1 hour from Forcella d'Alleghe. Lake Coldai is a few minutes away. This is the best place to spend the night.

Passing near the lake, continue into Val Civetta, dominated by the walls of the mountain. At the end, climb to Forcella di Col Rean and turn right to *rifugio* Tissi, at 2,250 m and 2 hours from Sonino. Views are great again, and open now towards the group of huge limestone towers south of the Civetta main chain; Torre Venezia Busazza, Torre Trieste.

From Col Rean, the trail descends through a wide grassy valley, then

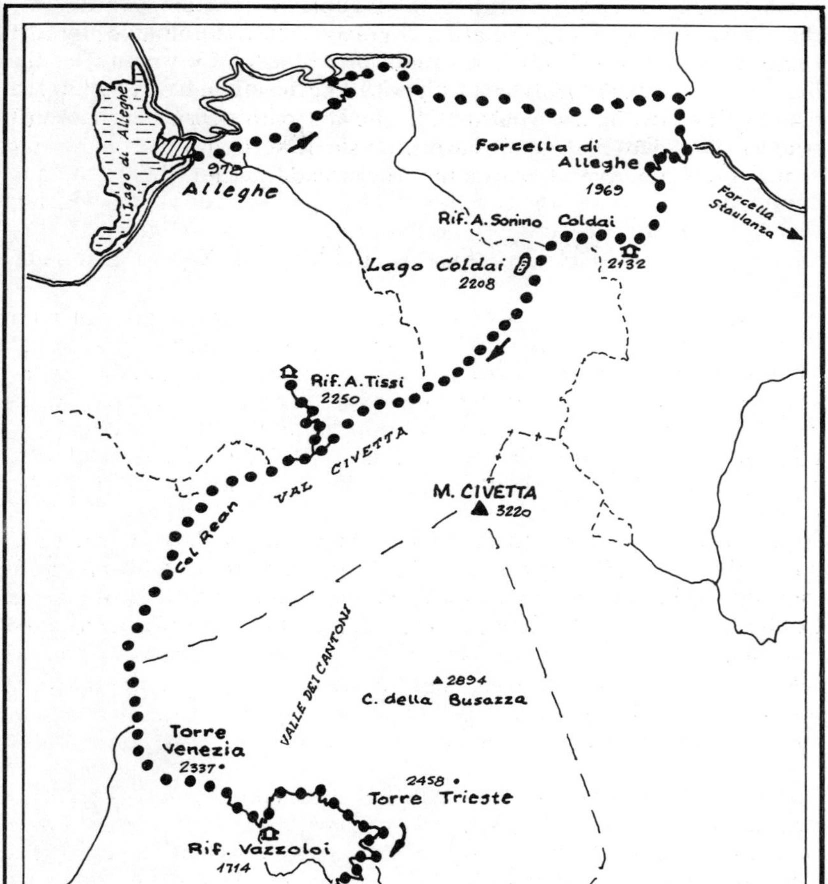
Lago di Alleghe
978
Alleghe
Forcella di Alleghe
1969
Forcella Staulanza
Rif. A. Sonino Coldai
2132
Lago Coldai
2208
Rif. A. Tissi
2250
VAL CIVETTA
Col Rean
M. CIVETTA
3220
VALLE DEI CANTONI
2894
C. della Busazza
Torre Venezia
2337
2458
Torre Trieste
Rif. Vazzoloi
1714
VALLE CORPASSA
La Moiazza
Listolade
VAL CIVETTA
(6 hrs)

reaches a group of stables, and becomes a dirt road leading to *rifugio* Vazzoler, at 1,725 m, occupying a magnificent position overlooking the steep valley descending to Listolade, and dominated by the thousand metre walls of Busazza and Torre Trieste. Continue after the hut, along the road which descends with a series of large zigzags in the valley, and leaving on your left *Alta via no. 1* continuing towards *rifugio* Carestiato and Passo Duran.

The road reaches a restaurant at the bottom of the cwm, and continues through a gorge towards the Cordevole river valley, which is reached at Listolade, about 15 km south of Alleghe. *Rifugio* Tissi to *rifugio* Vazzoler takes less than two hours, Vazzoler to Listolade, almost three.

Chapter 6

Pianura Padana

Wide and almost completely flat, Pianura Padana, the Po river plain, stretches from the Western Alps to the Adriatic Sea, forming the only really lowland area in a country of mountains and hills. It is the most heavily populated area of the country, the region with the richest agriculture and the biggest industries. From Turin and Milan to Verona, Padova, Parma and Bologna, many of the country's most important cities are here.

Quite obviously, this is not a very interesting area as far as the walker is concerned. Cultivated almost everywhere, criss-crossed by one of Europe's densest road and rail networks, the plain is very cold in winter and very hot in summer. The big cities, then, are never far from the Alps or the Apennine mountains and foothills. From Milan, it is usual to go walking in the Valtellina high valleys or in the smaller hills surrounding Lakes Como and Maggiore. Hikers based in Turin have a wide choice of walks in their own western Alpine valleys. From Venice and Verona, the Dolomites are near at hand; from Bologna, the Apennines are just out of town.

However, the large plain does have many things to offer. Many small towns and villages have historical ruins and buildings and old and beautiful *cascine*. The large farms typical of the area are scattered amongst the maize fields and the pastures. Quiet dirt roads follow many of the rivers' banks, providing interesting cycling routes and some short, pleasant walks.

The area's many wildlife sanctuaries and refuges abound near the rivers. Small but dense riverside forests offer nesting and breeding places for herons, and both the Piedmont and Lombardy regions have established networks of wildlife sanctuaries and protected areas. The River Ticino marks the regional border and is protected by the country's best lowland natural park, less than one hour's drive from Milan. West of it, more interesting parks have been established along Piedmont's smaller rivers, Tanaro and Sesia being the most important ones.

East of Milan, another large-scale park is being planned on the River Adda, which flows from Lake Como to the Po. More wildlife sanctuaries have been established on Oglio and Mincio, while the rivers crossing the Venetian plain directly to the sea (Adige, Piave, Brenta, Tagliamento) are generally less protected and flow through heavily populated areas.

Furthest to the east, one area ranks amongst the country's finest for the birdwatcher and the general nature enthusiast. It is the Po delta, occupying a huge area between Venice and Ravenna, criss-crossed by a complicated pattern of river tributaries, canals and lagoons. A national park is planned (as are many places in Italy!). But some smaller areas are protected already, and offer the birdwatcher excellent opportunities. The best ways of getting around here are by bicycle and boat. Away from the central part of the delta, some interesting hikes can also be had.

There are no long-distance trails in the area: the Milano–Genova part of E5 'European trail' starting from Bodensee is a 'theoretical' way mainly following surfaced roads, of no interest whatsoever – the *via del Ticino* will be dealt with below.

TICINO WALKS

Established in 1974, Lombardy's *Parco del Ticino* extends from Lago Maggiore to the Po, a 70 km stretch of territory marking the regional border with Piedmont for almost half its length. Another park has recently been established on the Ticino river's western bank: to the north west, on clear days, Monte Rosa's snowy summits can be seen, creating an impressive contrast with the lowland's maize and rice fields.

Apart from the urban areas, Ticino park is most effectively described as a wide area where general environmental rules (i.e. anti-pollution laws) are specially enforced, and where a series of smaller nature reserves are given special protection. These offer many interesting, if short, walks. The idea of a 'Ticino long-distance path' travelling all the way along the river still has a long way to go: it could become one of Italy's finest, certainly one of the most original ones.

We will give essential information about some of the possible walks. Let's remember that summer is not the best time of the year to hike there (mosquitoes are the only prevailing wildlife), and a pair of rubber boots could be useful companions on most occasions. Winter is cold, but it can offer unusual and very beautiful landscapes, whilst the best periods are around late autumn and late spring.

The park's headquarters and main information centre are in Magenta (phone 02/ 9797063), whilst *A piedi in Lombardia /I* (ITER) guidebook has some information about the area.

How to get there Immediately west of Milan, the Ticino area can be approached in many easy ways by public transport and by road. Novara is the best starting point for visiting the Piedmont bank of the river, whilst Vigevano and Pavia (both very interesting in themselves) make a good base for visiting the lower part of the Riva Po. From Milan, railways run to Sesto Calende, Somma Lombardo, Turbigo, Galliate, Magenta, Abbiategrasso, Vigevano and Pavia. From Novara, one more railway travels north on Ticino's west bank, whilst all smaller towns can be reached by bus from either Milan, Pavia or Novara.

Castelnovate walk Immediately west of Malpensa International Airport, is one of the Ticino's largest bends. The old village of Castelnovate is the starting point for a pleasant short walk: to drive there from Milan follow Malpensa highway to the airport, then pass near Caproni aviation museum (interesting) and drive through Vizzola Ticino. Vizzola can be reached by bus from Busto Arsizio.

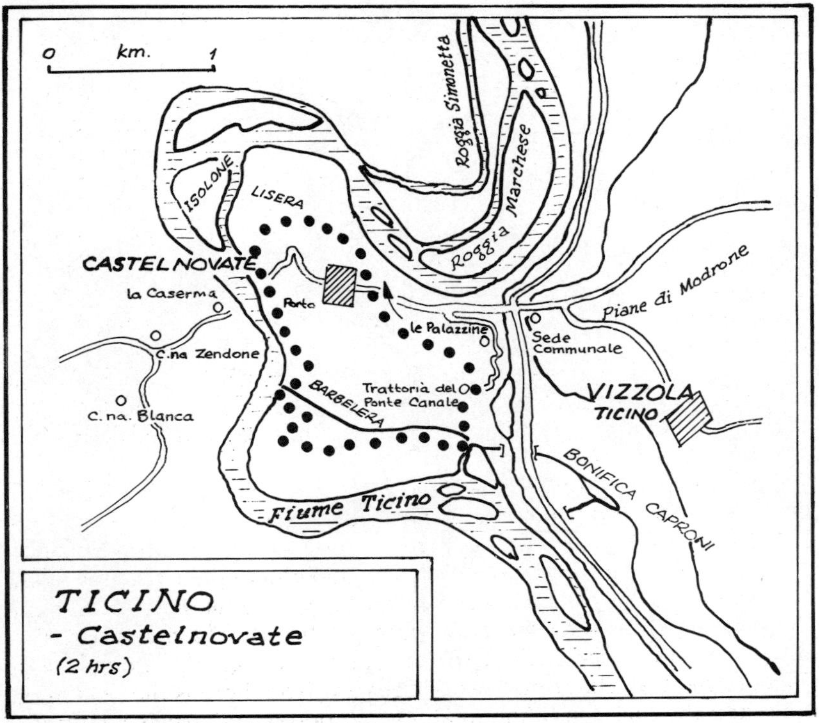

BWI-F

From Castelnovate, follow the dirt road descending north to the river: the loop starts and ends near to a small religious statue. At the junction you turn left, crossing a small wood and emerging near to the river: on your right, you can descend to one of Ticino's best beaches. Back on the same dirt road, continue as far as a surfaced road near to an old ferry's departure point, cross it, and continue south, keeping on the right hand road for about 1 km. When the road turns left towards an industrial estate, continue along a smaller path and cross another canal, the Roggia Molinara.

After crossing this, follow a trail on your right, which eventually becomes a dirt road. Keep right at the first junction, then left at the following two. A pleasant walk along the canal will lead to a crossing and to a nearby restaurant. A short climb is needed to reach Castelnovate. The walk takes 1½ to 2 hours.

Zelata to Bereguardo A few miles north of Pavia, Bereguardo's bridge lies right in the middle of the park's most interesting and most visited area. The Zelata to Bereguardo walk is a very pleasant one, whilst the beach area near to the bridge becomes quite crowded in summer. By car, you can start from either point. The bus starts from

Paradise Lily

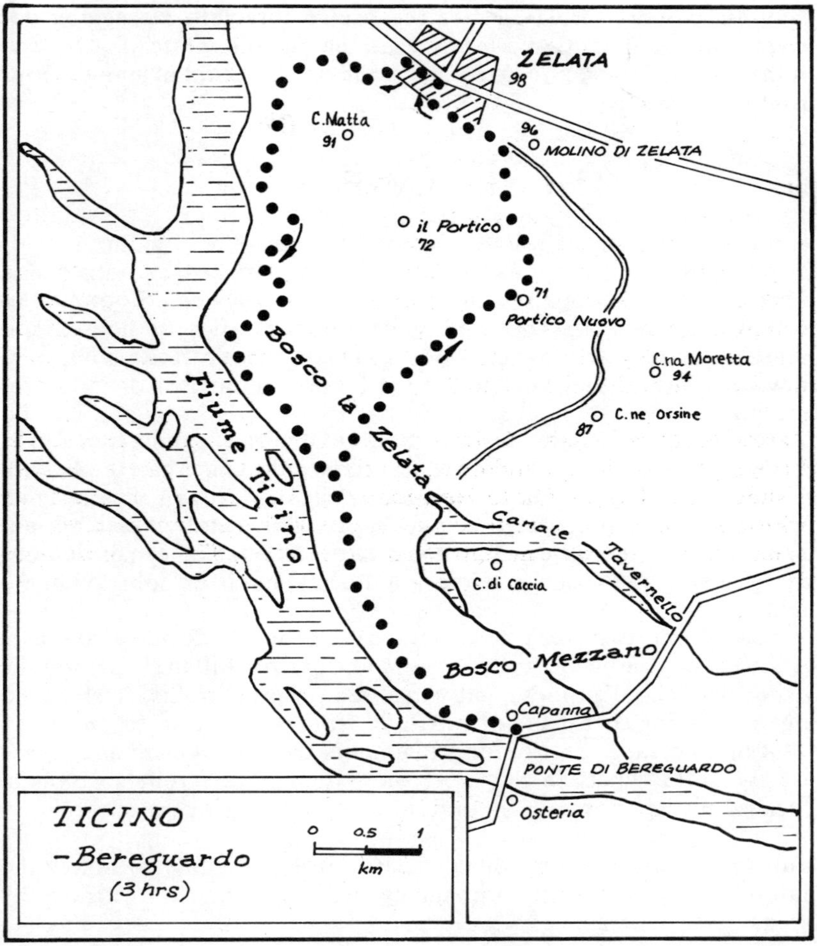

Pavia and continues directly to Bereguardo; the walk to Zelata on the surfaced road is pleasant and requires less than 30 minutes.

Zelata itself is a charming little town. You cross it, and start walking westwards, towards the river. After 200 m turn left, onto a smaller dirt road, descending to the Ticino's banks. These are reached near to a flat area where many birds can be spotted; before reaching the fence walk left on a smaller path, cross a small wood and continue along the river bank. After about ½ an hour (1 hour from Zelata) you come to a junction.

To reach Bereguardo bridge you must keep on the right hand trail; it continues in pleasant surroundings, with no possibility of making a mistake and reaches the bridge in about 45 minutes. If you have to walk back to Zelata, it is a good idea to turn right at the junction, passing a gate and then the Tavernello canal, which is crossed by a beautiful wooden bridge. After the bridge turn left, zigzagging between cultivated fields and farms. Pass the old and interesting Molino (mill) della Zelata before arriving at your starting point in about 1 hour from the junction.

THE GROANE WALK

A few miles north of Milan, Groane Park is quite a feature: it includes woods and marshes of great interest and beauty right inside what is one of Europe's largest urban areas. Between Saronno and Rho to the west and the almost continuous series of houses and buildings on the Milano–Seveso–Como highway, it offers a glimpse of how this part of the country looked before the arrival of industrial growth.

Groane Park includes several different kinds of landscape. Of its 3,200 hectares, about 500 consist of woods: oaks, pines and birches are the most important native species. *Brughiera*, open heath land, occupies the greater part of the park's area: it is scattered with ancient quarries and brick furnaces. A dense network of small canals demonstrates how long the struggle to drain the land has been going on in the area.

Apart from its historical importance, Groane Park has a role as a visiting centre, it being only a 30 minute trip from Milan. It is normally visited by school groups, and can offer pleasant walks, if short, to anyone staying in Milan for anything from a few days to one year, wanting to escape the city for a few hours. *Seveso*, *Bollate* and *Cantù* are the IGM sheets to the area: they are not very reliable though, because of the enormous amount of new buildings in the area.

How to get there From Milan's centre, it is quite easy to follow the Saronno–Varese road to Garbagnate. It is much quicker to travel by train.

The trail From Garbagnate's centre, start walking along the road to Cesate. Turn right at Via dei Tigli, follow it to the end and climb a few steps into a small pine and oak wood. Walk through it towards a concrete pillar, cross a small canal by a wooden bridge and turn right on a trail to reach a pine with a large white paint mark.

Turn left here, enter another small wood, and follow a dirt road to the right. Near to a fence, turn left following more marks, pass by an abandoned quarry and reach a house. Here you have to leave the trail, turn left and then right onto another trail, across a heath area and then into the wood again. Turn right on another trail, then left, and cross over the surfaced road. The trail continues a little to the right, and then enters a beautiful oak forest with fern undergrowth; pass through a first clearing and turn left at a second one, reaching the start of a *sentiero naturalistico*, a short nature trail.

Follow this, continue straight on after a small fountain, and carry on

keeping left at all the junctions. The best protected area ends here. Reaching the surfaced road, turn right, then left on the Via Trento, and then take the road to Senago for a further 400 m to the start of a trail: follow this into an interesting pine wood, exit close to a quarry and turn left amongst clay mounds. When these end, cross another short pine area to reach the starting part of the trail, which is followed to Garbagnate. The whole tour requires 2 hours.

BOSCO DELLA MESOLA

As I said before, the Po delta proper is a magnificent area, but not an ideal one for the walker. From Argenta and Comacchio, the best wildlife sanctuaries (Valli di Campotto, Valli di Comacchio) can be reached by car and afford only very short walks. Nearer to the open sea, Bosco della Mesola is a pleasant area for a walk through beautiful vegetation, in a forest where deer are very easily seen. This is strictly a weekend walk; the area is a nature reserve and can be visited on Saturdays and Sundays only.

Although the forest is old, it is mainly a man-made one. Its creators were probably the Etruscans: their city of Spina was a few miles away to the west, and the lack of wood in the area has been a problem for every ruler of the area since then. The Mesola forest was cited by Dante, Ariosto and Byron: the Estensi rulers of the area were the forest's best friends and developers. The area was ideal for hunting.

Later on, Mesola was used as a source for industrial wood: it was heavily logged up to this century, when it was established as a nature reserve. Today the forest is composed mainly of oak, ash and ilex (holly), whilst the area facing the sea consists of tall maritime pines. The walk is pleasant, and absolutely level: you can also enjoy Mesola in a different way, by renting a bike.

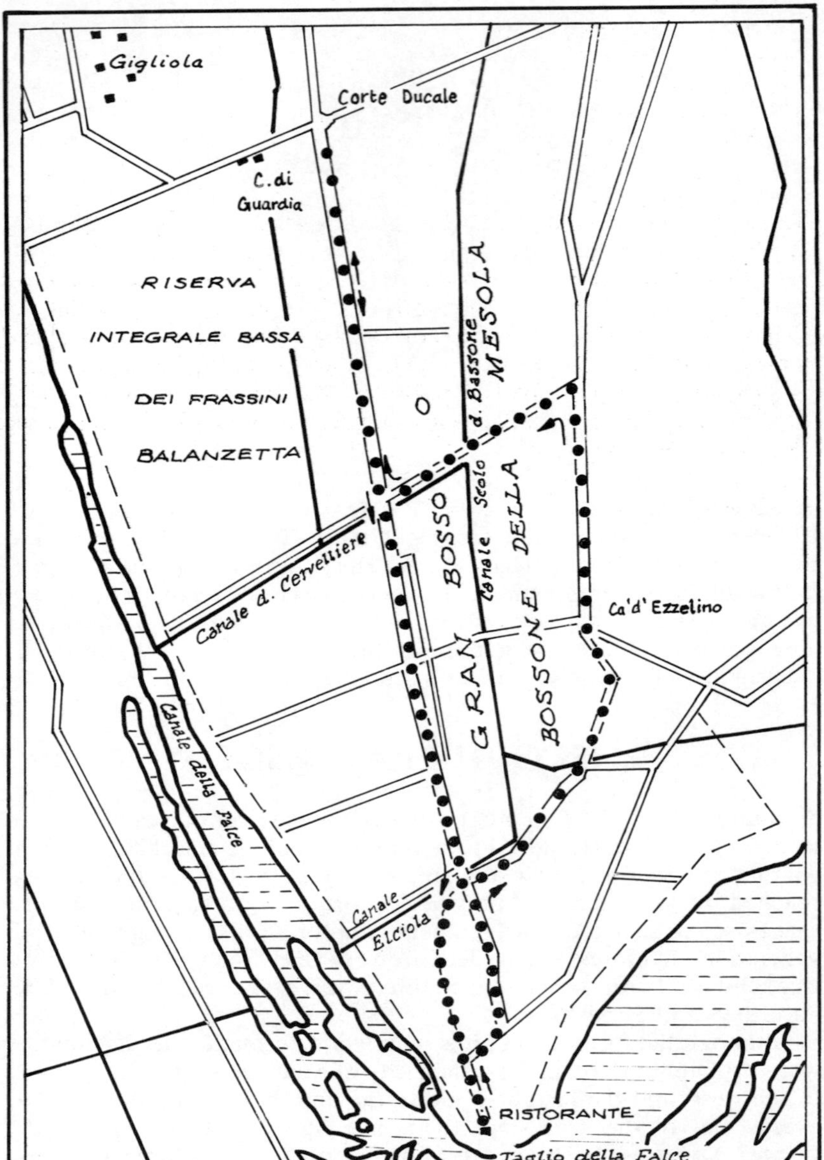
Gigliola
Corte Ducale
C. di Guardia
RISERVA INTEGRALE BASSA DEI FRASSINI BALANZETTA
MESOLA
d. Bassone
Scolo
BOSSO
GRAN
BOSSONE
DELLA
Canale
Canale d. Cervelliere
Ca'd' Ezzelino
Canale della Falce
Canale Elciola
RISTORANTE
Taglio della Falce
BOSCO MESOLA
(2 to 3 hrs)
0 km 1

How to get there Access to Mesola is from the Venice–Ravenna road, the *via Romea* used by eastern European pilgrims travelling to Rome. From Mesola drive a further 2 km south, and then 2 km to Bosco Mesola village. The entrance to the forest is 2 km further to the south. There are buses here to Bosco Mesola but not to the forest itself. Another road starts from the magnificent abbey of Pomposa, one of the area's most striking medieval monuments.

The trail Into the Mesola forest, a series of dirt roads are open both to the walker and to the cyclist. (You can rent a bike right at the forest's entrance.) Start walking straight for a few hundred metres, then turn right at the first junction; head towards the sea, which you can reach in about 1½ hours on foot. At the end of the track is the small Taglio della Falce restaurant, but direct access to the beach from here is prohibited. Almost half way along, you will pass near to a large fence: going left on smaller tracks is the best way to the area where deer are most abundant.

Chapter 7

The Tyrrhenian Riviera

Italy is a land of many seas, and each one has many stories to tell. The Adriatic has seen Venice's power, long struggles against Turks advancing from the South, wars between newborn Italy and the Austrian Empire. The Ionian sea is the one Greek settlers sailed, to found Naples, Syracuse and many more cities scattered along the peninsula's coasts.

The Tyrrhenian sea received its name from the people the ancient Greeks called *Tyrrhenoi*, and we now know as Etruscans. They reigned over the mainland of Tuscany and Latium (and for a shorter while, of Campania too) and they had Sardinia in their hands for almost a hundred years. Nowadays, the Tyrrhenian coast is Italy's longest, stretching from the French border at Ventimiglia to Reggio Calabria and Messina. Many places on this coast – from Portofino to Amalfi – are amongst the best-known areas of Italy, appreciated by foreigners from all parts of the world.

The Tyrrhenian coastal beauty was wonderful, and it still is in some parts of the coastline. But Italy is an overpopulated country, building industry has always had strong links with power, and concern for the environment has been almost always very close to zero. As a result, a trip to this part of the country can be an interesting adventure only if you choose carefully when and where to go. Summer weekends can be more than heavily crowded almost everywhere, whilst winter winds

Portofino

bring solitude and atmosphere to many places scattered between Liguria and the South.

For walkers, as for nature enthusiasts, only a few places have been left intact. Northwest to southeast these are the Portofino promontory and the Cinque Terre coast, in Liguria, Populonia, and Punta Ala and the promontories between Livorno and Grosseto, Uccellina and Argentario south of this town. South of Rome, Circeo is another impressive sight. The coast of Naples and Campania will be included in this chapter.

THE LONG TRAILS

How to organize a long walk on the Tyrrhenian coastline? The choice is between short walks near to the sea – Cinque Terre traverse is one of the longest ones in Italy – or a longer trek overlooking the sea but set back from it. *Alta via dei Monti liguri* (see also Chapter 9) is the longest scenic trail of this kind.

A new trail is being organized in Liguria's eastern riviera. Its name is *Verdeazzurro*, and it is a 10 day walk from Genova to la Spezia, passing Portofino and Cinque Terre on the way.

PORTOFINO TRAILS

Immediately east of Genova, Portofino is one of the very best known villages of the Ligurian riviera. Its *porticciolo*, a small harbour flanked by beautiful old houses, is one of the best places in the country to sit in a café and have a drink, expensive but recommended even to budget travellers.

Towards Portofino harbour and the coastal road zigzagging to Santa Margherita Ligure, descends a steep, heavily forested mountain, on the top of which is perched S. Maria di Nozarego sanctuary and – more to the west, on the highest summit of a long ridge – a big complex of radio and TV antennas. The southern slopes of the mountain, directly overlooking the sea, are wilder still. The magnificent San Fruttuoso abbey, a medieval building in an astounding setting, can only be reached by boat – or on foot.

Monte di Portofino – this is the whole area's name – is preserved by one of Italy's oldest protected areas, and is criss-crossed by a magnificent network of trails. This is partly due to the importance of the area, and partly to the fact that Liguria has always had a huge population of hikers. For the visitor coming from abroad, there is the possibility of walking at leisure, on trails ranging from 2 hours to a full hard day, without the navigational problems that can be had on many other coastal paths of Italy. Scenery is truly glorious – let me stress that again. Of course, during spring and summer weekends, solitude is the one thing you will not find. *Golfo Tigullio* 1:25,000 map, though not very detailed, is good enough for exploring and it can be found everywhere in the area. IGM's 1:50,000 *Chiavari* map is more detailed, but it lacks information about the trails.

How to get there A winding, beautiful coastal road connects Portofino village to Santa Margherita Ligure, on the Aurelia coastal road and on the main Genova–Pisa railway line. There is parking in Portofino, but during summer and spring weekends, you are warmly advised to leave your car in Santa Margherita and to take a bus to Portofino. On the western side, Camogli is also very well connected (trains and buses) to Genova, while from both Camogli and Santa Margherita frequent buses reach the village of Ruta, your best starting point if you want to traverse the promontory. Regular boat services connect San Fruttuoso to Camogli and Portofino.

The trails The simplest walk of all is the Portofino–San Fruttuoso trail, an easy path requiring less than 2 hours. As there can be small route-finding problems when leaving Portofino, my suggestion is to reach San Fruttuoso by boat, and then hike back. Longer expeditions include a tour starting and ending in Portofino (best for motorists) and a traverse from Ruta to Portofino (best for those who rely on public transport). The Camogli to San Fruttuoso trail has some exposed and difficult parts while crossing Punta Chiappa area.

San Fruttuoso to Portofino The trail starts right from the abbey: you have to walk to a smaller cove with some attractive fishermen's houses, then start climbing through dense bush, passing by a helicopter-landing pad. More zigzags bring you out of the forest, onto a spectacular part of the trail overlooking Punta Carega, with magnificent views onto Punta Chiappa and San Fruttuoso Bay. A long traverse follows, with short ups and downs, to a junction. Follow the right hand trail (left one climbs to Pietre Strette), and cross a deeply incut valley (Valle Rufinale) in order to reach the sparse houses of San Sebastiano, directly above Portofino village. You cross these, and then descend on small roads and steps to Portofino's car park. This trail, taken at leisure, requires 2 hours.

Ruta to San Fruttuoso The trail starts on the right of the paved road to Portofino Vetta hotel (you can also follow the road, but it is longer). From the hotel you follow a dirt road on the left, passing close to the radio and TV complex, and then entering a magnificent forest. A pleasant, level and cool walk will bring you to Pietre Strette, a group of volcanic rocks where there is an important trail junction. Turn right, and follow the long series of zigzags that will bring you to San Fruttuoso in 1½ hours from Ruta. Going up, this is a strenuous walk.

Portofino to Pietre Strette and San Fruttuoso This is the trail allowing you to make the complete, 4½ hours tour from Portofino to Portofino. You start from the car park, pass through the upper part of the village (some paint marks), continue upwards to the San Sebastiano houses.

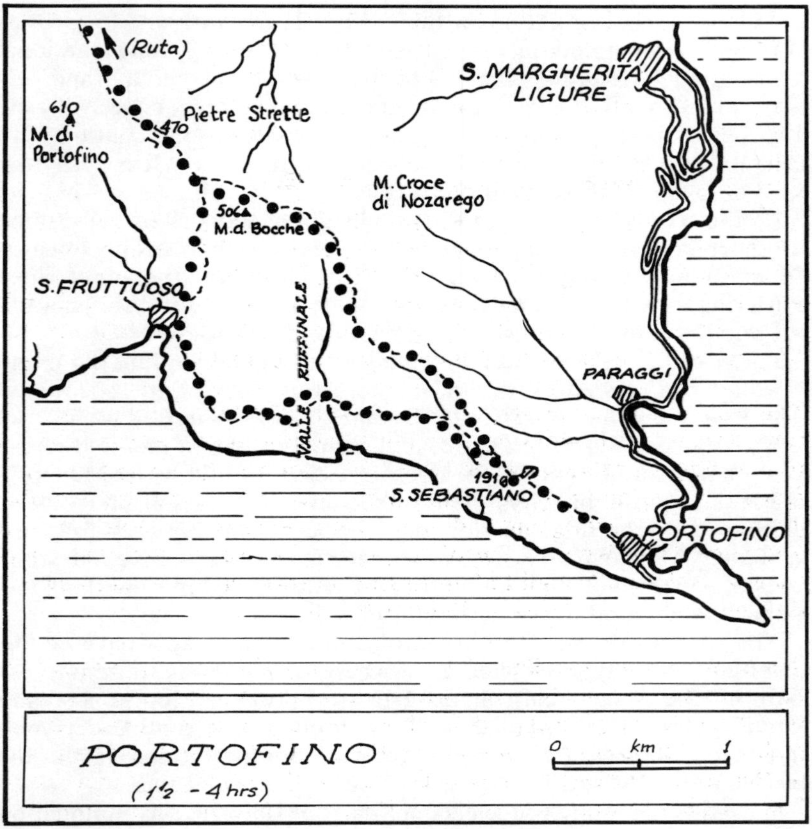

At a junction, you leave the left trail to San Fruttuoso and climb through the pine forest towards Pietre Strette and Ruta. When you reach Pietre Strette, you turn left and start the long descent to San Fruttuoso. Allow 2½ hours.

ACROSS THE CINQUE TERRE

At the southeastern tip of Liguria, the Cinque Terre boast some of the most beautiful areas of the Italian Riviera. The five villages themselves – north to south, Monterosso, Vernazza, Corniglia, Manarola and Riomaggiore – have been celebrated over the centuries by writers and poets, and have become a must for tourists seeking a peaceful beach, or a traditional fishing village perched on one of the best streches of the Tyrrhenian coast.

Access to the villages is difficult by car – small zigzagging roads descend from the mountainside, and travelling this way is an adventure in itself. It is much easier by train. The main railway line between Pisa and Genova passes right under the Cinque Terre, with one long series of tunnels interrupted only by village stations. ANAS, Italy's national road-building agency, is planning to spoil everything with a brand new coastal road. Until this one comes (and quite possibly it never will) the trail passes through the five villages themselves and continues to Levanto in the north and to Portovenere in the south. It is easily the most enjoyable coastal path of all Italy.

All the area is criss-crossed with a substantial network of trails: some are short paths descending to the beaches, others climb steeply towards the mountains above. The longest path of all follows the whole ridge bordering the Cinque Terre towards La Spezia: a beautiful scenic walk, but one that misses the five charming villages themselves.

The so-called coastal path, involving a substantial amount of up and downhill work, is easily the most interesting one for the occasional visitor to the area. It starts in Levanto, skirts beautiful Punta del Mesco, descends to Monterosso, and continues with a scenic traverse to Vernazza and Cogniglia. A less interesting bit follows to Manarola and Riomaggiore, but then the trail becomes first class again. A steep climb leads to the ridge overlooking La Spezia, which is then followed to medieval Portovenere, skirting on the east the impressive limestone faces of Muzzerone. The whole trail is easily walked in something less than 10 hours, and is normally split into 2 days.

Apart from Corniglia and Manarola, all coastal villages have hotels. Camping is strictly prohibited everywhere, and anyway quite impossible on the steep, cultivated terraces between Monterosso and Riomaggiore. Many travellers still try to pitch their tents every year, and this periodically triggers serious confrontations with the *carabinieri* or the local population. You should avoid this.

Since this is not one of the cheaper parts of Italy the accommodation solution for the impecunious hiker can be the train: from Corniglia or Manarola (in fact, from any village you choose) the 'commuting hiker' can easily board a train and land twenty minutes later in Levanto, where a comfortable camping site exists. Next morning, another trail will lead you back to where you interrupted your hike, and off you go again.

The train, however, allows you to hike only a small part of the trail. If you have only one day available, I would recommend walking from Levanto to Corniglia, or to Vernazza if you prefer a shorter day. Whatever the length of your walk, bring a water bottle, a hat, and a swimsuit in summer. But remember that the best times to walk the Cinque Terre are the months from October to April, well away from the heat and summer crowds. *Carta dei Sentieri delle Cinque Terre* (1:40,000 scale), published by la Spezca's section of CAI, can be bought in many shops.

How to get there As one of the main lines of Italy passes right through the Cinque Terre, the train is the best way to get there. Just remember that *espresso* and *rapido* trains normally stop only in La Spezia: if you are coming from Pisa, you will have to change to a local train in La

Spezia; if you're coming from Genova you can either change in Sestri Levante, or reach La Spezia and then travel back.

If you are driving a car, you can park it either in La Spezia (an industrial town of no interest to tourists) or Levanto, which is reached by a reasonable 12 km road from the Carrodano exit on the Pisa–Genova autostrada. From Portovenere, frequent and fast buses travel to La Spezia's railway station.

The trail Levanto is the starting point, and a nice little town that deserves exploration. After a look at the beautiful medieval church, you will be ready to start. From the centre you keep the sea on your left and find the first arrows pointing to steps on your left. Walk up these, cross the southernmost part of Levanto, and follow a paved road going south. Then the trail branches off, on the right and enters a heavily vegetated area leading towards Punta del Mesco. After crossing an attractive pine forest, you will reach (2 hours from Levanto) a junction; the abandoned lighthouse of Punta del Mesco is just a few

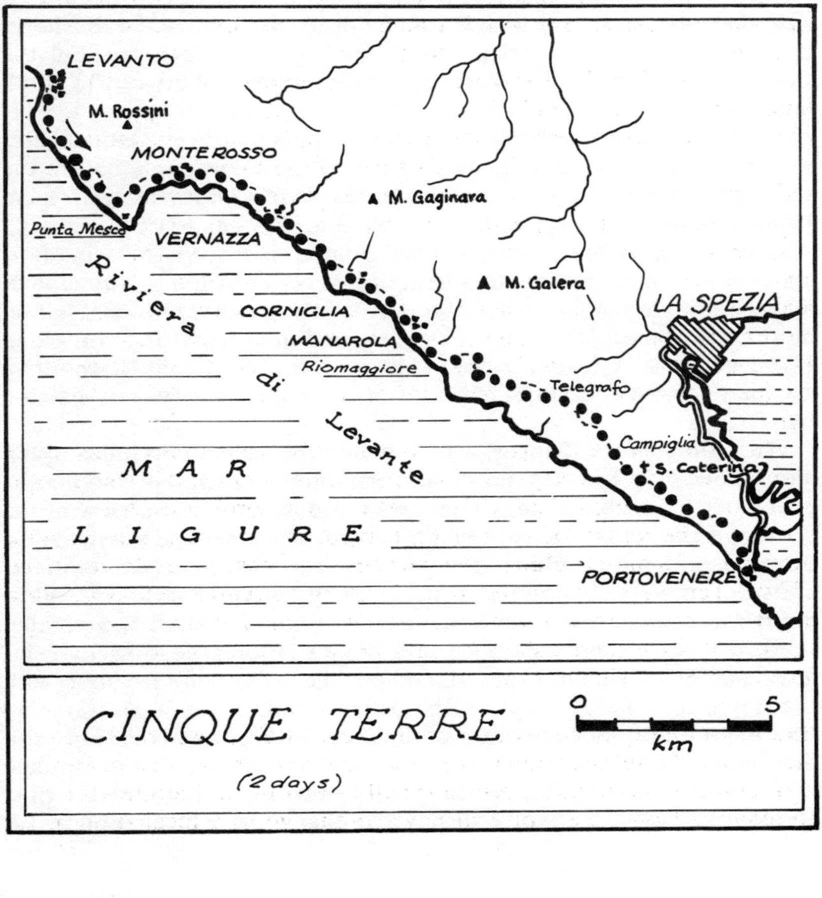

minutes' walk on your right. It is worth a look because you discover from here the Cinque Terre coastline. Then you get back to the junction, and half an hour's walk brings you to Monterosso, the biggest of the five villages, with a nice big beach waiting for you. Before descending to Monterosso, you leave behind on your left the main ridge trail, which you will meet again between Riomaggiore and Portovenere.

At the opposite end of the village start going uphill again along a series of very steep staircases, after which the path levels out between the vineyards, some 200 m above sea level. Slowly, the vineyards give way to steeper slopes, where the trail is often cut into the mountain-side. You get magnificent views of the sea, and better still, glimpses of Vernazza, the next village you will meet. This is the most impressive one in the Cinque Terre, with a striking circular tower dominating a tiny harbour: you will reach it, at the end of another steep descent, in 2 hours from Monterosso.

The following bit starts in the centre of Vernazza, right in front of the small road you have just come from. You climb steep steps again, have another beautiful view of Vernazza behind you, then cross a pleasant chestnut and oak forest. Your next encounter is with Corniglia's vineyards, and then with Corniglia itself, high above the seashore: the village is less interesting than Monterosso or Vernazza, but the view is outstanding. From Vernazza, walking time is between 1½ and 2 hours.

A modern staircase brings you to Corniglia's railway station, after which you will have a boring walk near to the railway line before the short, pleasant path brings you into Manarola in 1 hour from Corniglia. From here to Riomaggiore, you will find the celebrated 'via dell' Amore' which is pretty deceiving: the 'love path' consists of a short walk along a promontory, in a beautiful setting spoiled by the crowds and the marble plaques where famous love verses are carved. Half an hour from Manarola, including time to read the verses, and you are in Riomaggiore – a bigger place, with an attractive, small harbour, a substantial railway station and a lot of noise from every train passing by.

The trail follows Riomaggiore's main street, then continues uphill along a beautiful old paved path, turning right to reach the Madonna di Monte Nero sanctuary, at 340 m, commanding a beautiful view of the coast. To the south, you will be able to see the coastline stretching to Portovenere, partly hiding Palmaria island. On clear winter days, Corsica can be spotted in the distance. From the sanctuary, you follow a dirt road going uphill again (for a short while there are two parallel marked trails – both are good) to a beautiful forest leading to Telegrafo pass (511 m). On your left, you can see La Spezia's harbour, with the imposing Alpi Apuane on the background. There is also a small *trattoria* – the only one you will find before Portovenere. Here you meet again the 'upper' trail that you left behind near Punta del Mesco.

Then the trail goes on, perfectly marked and visible through a pine forest, right on the crest, entering the tiny village of Campiglia, at

380 m above sea level and 1½ hours' walk from the Monte Nero sanctuary. On the far side of the village you reach a small viewpoint where you will have to veer left (paths can be confusing here) to reach a dirt road. When it turns left your trail branches again to the right, starting an exciting traverse towards the white Muzzerone cliffs.

For a while, views get better and better again every metre you proceed, then a short descent leads you to the col that precedes the Muzzerone itself. You follow the road for a short distance, then start going uphill again on a short-cut, after which you are on the level again. Portovenere is now right below you; a very steep descent leads to the castle and then to the entrance of the old fortified village, a few feet from the bus stop to La Spezia and 1½ hours from Campiglia.

Before boarding the bus you must have a look at Portovenere: perched on the cape's last rock, the church of San Pietro is one of the most impressive monuments of all the Tyrrhenian coast.

UCCELLINA PARK

South of Grosseto, a magnificent line of hills borders the Tyrrhenian sea between Alberese and Talamone. Old towers are perched on the highest summits, wild boar, foxes and deer roam the hills, and the beach is one of the very best in the country. Unlike the nearby areas of Porto Santo Stefano and Punta Ala, there are no hotels nor roads: the park is strictly controlled, and the park's administration is making Uccellina one of the best nature sanctuaries in Italy.

Started in 1975, *Parco regionale della Maremma* has been established by Tuscany's regional government. *Maremma* is the southwestern part of the region, mainly included in Grosseto province. However, almost everybody continues to refer to the area as *Parco dell'Uccellina*, from the name of the hills forming the park's backbone.

When the park was established, there was a long struggle to eradicate poachers from the area: nowadays the park's fauna is safe, and the administration is working to implement tourist facilities in the area, and to continue with scientific research. Right in the middle of a heavily crowded series of beaches, their task is not easy: access to the park has been restricted to 3 days a week with a planned number of visitors. Access from the sea is forbidden, and only a fixed number of cars is allowed on the small road reaching Marina di Alberese north of the Uccellina hills and on the edge of the Park itself.

Spring is the best time to visit Uccellina to admire the flowers in the hills and to appreciate the scents of the vegetation. Winter can be very interesting: from the hills, you can enjoy incredible views: from nearby Giglio island, the eye travels to Montecristo, and then to faraway Elba and Corsica. In summer, you still can enjoy yourself because of the beach: but this can be crowded, and this is the time of the year when the 'fixed number' of visitors rule proves necessary. You have to arrive early in the morning and wait for the afternoon breeze before walking around.

How to get there With a car, you must follow the Aurelia highway: 12 km south of Grosseto you will turn on a smaller road to Alberese. By public transport this is a perfectly easy area to reach; every train on the Roma–Pisa–Torino mainline stops in Grosseto, and buses to Alberese start a few minutes' walk from the station. On open days (Wednesdays, Saturdays and Sundays) you must buy a ticket in Alberese, and then wait for one of the Park's minibuses to carry you inside the area. Entrance is allowed from 9 a.m. to one hour before sunset. Camping or bivouacking in the park is strictly forbidden, as is landing from the sea. One important hint: In Alberese, it is easy to find sandwiches to carry with you in the park. There is also a water fountain; remember that there is no water at all inside the park! Groups can arrange visits on different days, by phoning (0564) 407098.

The trails There are 4 different trails in the Park and you must not deviate from them. My favourite one is the *San Rabano* trail, starting right from the Pratini area where you get out of the minibus. In a day you can easily combine this with the beautiful *Torri* trail and a substantial stop on the beach. *Cala di Forno* trail is long and not very interesting, while the *Grotte* trail reaches a seldom-visited area of the Park.

From Pratini, you start on the left of the road, near a sign: you cross a large meadow, enter the forest, and start climbing quite steeply for about half an hour. Then the path starts to level out and reaches the main ridge of the Uccellina hills: views start to be very interesting. You descend for a while, climb up again, and reach a magnificent grassy terrace overlooking the beach and most of the Park. You can stop for a while, but the best surprise is a few minutes away. The path turns left, descends again, and then reaches the *San Rabano* abbey, in a large depression on the main ridge, and 1½ hours from Pratini.

The magnificent abbey was built in the XI century, and abandoned around 1650. The church is partly ruined, but the tower is still imposing and beautiful seen beyond a dense 'jungle' of bushes and oaks. Starting from the church, the return path traverses the western slopes of the hills, and descends to the access road about midway between Pratini and the beach. It takes 45 minutes to get here from San Rabano. Turning left, and following the main road, you will reach a drainage channel and then, to the left, the splendid beach. A stop here would be welcome.

From the beach you must walk along the right side of the limestone cliffs: the path starts climbing again, and in a few minutes reaches the Collelungo tower, partly ruined, from where you have another beautiful view. Continuing along the trail, you descend to the road and follow it bearing right as far as a wooden enclosure. Immediately after this you turn left, following the *Torri* path on the left of a meadow full of olive trees. Then the path veers left, and climbs gently, along a large ridge, to the Castelmarino tower. The view from here is the best in the park, and the one you'll find in almost all books and articles dedicated to the area.

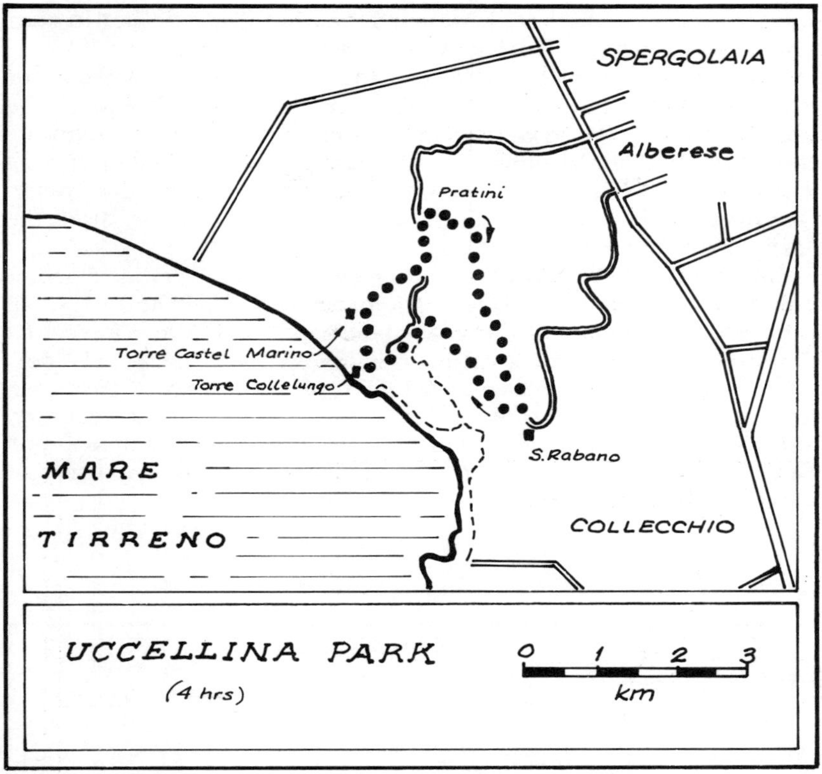

On the way down, you follow the same path to a sign (the only one on the trail). Here you turn left, and in a few minutes find yourself again on the paved road. You follow it bearing left, and continue to the Pratini. The whole tour, including both trails, requires 4 hours' walking. The length of the beach stop, obviously, depends on you and the weather!

THE CIRCEO WILDERNESS

Midway between Naples and Rome, Circeo is a true mountain, right in front of the sea. It is isolated and impressive. On the side overlooking the Tyrrhenian sea, a 200 m limestone face dominates a thick, impassable 'jungle' of mediterranean vegetation. On many clear days, Ponza and Ventotene islands can easily be spotted far away in the sea. Around the mountain itself, lies one of Italy's most interesting national parks.

The hike up the mountain's 541 m is short – perfectly suitable for half a day. Winter or early spring are the best and wildest times of the year: the thin ridge which the trail follows is fully exposed to the wind and white crests can be seen on the waves. In summer, the breeze manages to make the heat less oppressive, but it is wise not to start before the afternoon. The hike's length allows this perfectly.

Different seasons offer the hiker a choice of things to do before or after the walk. In winter, explorations into the forests and in the marshes forming the lower part of the park can result in interesting encounters with the wildlife. In summer, the long beach stretching north of Circeo is one of Italy's very best. All the year round, Fossanova Abbey and Terracina's Giove Anxur temple offer the possibility of more cultural stops along the way.

Circeo National Park is all that survives of the huge Pontine marshes and forests, destroyed to make room for fertile land in the 1930s. All around, and notably on the coast between San Felice Circeo and Terracina, cottages and apartment buildings have completely destroyed what was one of the country's finest pieces of scenery. If you can spare another day, and want to enjoy more of this part of the country, just board a ferry in Anzio or Formia, and spend as much time as you want in Ponza, Ventotene or the nearby islands. There are plenty of walks there, too!

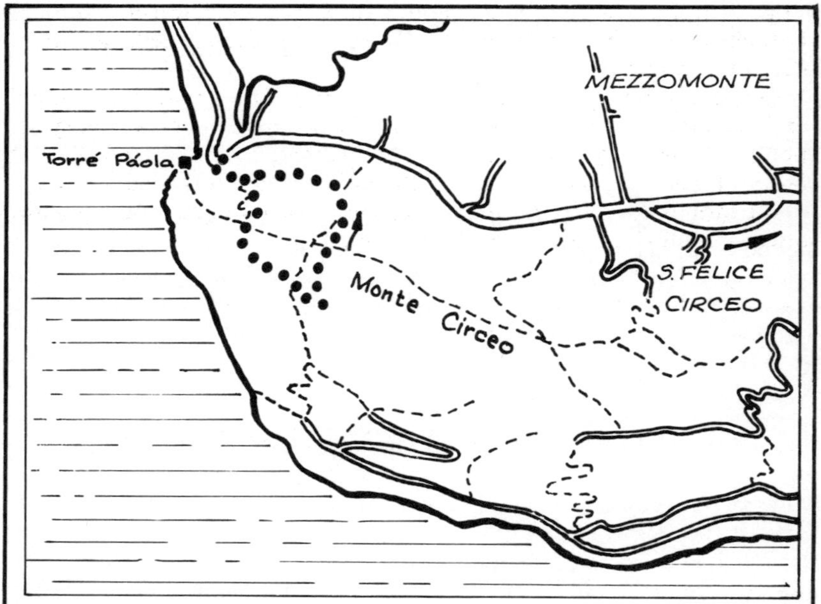

CIRCEO
(3 hrs)

How to get there If you are driving access to San Felice Circeo from Naples or Rome is straightforward, once you've managed to get out of the towns. With public transport, from the southern side of Rome, in an area designed by Mussolini in the 1930s called EUR, you must board an ACOTRAL bus to San Felice: they run every hour or so. From Naples, your best bet is a train to Formia, and a bus to Terracina and San Felice from there. From San Felice, you must follow a 3 km paved road to Torre Paola. It is not very pleasant to walk, and you would be better off hitching a ride if you can.

The trail From Torre Paola (the tower is private, and closed), a dirt road enters the dense forest of the mountain. It is best to walk it from the beginning. You keep right at the first junction, then reach a small clearing on the side of the road. A narrow and very steep path starts from here, leading directly to a small terrace. Here the yellow painting marks the start, and the trail becomes much easier. It goes right, climbing again, to reach the rocky ridge of the mountain and an exceptional view.

The trail continues zigzagging between the large boulders of the ridge to the first summit; in front you can now see the main summit, and on the right – west – side the face of *Il Precipizio*. The ridge descends for a while, then becomes exposed and steep again. A larger ridge continues as far as a small saddle, where a red-marked trail branches off to the left. A couple more zigzags lead to the large summit (2 hours from the start).

On descending, you reach the saddle immediately under the summit, and must follow the red-marked trail. This is steep, quick and easy, and peters out when you emerge from the forest. You must keep left on fainter tracks, to reach a larger path leading to the dirt road at the base of the mountain. On this, keeping left, you reach the starting point after a few minutes (1 hour from the summit).

Chapter 8

The Etruscan Hills

Centuries before the Roman conquest, the Etruscans ruled over a large part of Italy. East of Bologna, the town of Spina was the gateway to Greece and the Middle East, and the Apennines were crossed by merchants along the Etruscan roads. To the south, their influence extended throughout a large part of Campania whilst to the west a bitter rivalry developed between the Etruscans and Phoenicians and Greek ships and other traders. Conquered and in many cases destroyed by Rome, the Etruscan cities disappeared into oblivion. Roman historians forgot a people who had taught Rome so much, and archaeologists only started having a real interest in the Etruscans during the late eighteenth century.

Nowadays, some of the most interesting Etruscan necropolises are amongst central Italy's most visited areas: Cerveteri, Tarquinia, Vetulonia and Populonia are compulsory stops for every traveller making his way along the Tyrrhenian coast. The most important Etruscan towns were built along the coast of southern Tuscany and northern Lazio and on the inland hills of the area. Wild and inspiring, this is still one of the most attractive parts of the country. Scarcely inhabited, it offers the hiker many possibilities.

There are no real mountains here. Hills are sometimes barren and sometimes covered with thick forests, where once the Etruscan roads were opened. In the volcanic soil and rock, rivers have dug a series of

Abbey of Monte Oliveto Maggiore

impressive canyons, which were used as natural ramparts, defending fortresses and towns, or as walls where richly decorated tombs were carved. To the west, from the tops of many hills, the Tyrrhenian coastline can be spotted, whilst snowcapped mountains can be seen on the opposite side during winter.

On the whole, the area is amongst the country's finest as far as lowland and hill hiking is concerned. Easy to reach from Florence or Rome, it can also be approached from the Rome to Florence motorway or from the ancient Via Aurelia, the highway following the Tyrrhenian coast. As usual, mid-season is best for the walker. Autumn can be muddy, while spring is truly magnificent, April being probably the best time of all. Later in the year, a few more miles can lead you to the seaside and a swim.

ACROSS THE CRETE SENESI: MONTE OLIVETO TO S. ANTIMO

South of the beautiful, medieval town of Siena, an impressive landscape of hills extends to the foothills of Monte Amiata, a long-time extinct volcano which is southern Tuscany's only real mountain. A few dozen miles from some of the best known areas in the country, it is still a wild, interesting place, and an ideal one for low altitude walking which is at its best during spring or autumn.

This is not the best area for Etruscan remains, although Siena was certainly an Etruscan city and smaller settlements were scattered on the hills. Almost nothing is left of the Etruscans here, but the medieval buildings, towers and ruins give the countryside an interesting flavour. The via Cassia connecting Siena to Viterbo and Rome, was built by the Romans immediately after the Etruscan cities were defeated. It retained its importance throughout the Middle Ages, when it became part of the pilgrims' route to Rome. Travelling north to south, it reaches the starting points of many interesting walks.

The distance between Siena and Monte Amiata can be walked in 3 to 4 days. It is better to start from Monte Oliveto Maggiore: a beautiful and interesting abbey where it is possible to spend the night, avoiding the first stretch that should be walked on surfaced roads. Montalcino's tower (and Brunello, one of the country's best wines) and the isolated abbey of Sant'Antimo give the walk a unique character. Continuing towards Monte Amiata, you pass the impressive Castle of Rocca d'Orcia. Amiata itself offers a series of pleasant walks, mostly through a thick forest, recommended during summer's hottest weeks.

The Monte Oliveto to S. Antimo walk, on the opposite side, is a classic mid-season walk. The best times of the year are probably April and October; summer is really *too* hot and winter muddy and cold, but still possible for adventurous hikers. IGM maps are useful, and can be bought either in Siena or in Florence. You will need the *Asciano*, *Buonconvento* and *Montalcino* sheets.

How to get there Siena is very easily reached from all parts of central Italy. Buses are best from Florence, whilst from Rome you should board a train to Chiusi and then a slower one to Siena. To reach Monte Oliveto, you have a choice between buses and hitch-hiking, or you can take another slow train to Asciano and start from there. The 6 km walk is not really unpleasant, but it is almost all on a surfaced road. It is possible to sleep in Monte Oliveto's guest rooms but you should inquire first, by phoning (0577) 707017.

The walk From Monte Oliveto, you start on the surfaced road to Asciano. When this turns left, you turn right onto a short-cut towards Chiusure, a small village overlooking some beautiful clay calanques and gullies. Passing another road to Buonconvento on the left, continue on the dirt road passing near the eroded area and climb up as far as the dividing ridge between the Serlate river valley and the parallel one which the via Cassia runs through.

When you reach the houses at Fornacino turn left, onto a smaller track: this continues along the ridge, passing houses at Gre, Renaiole and Poggio Saltarello before reaching a large dirt road connecting Buonconvento to S. Giovanni d'Asso. Follow this along the right for 100 m and then start following the ridge again along another small dirt road. At a junction you must keep right, then continue, passing on the left of a rounded hill. You will reach a point from where both via Cassia and Montalcino's towers can be seen. In front of you is a big farm. Before reaching it, turn right towards the houses at pannone, then continue along a descending road to reach the Via Cassia in about 4 hours from Monte Oliveto.

To the left, follow the main road (this is an unpleasant stretch!) for 700 m, to the 194,600 km marker. Here you turn right again onto another dirt road, reaching Risveglio and the Colle Sassi farm. Here you must continue towards the hill's summit, where there is another dirt road. Follow it to the right, passing a small graveyard and descending again to the Montalcino–Buonconvento road, near Val di Cava.

You cross the road, follow a sign to Badia Ardenga and then turn left at two junctions. A steepish climb leads to a chapel and then to Montalcino's medieval walls, which are entered through a beautiful gate, after about 2 hours from Via Cassia. Apart from drinking Brunello, an overnight stop in Montalcino is recommended because of the impressive castle, and the quiet atmosphere of the old town.

On day two, you should start on the surfaced road to Grosseto: this is a 2.5 km stretch. To partly avoid it, start off walking through a small pine forest and then turn left across the Poggio Civitella hill. From Ragnaie junction, follow a pleasant dirt road left, passing Cocco farm, to the small village of Villa a Tolli, a tiny fortified town with a beautiful church. The same road continues, amongst olive trees, to Sant'Antimo church, one of southern Tuscany's romanesque masterpieces. To visit, you can either arrive when a mass is going on (usually twice a day), or walk to the village nearby and ask for the warden. From Montalcino, you need 3 hours.

From S. Antimo, there are various possibilities. You can walk for about 1 hour on a surfaced road descending to Monte Amiata railway station (check timetables beforehand!), or hitch-hike towards Montalcino. A third possibility is to follow a dirt road climbing from Castelnuovo village to the ridge behind, and then descend to the Orcia river. Ford this, reach a bigger dirt road near two yellow silos, and follow it right on a long ascent to Castiglione d'Orcia, which is reached after a further 3 hours from S. Antimo. Here you will find the beautiful Rocca d'Orcia castle, an hotel and buses to take you back to Siena.

THE VULCI WALK

Looking at a map of Italy, the area between Viterbo and the Tyrrhenian sea looks very empty by Italian standards. Towns are few and far between, roads travel for dozens of miles without a single house in sight. The border between Tuscany and Latium (i.e. the ancient border between independent Tuscany and the Papal territories) lies a few kilometres north of Vulci. The ancient bridge crossing the Fiora river canyon was one of the border's crossing points.

Vulci itself was one of the most powerful Etruscan cities, and was destroyed by Rome in 290 BC. The ruins which can be seen today are mostly Roman, but the remnants of an Etruscan temple can clearly be seen and are one of the site's most impressive monuments. The big necropolis lies on the Fiora's left bank, and it was one of the very first ones to be explored (and sacked) around 1800 BC.

North of Vulci, a few yards from the bridge, is Abbadia di Castro; an impressive fortress first mentioned in 890 AD, built on the site of an ancient castle. The Abbadia can be seen from many miles away, hosts a small but interesting museum, and is a good starting point for a 2 to 3 hour walk including the old town and the biggest tombs in the area. These are impressive but empty, having been ransacked in very ancient times. Most of the nearby sepulchres were emptied and then destroyed in the first period of Etruscan archaeology: this was private land, and the useless tombs had to be eliminated to allow more soil to be ploughed!

Approaching Vulci, many interesting sights and monuments can be visited, Tuscania and Tarquinia being the nearest and most interesting. Castro, hidden in nearby Selva del Lamone, and Norchia offer walks very similar in character and style to those at Vulci. A little to the north from Abbadia di Castro is Vulci's WWF wildlife sanctuary; apart from housing numerous birds, it is one of the very last places in Italy where otters live. It can be included in the walk but to visit it, you must ask the permission of WWF's Latium branch in advance (06) 844010.

How to get there Best access to Vulci is from the Via Aurelia. One kilometre north of Montalto di Castro (exactly 100 km from Rome) a road branches off, and after another 11 km arrives at a junction. Abbadia di Castro can be seen clearly on your right: turn right and follow the road to Canino, passing on the way the WWF sanctuary's

entrance. From Florence, you can drive to Siena, then on scenic Via Cassia to Lake Bolsena, and then right to Valentano, Canino and Vulci. Or you can drive to Orvieto, then to Bolsena, pass north of the lake and continue as above. There are no buses to Vulci; once you reach Montalto, you can hitch-hike; it should not be difficult.

The trail From Abbadia's car park, start by crossing the impressive bridge over Fiora river canyon. Turning left at its end and you will find a small steep path leading to the bottom of the canyon, offering an interesting view on the bridge. Continue on the dirt road that passes the bridge, soon reaching a crossroads. Turn left, passing near a restaurant, descend and climb up again to reach the old town's entrance.

A beautiful, paved Roman road crosses the area, and leads the way to the old city. Many interesting sights include some beautiful mosaics, an Etruscan temple basement and the big Roman baths. Continuing along the paved road, you descend to a meadow flanking the river. You must ford the Fiora (normally easy and you do not even get your feet wet, sometimes awkward and on rare occasions impassable), climb a small dirt road and reach the plateau of the necropolis, in sight of the biggest tomb of all, nicknamed *Cuccumella*. With a flashlight you can explore its interesting corridors and rooms; Cuccumella's interior was completely ransacked a long time ago. In the surrounding area are more tombs worth some exploration.

Now continue on another dirt road amongst olive trees, keep left at a junction, reaching the paved road coming from Canino. Follow it to the left, back to the walk's starting point. If you have arranged for a visit to the WWF sanctuary, you can reach it again on foot; cross the bridge once more, reach the junction where you turned left, turn right and continue to the entrance. The normal tour, sightseeing included, requires 3 hours, the walk to WWF sanctuary not more than 15 minutes one way.

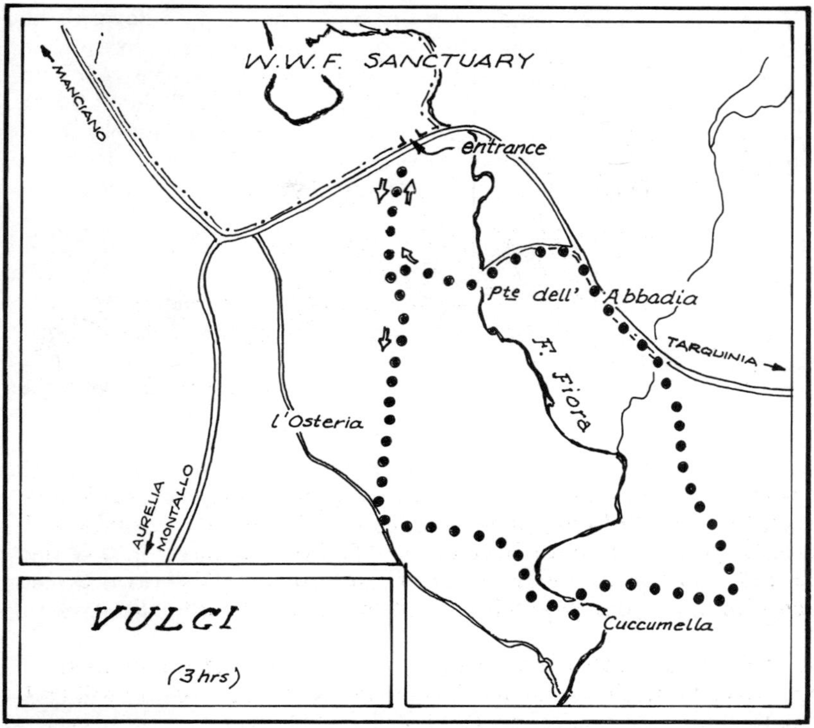

BLERA NECROPOLIS AND THE BIEDANO CANYON

Deep and impressive, the Biedano river canyon crosses the volcanic rock plateaux west of Lake Vico, offering some of Etruscan Latium's wildest scenery. West of the canyon's lowest point lies the most interesting of Blera's several necropolises. Carved into the reddish rock, the tombs open amongst a lush vegetation, near to the ancient (Etruscan, then Roman) Via Clodia, now transformed into a modern dirt road.

Easily reached both from Rome and the Tyrrhenian coast, Blera and nearby Barbarano are also two of the best examples of the area's small medieval towns, perched upon low ridges naturally defended by canyons. A small nature reserve has been established near to Barbarano by the regional government in 1985.

Many walks are possible in the area; the abandoned railway which once linked Civitavecchia to Capranica offers the longest and most varied one, requiring 2–3 days to the Tolfa hills and the seaside. A few miles to the east, Lake Vico is another extremely interesting Lazio nature spot and offers a choice of interesting short walks, as well as many opportunities for the birdwatcher.

From Blera, a very good 2 hour walk can be had towards the Biedano canyon and the best-known necropolis. The return, over the canyon's southern rim, offers magnificent views across the valley and the modern town. East of this, a slightly longer walk leads to the Barbarano crossing and all the length of the canyon: a magnificent hike which is rightly becoming one of the region's best known and appreciated. IGM map (useful, but by no means necessary) is *Vetralla*.

How to get there Both Blera and Barbarano can be easily and quickly reached from Rome on the Via Cassia (one hour trip), or from Viterbo or Tarquinia. The latter approaches involve passing near many more interesting Etruscan sites (Tarquinia, Norchia, Castel d'Asso). Direct ACOTRAL buses leave from Rome and Viterbo to both towns, or you can travel by train to Vico or Cura di Vetralla stations, and then hitch-hike or wait for a bus.

Blera necropolis trail From the town's entrance, start walking all the length of the main road; on the left is an Etruscan inscription carved on a black rock. Pass through a gate, descend a little, and then start a level traverse where the first, smaller tombs are found. You pass a small canyon (this is the old Via Clodia), to reach a beautiful bridge crossing a smaller stream. A few metres ahead, you enter the most interesting

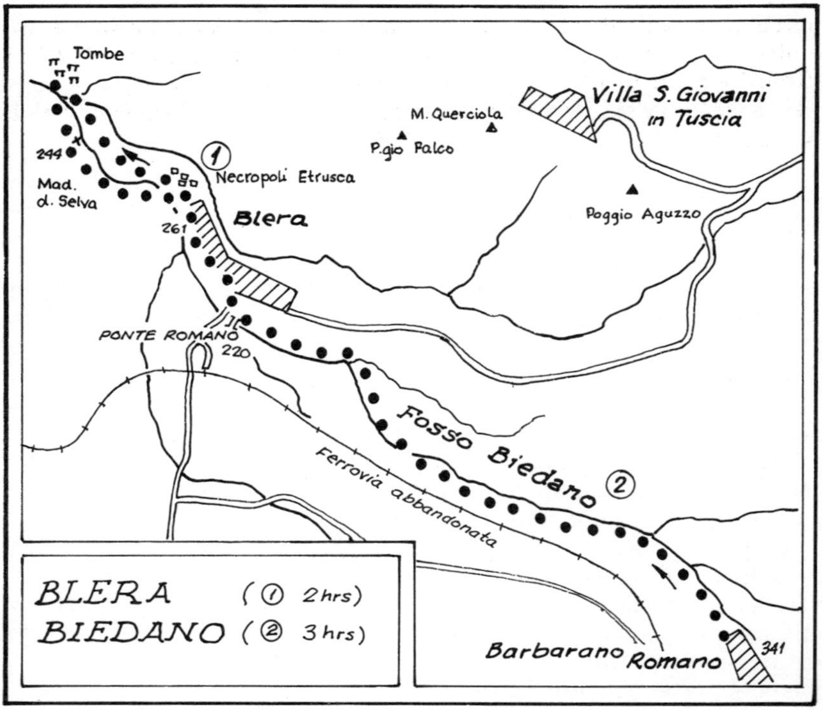

area of the necropolis. To reach the best tombs keep to the left (descending) road, and then turn right onto a small path and staircase: the area is worthy of as much exploration as you want to give it.

When you return to the descending road, you continue for a few minutes on it and then leave it to cross the River Biedano and reach a remarkable red rock face, with a small fountain at the foot of it. A narrow path climbs to the right and reaches the plateau above. Follow this left, to reach a small church; after this you turn left again, descending onto another dirt road to the Biedano right under Blera. On your right is another, much older bridge. Allow 2 to 3 hours for a return to the town, obviously more if you are an archaeology enthusiast.

The Biedano canyon trail Another beautiful trail, this can cause some problems because of the dense vegetation. Wear long sleeves and trousers! From Blera, you can start by walking the first hike described, or by directly descending to the river. Pass under the new bridge, near to the old one, and continue walking through the canyon. You pass the last fields and fruit trees, leave an interesting cave on the left, and enter the most heavily vegetated area. The trail is quite indistinct for about half an hour, after which you find on your right a small, impressive passage. This becomes a tunnel, and leads near to an ancient dam, after which the valley becomes larger. Red lava cliffs mark the most impressive part of the walk: Barbarano is not far.

A better trail continues along the right of the valley, passes by a very large cave, and then reaches the foot of the rocky spur where the village is perched. A short climb leads to Barbarano; allow for $2\frac{1}{2}$ hours from Blera. If you have a car there, hitch-hiking is definitely the best way to return to it: instead, you can have a rather dull 5 km walk on the surfaced road.

Chapter 9

Northern Apennines

The Apennines are the 'southern half' of Italy's mountains but a half extending well into the country's northernmost regions. The chain extends for some 1,200 km from Liguria and Piedmont to Reggio Calabria, touching on the way 13 out of the country's 20 regions. Later in the book, we will deal with the central (highest) and the southernmost part of the chain.

For many Anglo-Saxons the Northern Apennines are associated with memories of the bitter fighting in the last year of the Second World War. The part of the chain stretching from Liguria to Tuscany and Emilia saw fierce fighting between the Allied troops and the Germans. Italian *partigiani* fought an intense guerrilla action against the occupying troops and this led to many mountain villages being destroyed in revenge.

Other areas recall more pleasant memories. Alpi Apuane, directly overlooking Massa and Carrara on the Tyrrhenian coast, is the birthplace of marble: Michelangelo's statues were first conceived here, with the sculptor himself carefully choosing the best blocks for his work. Further to the east, on the border between Tuscany and Umbria, the thick forests of Casentino have some of the most fascinating scenery in the country. Camaldoli and la Verna abbeys are where St. Francis preached.

The chain is easy to reach for a lot of Italians. Distances from the main cities are not great, even if the mountain roads are always long

in the Apuane

and devious. Traditionally, hikers from Turin and Milan (and also, on a lesser scale, from Genoa) have preferred the Alps. Mountaineers from Tuscany and Emilia have made Apuane, Cusna, and the peaks around Abetone some of the most popular massifs in the country. Elsewhere, many valleys and summits are very little, if ever visited.

The visitor has a choice to make. Some of the mountains offer a real mountain flavour – subtle ridges, exposed summits, rock faces – whilst others, lower in height, are essentially heavily forested plateaux. Rock is generally schist or (arenaria), making the trails slippery when it rains, and the rock poor in any weather. The Apuane are a limestone and marble 'island' of steep mountains, with better options for the rock climber in summer, and for the ice man in the cold season.

In the northwest, from the boundary with the Alps at Colle di Cadibona (between Savona and Mondovì) a low chain separates Liguria from Piedmont and then from Lombardy. In the north, Monte Penice (1,460 m) and Lesima (1,724 m) dominate the rolling hills of Oltrepò, while the first serious summit in the Ligurian Apennines, Monte Maggiorasca (1,799 m) lies on the border with Emilia. More to the south, already in Tuscany, the Alpi Apuane are separated from the main chain by Lunigiana and Garfagnana's lush green valleys. Apuane's highest point is Pisanino (1,945 m), nearby Pizzo d'Uccello (1,781 m), Tambura (1,879 m) and Pania della Croce (1,858 m) providing the best routes to the climber.

On the main chain, the stretch between the Cisa pass and the old Bologna to Pistoia road boasts almost all of the chain's important summits. Ridges are exposed, slopes are steep; this is the area to go if you want to look for a 'real' mountain atmosphere. West to east, the main summits are Orsaro (1,830 m) overlooking beautiful Lake Santo Parmense, Sillara (1,861 m), Alpe di Succiso (2,017 m) and Cusna (2,120 m), the most interesting summit of the chain. Nearby Monte Prato (2,053 m) is the highest point in Tuscany.

A little to the southeast, is the important range of mountains flanking the Abetone pass and ski area. Giovo (1,991 m), Rondinaio (1,964 m) and Libro Aperto (1,937 m) are the most important summits, while nearby Cimone (2,165 m), the highest of all, is spoiled by roads, téléphériques and radio stations. Corno alle Scale (1,945 m), overlooking beautiful Lago Scaffaiolo, is very popular amongst hikers based in Bologna.

More to the east, on the border between Tuscany and Romagna, summits get much lower in height. Futa and Alpe di San Benedetto hills are rolling and gentle, with summits not exceeding 1,200 m. Monte Falterona (1,604 m), well known as the source of the River Arno, is another impressive mountain. To the south of it is the magnificent Foreste Casentinesi area, including some of the most interesting natural forest reserves of the country. More forests and hills lead to the border with Umbria.

Where and when to go The chain is huge, and suggestions can only really be minimal! Access to the main areas is quite evident from a

Hoopoe

road map. From Genova, Bologna, Firenze (Florence) and many more cities the Apennine mountains are always near at hand. Just remember that mountain roads are normally small and winding and distances can be long and tiring to negotiate.

The relative lowness of many summits can be misleading. Being very exposed to the Tyrrhenian winds, all the highest part of the chain (including the Apuane) are covered with heavy snow, and mountaineering equipment and experience are required to walk on many trails until June. The first snow makes the mountains difficult again at the end of October. The lower mountains east and north of Florence provide interesting walks, also in April and May. The heavy forests of Casentino make many low altitude hikes pleasant even in August. The sea nearby makes fog a frequent companion on many summits and ridges. However, nearly all the trails are really well marked.

THE LONG DISTANCE TRAILS

Two of Italy's most important trails are found in the northern Apennines region. Both follow the chain's main ridge, on the dividing line between Liguria and Tuscany to the west, and Piedmont, Lombardy, Emilia-Romagna and Marche to the east. Tuscany's *GEA*, because of its proximity to Florence, has become one of the country's most popular long trails amongst foreigners.

Alta via dei Monti Liguri follows the whole arc of the region's mountains. These are the Alps in the first part, and then Apennines, but the walk's character is the same all the way along. With beautiful views over the sea in many places, the trail starts at Ventimiglia on the French border and ends near la Spezia; at Passo dei Due Santi it connects to *GEA*. The whole walk requires 25 days, and the going is normally not hard.

Tuscany's *Grande Escursione Appenninica*, again, follows the region's mountains all the way, from Passo dei Due Santi to Bocca Trabaria in the southeastern corner of the region. It is another 25 day hike and another one which does not require a tent. In the north it has a distinct 'mountain' flavour, crossing exposed ridges and open pastures. The southern part is lower, accessible for a longer period, and less tiring.

Two shorter trails complete the area's network. *Apuane trekking* is a 6 day loop around this chain, while *Garfagnana trekking* is a 360° and 7 day tour of this beautiful green valley. The western part of the trail is on the Apuane side (so following *Apuane trekking* for a while), as the eastern part follows the main Apennine's *GEA*.

BOBBIO: LOOKING FOR THE OLD PILGRIMS' ROUTE

This is a short hike in a very pleasant area, near to a much longer and very ancient trail. Bobbio was an important stop on the medieval pilgrims' route from northern Europe to Rome, and the pilgrims' way came up from Varzi to Passo del Penice, to descend steeply towards Bobbio itself. The small town is a very attractive one and a place seldom visited by tourists. Irishmen come here quite often, because the town's abbey was founded by St. Columba in 615. The Saint's sepulchre was another reason for the town to become important for catholic pilgrims slowly walking through Europe.

Monte Penice is the highest summit around and it commands an incredible view across the Padana plain; Monte Rosa's glaciers can be seen in the distance on clear days. But Penice has been spoilt; radio and TV equipment and a huge new concrete tourist hotel give it an ugly appearance. It is interesting to follow the road by car to the top, have a look at the view, and then descend back to Passo del Penice and walk on the col's other side.

Geographically, both Penice and Bobbio are on the border of many different regions, cultures and landscapes. Northeast, the Trebbia river valley descends to Piacenza and Emilia. North, the rolling hills of the Oltrepo' Pavese, rich in castles and good wines, descend towards Milan and the Po. A few miles to the south, steep valleys start their winding descent towards the Ligurian Riviera. Dialects, flora and landscape make this part of the country unique, a special and interesting blend of many of northern Italy's facets.

North of Passo del Penice, a long forested ridge forms the Apennines' northernmost point which juts towards the plain and Oltrepò. You can walk pleasantly here from half an hour to a day. If you are looking for a longer trip, and travel by public transport, you can try to reach Zavattarello by bus from Pavia, climb up a road and then a small path to Calenzone, continue on this trail, reach Penice, and then descend directly towards Bobbio on the dirt roads and mule tracks a little south of the road. This is an interesting 2 day trip.

How to get there Many roads lead to Passo del Penice. The shortest one from Milan goes through Voghera and Varzi, but the slightly longer tour through Piacenza and Bobbio is recommended because Bobbio is an interesting place. From the south, you can follow a very winding, long and interesting road from Genova, through Torriglia and Ottone, or another one from Chiavari through Santo Stefano d'Aveto. By bus your best bet is from Piacenza, but buses to Penice seldom operate from Bobbio.

The trail From the Pass' 1,100 m, follow a small, unmarked dirt road northwards, climbing by way of a couple of zig zags through a deep fir forest. You can park near a small Corpo Forestale hut, or a little after this, at the beginning of a long series of meadows and

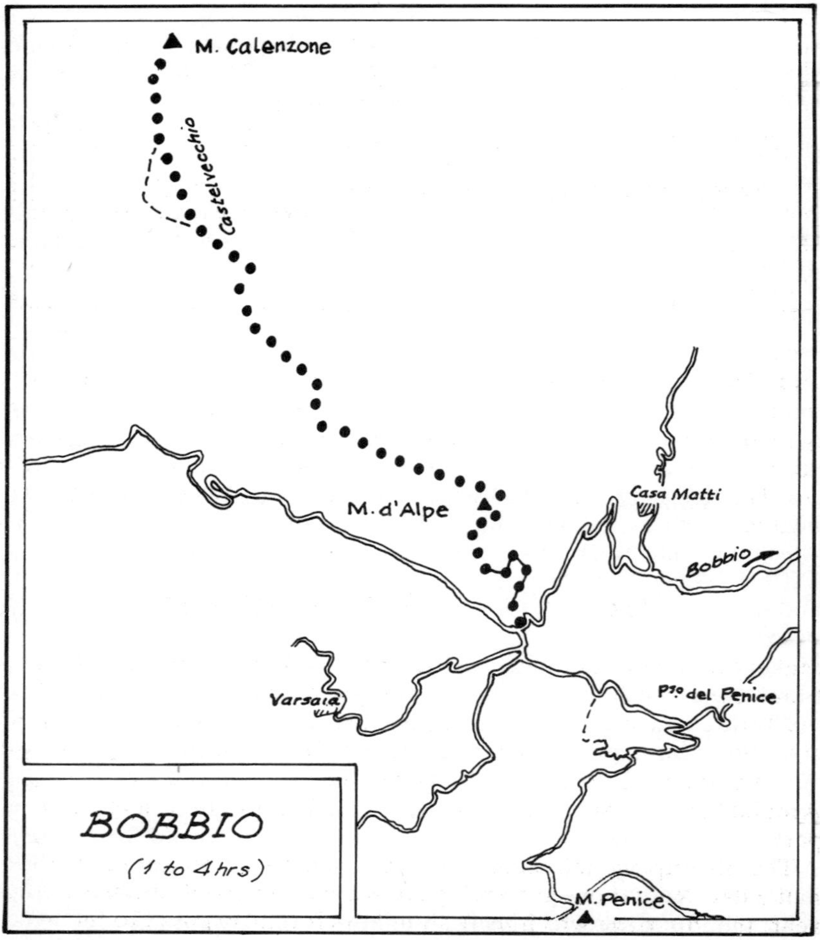

pastures. Monte d'Alpe's large summit (1,253 m) is a few metres away to the south. On foot, you can walk here in 15–20 minutes from the main road.

Now you have to walk on the small dirt track that more or less follows the ridge's crest, continuously in and out of the forest. You can walk as long as you want. In less than an hour you reach a junction. Follow the right hand track, exiting again from the forest on the Costa Castelvecchio. To Monte Calenzone, the ridge's next outcrop, you need 1½ to 2 hours. Allow the same time for the return trip.

MONTE CUSNA AND ABETINA REALE

Between the Firenze–Bologna motorway and the Cisa pass between la Spezia and Parma, stretch the highest and most rugged part of the northern Apennines. The area's loftiest peak, Monte Cimone, 2,165 m, lies right on the border between the provinces of Bologna and Modena and is not an attractive area for hikers and nature lovers. Ski tracks, roads and cablecars climb straight to the top and criss-cross the mountain's slopes, whilst a huge radio transmitter lies on the highest summit.

Monte Cusna, at 2,120 m the area's second highest mountain, is by far the most interesting destination. It lies in Reggio Emilia province, a little to the north of the main ridge; the latter culminates in nearby Monte Prato, at 2,045 m the highest summit in Tuscany. Deep forests, excellent views, and a good network of pleasant huts make Monte Cusna a very interesting proposition for a few days of hiking or just for a rest. The area is not far from a lot of well-known tourist destinations, from Lucca and Versilia to Cinque Terre and the Emilian cities. The access roads, however, are always long and quite tiring.

Cusna itself consists of a long ridge, reached at one point by a téléphérique coming up from Fanano (and only open in winter, during the ski season). The large Lama Lite ridge connects Monte Cusna to Monte Prado and the main ridge, thus dividing the two most interesting valleys of the area. Both are heavily forested; Bargetana valley slopes northwards towards Ligonchio, Abetina Reale drops southwards towards Civago. This small village is the best starting point for most walks in the area.

At Lama Lite, *rifugio* Battisti is a very good place to stay, even for more than one day. It is owned by the Reggio Emilia's section of CAI, and is normally open from the beginning of July to mid-September. It is sometimes open for longer periods at weekends, and can be open for groups all the year round. In winter, the area becomes good for cross-country skiing (up to the hut), ski-mountaineering (to the summits), and even for some ice-climbing on Monte Prato and Cusna. The hut's telephone number is (0522) 800155.

If you are interested in longer walks remember that the area (as with all of these mountains) is crossed by GEA, that uses *rifugio* Battisti as an overnight stop. The long trail section between Abetone and Cisa passes is by far the most 'alpine' of all, traversing deep forests and commanding extensive views both towards the sea and the Po plain.

How to get there Civago, the trail's starting point, is normally approached from Reggio Emilia through SS. 63 and Villa Minozzo, or from Modena through Sassuolo, SS. 486 and Piandelagotti. If you are looking for public transport start from Reggio. From the Tuscan side, a long road from Castelnuovo Garfagnana winds up to Foce delle Radici, where you turn left to Civago.

The trail From Civago to Abetina Reale hut, there is a choice between two trails. The first one is longer, nicer, and recommended if you are planning to spend a night either in Abetina or in *rifugio* Battisti. If you are here for a day walk, the shorter approach will leave you time for some exploration higher up.

For the longer trail, from Civago's 1,011 m, follow the road on the right side of the valley to Case di Civago, and then to the road's beginning (if you prefer walking, this is a mere 20 minutes from the village). Start walking up a gently climbing trail, in the forest, with some interesting views on Sperone di Monte Prato's rock on the far side of the valley. At a fork, keep to the left (*sentiero basso*), reaching a

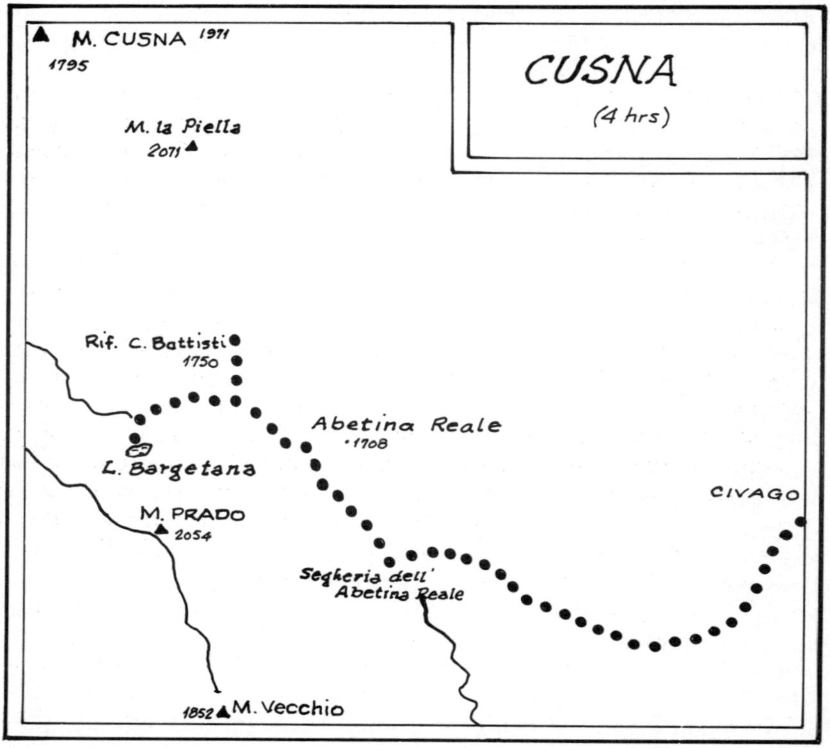

ford where a dirt road goes left. Continue straight on, climbing through a beautiful fir forest to a large building at Abetina Reale (1,401 m and $1\frac{1}{4}$ hours from the start). If you need to save time, follow the road from Civago do Passo delle Radici, cross the river, and turn right onto a large, unmarked dirt road. From where private cars are forbidden you will need little more than 30 minutes to Abetina Reale. The *rifugio* is an old building and is the starting point for horse-back tours.

The marked trail keeps climbing to the right, partly on a dirt road, to the tree-line. Through beautiful pastures, you keep climbing to Lama Lite Pass (1,791 m), from where you can see Monte Cusna. Turn right on a large dirt road, then left to *rifugio* Battisti (1,750 m) and again $1\frac{1}{2}$ hours from Abetina Reale. From here, you have a large choice of trails.

The climb to Monte Cusna takes 3 to 4 hours for the round trip. Follow a large trail to the Cusna's ridge at Passone, and then go along the ridge, passing the téléphérique's station on the way. The hike to the summit is easy but watch out for slippery rocks. On the other side of the valley, a shorter and perhaps nicer walk leads to Monte Prato (2,053 m, 2 hours return), passing by the magnificent Lake Bargetana. The latter is a good destination for a short but interesting walk.

BETWEEN QUARRIES AND SUMMITS: THE PANIE HIKE

Marble has always been important in the economy of the Apuane people. It has also been a menace. Both old and modern quarrying techniques have claimed a heavy toll of lives every year, and you cannot avoid shivering when you see one of the ill-famed *lizze*, the very steep corridors where marble is lowered on long ropes and a man descends under the block to put grease on the track!

Around Carrara, a visit to the biggest quarries is a very interesting one, and a completely different experience from admiring Michelangelo's statues or any other masterpiece in the churches and museums of Rome and Florence. Nowadays there is another big problem. With new, powerful quarrying techniques, whole mountains are bound to disappear; even the so-called 'Park' recently established by Tuscany's regional government has completely failed to deal with this problem.

Amongst the most endangered area is Monte Corchia, dominating the small village of Levigliani. It is a surprising mountain as Antro del Corchia, Italy's deepest cave (950 m vertical drop) tunnels down through the marble. International teams, including English ones, played an important role in its exploration. Now a new quarry is being opened right on top of the mountain, and the cave itself is in danger.

Nearby, Panie massif is one of the highest and most interesting in the whole area. In winter, Pania della Croce provides classic snow and ice climbs to the mountaineer. In summer, pleasant and perfectly easy trails open up magnificent round tours to the walker. Two huts allow the walk to be spread over two interesting days. When choosing a time to start, remember that the initial ascent from Levigliani to Passo dell'Alpino can be very hot.

All around, the Apuane offer dozens of very interesting walks. South of the one described, my favourite one goes from Stazzema to *rifugio* Forte dei Marmi and Matanna, at the foot of the imposing Procinto and Monte Nona cliffs. To the north, in the wildest and highest area of the group, interesting, steep hikes lead from *rifugio* Donegani towards Monte Pisanino and Pizzo d'Uccello. Near to the Tyrrhenian again, another easy and beautiful path leads from *rifugio* Carrara to Monte Sagro.

How to get there The starting point for this trail is Levigliani, a small village close to huge marble quarries. To reach it, follow the road from Forte dei Marmi and Pietrasanta (nearby is the Versilia exit on the Genova–Livorno motorway), and continue through Ruosina to Levigliani. From the village, a steep dirt road continues along the north side of the valley, to a junction where the trail starts (3 km from the village). By bus, you can travel to Levigliani from Forte dei Marmi railway station, or from Massa or Lucca. Once you reach the village, you have to walk along the dirt road (3 km, or 45 minutes on foot).

The trail From the junction, you follow the left hand road for a few metres and then start climbing up a steep but beautiful old trail. Near the first bend, a hole in the rock is the lowest of the three entrances to the Corchia cave – this is for experienced cavers only!

The trail goes on zigzagging for a long way, with interesting views on the left towards Monte Corchia. You cross a level ridge (Passo dell'Alpino) and continue traversing, with views on Pania della Croce, to a large grassy saddle. Turning left, in a few minutes you reach *rifugio* Del Freo (1,180 m, 1 hour from the dirt road), a convenient place to spend the night.

Next morning you go back to the saddle, and then follow the trail climbing on the left side of the grassy ridge of Pania della Croce. You reach a small saddle (le Gorfigliette), and then continue on the steep trail to the summit ridge. Following this on the right, you reach Pania della Croce's 1,859 m (1½ hours from the hut). The view is extraordinary.

Another trail leaves the summit ridge on the opposite side. Follow it by descending a large stony cirque, Vallone dell'Inferno. The path descends, veers left, and crosses the Focetta del Puntone saddle. A few minutes' walk leads to *rifugio* Rossi (1,600 m, ¾ hour from the top). If you have only one day, you should stop here, or even on the Pania's summit. The return trip from the dirt road to the Pania requires about 4 hours.

Continue descending on the eastern (Garfagnana) side of the mountain, along a beautiful trail amongst much greener scenery. Enter the forest, and continue descending quite steeply for about an hour. From a small rocky outcrop (a few more minutes on the main trail lead to the

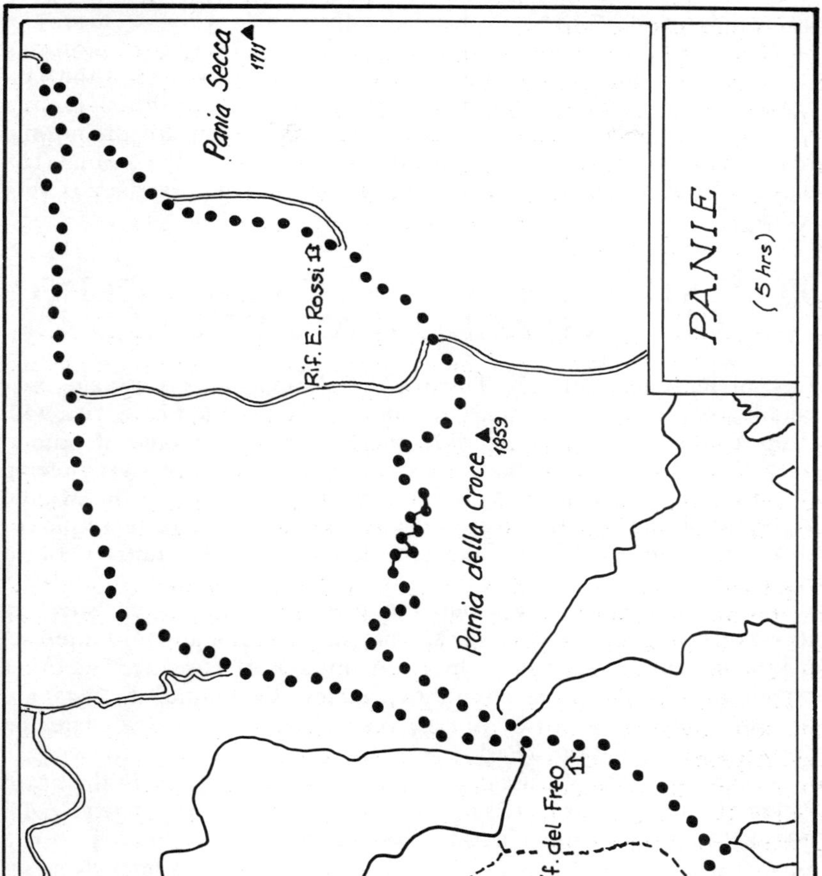
PANIE
(5 hrs)
Pania Secca
1711
Rif. E. Rossi
Pania della Croce
1859
Rif. del Freo
M. Corcha
1677
Marble Quarries
LEVIGLIANI

road coming from Castelnuovo Garfagnana), a well-marked trail turns left, starting a long traverse under the eastern slopes of the Pania. Pass under a large gully (Borra di Canala), turn on to a rocky ridge, and enter another large grassy valley traversed by another big trail coming from Isola Santa. You follow the trail to the left, to reach the first grassy saddle again and the nearby *rifugio* Del Freo. From Pania's summit to the *rifugio*, allow 3 hours. A direct descent for the normal route (the one you've been up on) requires no more than 1 hour. The descent from *rifugio* Del Freo to the dirt road from Levigliani is very quick.

FORESTE CASENTINESI: CAMALDOLI TO CASTAGNO D'ANDREA

East of Florence, between Tuscany and Romagna, is a strange, fascinating part of the Apennines. Mountains are rounded here, rich with deep forests, abundant in wildlife and flowers. It is a land of waters; both the Rivers Arno and Tevere are born here and start flowing towards the Tyrrhenian sea. It is a land of peace; during the Middle Ages, monks and hermits were attracted by the peace of these mountains, and founded abbeys which are still amongst the country's holiest places.

It is an interesting area, but also one which is rarely visited by foreigners. Camaldoli, Badia Prataglia and la Verna are very interesting old abbeys, and can be included in any tour of Tuscany. The other big interest is nature; the *Foreste Casentinesi*, Casentino's Forests, are protected by a series of State reserves, which will sooner or later be grouped into a National Park.

Along the whole of Tuscany's mountains, from Liguria in the north to Umbria in the south, runs *Grande Escursione Appenninica* (*GEA*), one of the most interesting long distance trails in the country. It is a very appealing idea indeed, requiring 25 days for the complete journey, but it can be split in many different ways. Its excellent guidebook, *GEA* by Alfonso Bietolini and Gianfranco Bracci, published by Tamari, has extremely detailed maps, making it easy to use for foreigners who do speak Italian.

My suggestion is a 2 day hike along the GEA from Camaldoli to Castagno d'Andrea, across the most interesting part of the forests and the imposing Monte Falterona massif. If you have more time, it can be interesting to start from la Verna, on the Bibbiena–Pieve S. Stefano road. Shorter walks can be taken simply by turning back when you want to. You can also choose your own hike apart from the guidebook's maps. The 1:15,000 *Carta turistica*, published by Comune di Poppi, can be used for the first part of the hike.

How to get there The trail follows the main Apennine ridge dividing Tuscany from Romagna. Buses are slow, but they allow hikers to walk without having to come back the same way. SITA, LFI and Francioni lines drive from Florence and Arezzo to Chiusi della Verna, Badia Prataglia, Passo della Calla and Castagno d'Andrea. By car, you have the choice between leaving it in Florence or Arezzo, travelling back to pick it up again at the end of the walk (a long business), or retracing your steps. Both days are quite short: you can do the round trip from Florence in two complete days.

The trail The bus will drop you a few metres from the main Camaldoli Abbey, which is worth a visit. If you get here the day before starting your hike, you have the choice between two hotels and the camping area near the small village, where there is also a *Posto tappa*, a small hostel where GEA hikers can sleep for a small fee.

You start your hike with an hour of steepish ascent, from the abbey's 816 m to Eremo di Camaldoli's 1,104 m. The trail goes straight up, cutting off the small paved road's many bends. Then you follow the trail ascending on the left of the building, which is easily followed because of the GEA's red and white marks. You reach a dirt road following the ridge almost exactly, and continue along to the left. At Giogo Secchieta pass you turn right, continuing on the Romagna side of the mountain; a short uphill walk leads you to Passo Porcareccio, at 1,456 m and another half hour's walk. Another short climb brings you to Poggio Scali at 1,520 m; this is an excellent viewpoint over the whole of the area (around 1½ hours from Eremo). In the early morning, it is not impossible to spot wild boar and deer. From here, the trail alternates between short ascents and longer descents to Passo della Calla, at 1,296 m, on a paved road connecting Stia (Tuscany) to Campigna (Romagna). On a smaller road, continue to *rifugio* la Burraia, at 1,358 m, a friendly inn where you can spend the night. The walk does not take more than 4 hours. La Burraia's phone number is 0543/ 980053 and nearby is another *rifugio*, owned by CAI.

On day two, start climbing along the ski run, turn right near a couple of trees, and continue to a military transmission point. Continue on the ridge to Monte Falco (1,658 m, the area's highest mountain), descend steeply to a fork at 1,510 m (on the left you can descend to the source of the Arno), and climb steeply again to Monte Falterona (1,634 m, 2–2½ hours from la Burraia).

After stopping to appreciate the view, follow the trail which starts 50 m north of the summit, and descends steeply to Fonte del Borbotto, at 1,200 m, where there is an emergency shelter not far from the water fountain. Descend onto the small road, leave it at the first bend and continue on another steep trail descending to Castagno d'Andrea (716 m, and 2 hours from the top of Falterona). If you want to stop for the night, you can ask for the keys of *Posto tappa* at Osteria il Rifugio.

Chapter 10

The Central Apennines

The central Apennines, the *Appennino centrale*, is by far the highest and the most rugged part of peninsular Italy. The highest part of Italy's backbone starts in the north with the Monti Sibillini massif on the border between Umbria and Marche, stretching southwards with the beautiful and extremely little known chain of the Monti della Laga (this is shared between Abruzzo, Lazio and Marche), which leads to the highest massif, the Gran Sasso.

At 2,912 m, this is by far the tallest mountain in the whole chain, and has the southernmost glacier in all Europe. Its main summit, an incredible viewpoint, is perfectly easy to reach for the well-trained hiker once the winter snow has melted away. The Gran Sasso is entirely in Abruzzo region, and so is Maiella, the second highest (2,795 m at Monte Amaro) and probably the wildest massif in the whole chain.

Slightly more on the Tyrrhenian side of the peninsula are many other mountains; Terminillo (2,216 m), Velino (2,486 m) and nearby Sirente (2,358 m), the long chain of Monti Simbruini and Monti Ernici, which directly overlook the lowlands of Lazio. A bit more to the south, the *Parco Nazionale d'Abruzzo*, established in 1922, is one of the oldest and the second biggest national park in Italy. Its highest summit, Monte Petroso (2,249 m), is just slightly bettered by nearby Monte Greco (2,285 m), just outside the Park's boundaries. The Park is a

refuge for bears, wolves, chamois and deer, and it is well worth some exploration.

Travelling south again, the beautiful and very little known massif of Matese, reaching 2,050 m in the Monte Miletto, is at the southern end of the highest range. It is shared between the regions of Campania (where Naples is!) and Molise, and is followed, travelling south, by lower and very different mountains.

As the heights of the summits I have just mentioned tell, this area is to be taken seriously at all times of the year. Some mountaineers in the Alps, having never travelled this way, will probably explain to you that these mountains are 'nothing but easy hills'. They are not, and the proximity of the open Adriatic sea makes Gran Sasso, Monti Sibillini and Maiella the windiest parts of all Italy.

Here you will find almost no permanent snow (the Calderone glacier on Gran Sasso is very small) and almost all of the summits can be reached very easily. In the middle of summer, heat and the lack of water can cause the most serious problems. In winter, the whole area receives a heavy amount of snow and offers perfectly good downhill skiing, ski-mountaineering and cross-country skiing opportunities. In summer, the technical climber's interests are reduced to the sheer limestone faces of Gran Sasso, and to smaller-scale problems elsewhere. In winter, as in Scotland, all these mountains offer serious ice and snow climbing, which must obviously be tackled with proper equipment and experience. Beware of these mountains during late autumn: the first snows may have melted or been swept away by the wind on the sunny south slopes, but not in the northern gullies. Often poorly equipped hikers are found on summits where climbers arrive from serious ice-climbs: such conditions could easily become deadly for the inexperienced ones.

When and where to go A network of good motorways and roads lead easily into the mountains from Rome, Naples and the Adriatic coastal town of Abruzzo. Like many other mountain areas, this one is best enjoyed with a car: Abruzzo's mountains can offer the visitor a very interesting week in which mountain hikes and visits to churches and ancient monuments can be alternated. L'Aquila has some of the finest ancient churches of central Italy, and many more fine ones, usually set in very beautiful surroundings, are to be found along the L'Aquila to Sulmona road, or in the Pescara river valley.

If you are using public transport, stick to a single area, and spend a few days in it, without trying to travel too much; the Sangro valley in the Abruzzo National Park is possibly the best area for that. A railway line links Rome to Pescara crossing Avezzano and Sulmona, the AFA buses are very fast between the main towns, and reach almost all mountain villages: for information ring (06) 4742801 in Rome, (085) 51329 in Pescara and (0862) 20384 in L'Aquila.

As this is a true mountain area, the best hiking period goes from June to October, but there are lower paths where you can enjoy interesting hikes even in winter. But at this time of the year it is probably more interesting to try some hikes in Lazio or Toscana, and then move to the mountains for some skiing. Apart from the downhill tracks (quite good, but short as a rule, and not as interesting as in the Dolomites or Valle d'Aosta) you'll find here some truly excellent cross-country opportunities.

THE LONG DISTANCE TRAILS

There are not, at the moment of writing, proper marked long distance trails in this part of the country. You can easily organize hikes up to a week following Sibillini, Gran Sasso, Maiella and Abruzzo National Parks' marked trails. Two long unmarked trails have become quite popular in the last few years. Both are quite strenuous, require IGM maps and a compass, and can only be walked with a tent.

The northernmost one is the *Sibillini to Gran Sasso* hike: it starts by crossing Monti Sibillini, touches the Forca Canapine hut, crosses the Via Salaria at Accumoli, and climbs towards Monti della Laga's main ridge. Then it follows the main crest to the south, descends to Lake Campotosto, and enters Gran Sasso massif from the beautiful Chiarino valley. You can end on Corno Grande's 2,912 m, or continue more towards the east.

The second established trail is the *Simbruini to Parco d'Abruzzo hike*, starting around Carsoli and ending in Civitella Alfedena or Pescasseroli. It starts crossing the Simbruini chain (you can actually start walking from Camerata Nuova or Pereto), touches the chain's main summits (Autore, Tarino and Viglio), then drops from Monna's summit to the beautiful Trisulti abbey. Another climb leads to the Pizzo Deta summit, a long descent to Balsorano and then a further climb brings the hiker up to the Park's mountains, near Monte Cornacchia's 2,003 m. The chain is then followed south to any of the Park's main centres. On the whole, this is a magnificent 10 day hike, not to be walked in the hottest period of the year.

Probably a long system of trails will develop during the next few years. From Bocca Trabaria, *GEA* will continue along the border between Umbria dn Marche, to Monti Sibillini. After this, the trail will branch off at Forca Canapine. The western trail will touch Terminillo, Lake Salto, Carsoli, and continue following the *Simbruini to Parco d'Abruzzo* trail. The eastern branch will start on *Sibillini to Gran Sasso* trail, continue southwards across the Pescara river valley to Maiella, traverse this massif to Campo di Giove, and then continue through Roccaraso, Monte Greco and Barrea to the southern end of the Abruzzo park where the two trails will merge again.

EXPLORING THE SIBILLINI WILDERNESS

Where did *Sibilla* live? And what happened, in the very last stages of his life, to Ponzio Pilato, the Roman governor who was responsible for

Jesus' death? To look for an answer, you don't have to travel to the Middle East, or to Delphi. Instead, travel to the northernmost of the big mountain massifs of central Italy where the Monti Sibillini, stretching exactly along the country's backbone, and parting Marche from Umbria to find the answers.

It is a beautiful, wild area, of very steep grassy mountains, offering serious challenges here and there to the climber. To the average hiker, this is an extraordinary place to arrange 2 to 3 day backpacking tours. If you want a softer option, you can have a base-camp somewhere, and then travel around for easy day hikes. All the main summits and valleys are also within your reach this way. You can stop in Castelluccio, the highest inhabited village of peninsular Italy, or try and look for an hotel around Montefortino and Montegallo. I would suggest the CAI *rifugio* at Forca Canapine; my friends Lino and Giovanna are very friendly, the food is good and cheap, and the area is very attractive outside the main summer season. From December to March, you have beautiful and easy cross-country ski tours, and in June the flowers on Piani di Castelluccio are incredible.

North to south, the Sibillini massif rises into easy Monte Rotondo (2,103 m), then into the more difficult Priora (2,332 m). A little to the west is the imposing Monte Bove massif (2,169 m), while on the east Monte Sibilla was supposed to house a magician's cave. South again, and you find the highest massif of all; Monte Vettore (2,476 m) is taller, whilst nearby Pizzo del Diavolo (2,448 m) boasts the most impressive rock face of the area, directly falling into the blue Lago di Pilato, where, according to tradition, the Roman governor of Galilee was drowned.

The Sibillini area has long since been proposed as a National Park: hiking around, you can understand why! For a description of the hike and many others, you can rely on Kompass' 1:50,000 *Monti Sibillini* map, available everywhere in the area. Maursio Calibani and Alberico Alesi's *Guida dei Monti Sibillini* describes more than sixty hikes.

How to get there This is a difficult area to reach for those travelling by public transport. For those who travel by car the Monti Sibillini are very easy to reach from the beautiful and often-visited towns of Umbria (Perugia, Assisi), and from the lesser known, but magnificent medieval town of Ascoli Piceno. You can reach Castelluccio and Forca Canapine from the western side, and Montefortino (don't miss the Infernaccio canyon!) and Foce from the east. By bus, your best bet is a ride to Ussita from Visso, and then a walk up the beautiful but long Valle di Panico. Anyway, you can always hitch-hike!

The trail My suggestion is a 2 day hike into the Lago di Pilato area, and up Monte Vettore to enjoy a great, great view of rolling hills and mountains stretching in every direction. For this, your best starting point is the village of Foce, at 945 m above sea level, and about 30 km from Ascoli Piceno. You can take a bus to Montemonaco, and then hitch a ride. Foce itself is a small pleasant enough place to rest for a while.

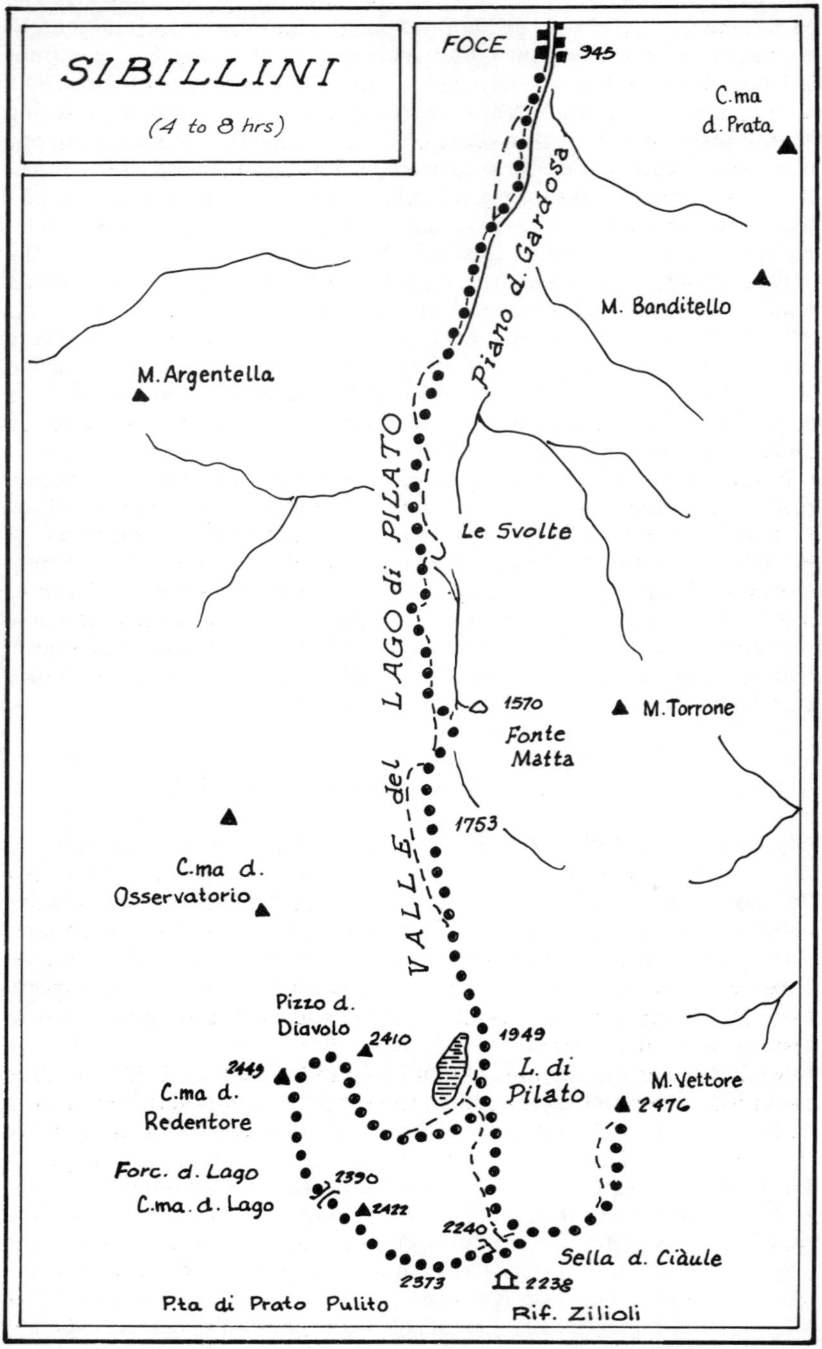
SIBILLINI
(4 to 8 hrs)
FOCE
945
C.ma d. Prata
Piano d. Gardosa
M. Banditello
M. Argentella
VALLE del LAGO di PILATO
Le Svolte
1570
M. Torrone
Fonte Matta
1753
C.ma d. Osservatorio
Pizzo d. Diavolo
2410
1949
2449
C.ma d. Redentore
L. di Pilato
M. Vettore
2476
Forc. d. Lago
2390
C.ma. d. Lago
2422
2240
Sella d. Ciàule
2373
2238
P.ta di Prato Pulito
Rif. Zilioli

From the village, follow the main path heading south across beautiful Piano della Gardosa, and towards rocky Pizzo del Diavolo. The path climbs steeply over the Svolte (means literally 'zigzags', so don't be surprised) and continues along a grassy valley, close to the rocks. Skirting these on the left, you get to the lake shore, at 1,950 m, which takes 3 hours from Foce. You can rest and return on the same day and even climb Monte Vettore if you have started early enough in the morning. There is a small patch of grass between the two halves of the lake for camping, and more sites are available on the far side. Don't camp too near to the scree slopes in case hikers and sheep cause stones to fall.

Next morning, climb a steep path on the east (left) across a rock band, to the grassy slopes leading to Forca della Ciàule, where *rifugio* Zilioli is. This has been heavily damaged and does not offer any shelter at all. On the left, a large grassy and stony ridge climbs gently to the top of Monte Vettore, at 2,476 m and 1½ hours from the lake. To return, retrace your steps. But if it's early enough in the day, you had better continue south, climbing (there is always a path) all the peaks in the horseshoe enclosing the lake. When you get to Cima del Redentore, a tiny ridge on the right brings you to Pizzo del Diavolo. Then you retrace your steps on the ridge, turn south (left coming from the Pizzo), and race down a huge scree slope, landing a short distance from the lake. From Vettore, taking it slowly, allow 2½–3 hours. The hike down to Foce will take a couple more hours. If you are carless, descend the main path from Forca della Ciàule going down to Forca di Presta, and continue on a gentle ridge flanked by unpaved roads to Forca Canapine. From the lake to *rifugio* CAI, allow 5 hours.

THE GRAN SASSO TOUR

High above the hills of eastern Abruzzo, clearly seen from many of central Italy's summits, Gran Sasso is a mountain of many surprises. On the northern side, it boasts Dolomite-like limestone faces, offering the rock climber a choice of beautiful climbs. On the southern side, Gran Sasso is the Apennines at their best; the 'big stone' of the Corno Grande massif mirrors itself into the huge plateau of Campo Imperatore, 20 km long, offering both the hiker and the motorist a surprising taste of Anatolia or central Asia.

With the western summit of Corno Grande reaching 2,912 m, Gran Sasso is a high mountain, and one to respect. It is not very well known by hikers and climbers from northern Italy, but in 1573 it was one of the very first mountains in Europe to be climbed by man. Today, it is the favourite playground for many hundreds of hikers and climbers based in Rome and in all the cities of Abruzzo, Marche and Lazio. Maiella is huge, and Velino or Terminillo are easily reached. But Gran Sasso is the only mountain in this part of Italy which shows visitors glimpses of the real, high summits of the Alps. Its ascent is perfectly easy and a must for the hiker happening to travel this way after the last snows of winter have melted.

The Gran Sasso massif is a 35 km long barrier stretching from east to west and parting Teramo and L'Aquila provinces of Abruzzo. Right in the middle, the Corno Grande and Corno Piccolo massifs are by far the highest and most visited of all. East and west of these, many other summits and valleys offer long expeditions for the backpacker. The round, 2 day trip I am describing here is a combination of many things. Vallone delle Cornacchie is crowded, but lower Val Maone much less so and the views vary from the rocky, Dolomite-like limestone faces to the endless chains of rounded mountains stretching to the south. From the summit, the Adriatic sea is easily seen on most clear days, on exceptionally brisk winter days, both of Italy's seas can be seen and a thin white line marks the far-away hills of Yugoslavia.

The ascent to Corno Grande's summit is nothing more than a hike; there is only a 10 m rock scramble on the way up, none on the descent. However, this applies only when *all* the snow has melted away, normally from the end of July to the end of September. With any snow around, the steep slopes around Passo del Cannone can be tricky, even to experienced climbers: in this case you should go the other way round, climbing up the Calderone glacier. You must take an ice axe and know how to use it.

In full summer conditions, you should bring only normal hiking equipment and dress taking into account that the climate can reach extremes in both directions. A sleeping bag is recommended but not necessary when sleeping at Duca degli Abruzzi. If you have a CAI or any other club card, it could be useful too. Remember that the Duca degli Abruzzi and Franchetti huts are open during summer, but the Garibaldi hut is closed. To know the exact opening times of the huts, ring (06) 6561011 for Duca degli Abruzzi, and (0861) 95642 for Franchetti. The best available map is IGM's 140 III NO *Gran Sasso d'Italia*.

How to get there The suggested trail touches both sides of Gran Sasso: it is described from the northern side, but can easily be reached from L'Aquila's side, driving up the road that reaches Campo Imperatore's hotel. From here, first walk half an hour to nearby Duca degli Abruzzi, and then simply reverse the two days which will be described as follows: day two becomes day one, and vice versa. If you are travelling by bus, you will have to start from Prati di Tivo, reached by bus from Teramo. If you are driving there are two choices: Campo Imperatore is nearer to Rome and the Tyrrhenian coast, Prati di Tivo is easily reached from the Adriatic coast, and offers a more impressive sight.

The trail Once you get there, Prati di Tivo will certainly deceive you. The lower old village of Pietracamela is quite attractive, but the higher Prati boasts only a series of big hotels that have destroyed a very beautiful spot. The cheap way to sleep is at the Jarkhun campground (phone: 0861/95616), a 20 minute walk or 5 minute drive on a side road to the left: they also have cabins. The cheapest way of all, much used by young climbers, is to bivouac in the chairlift's lower station.

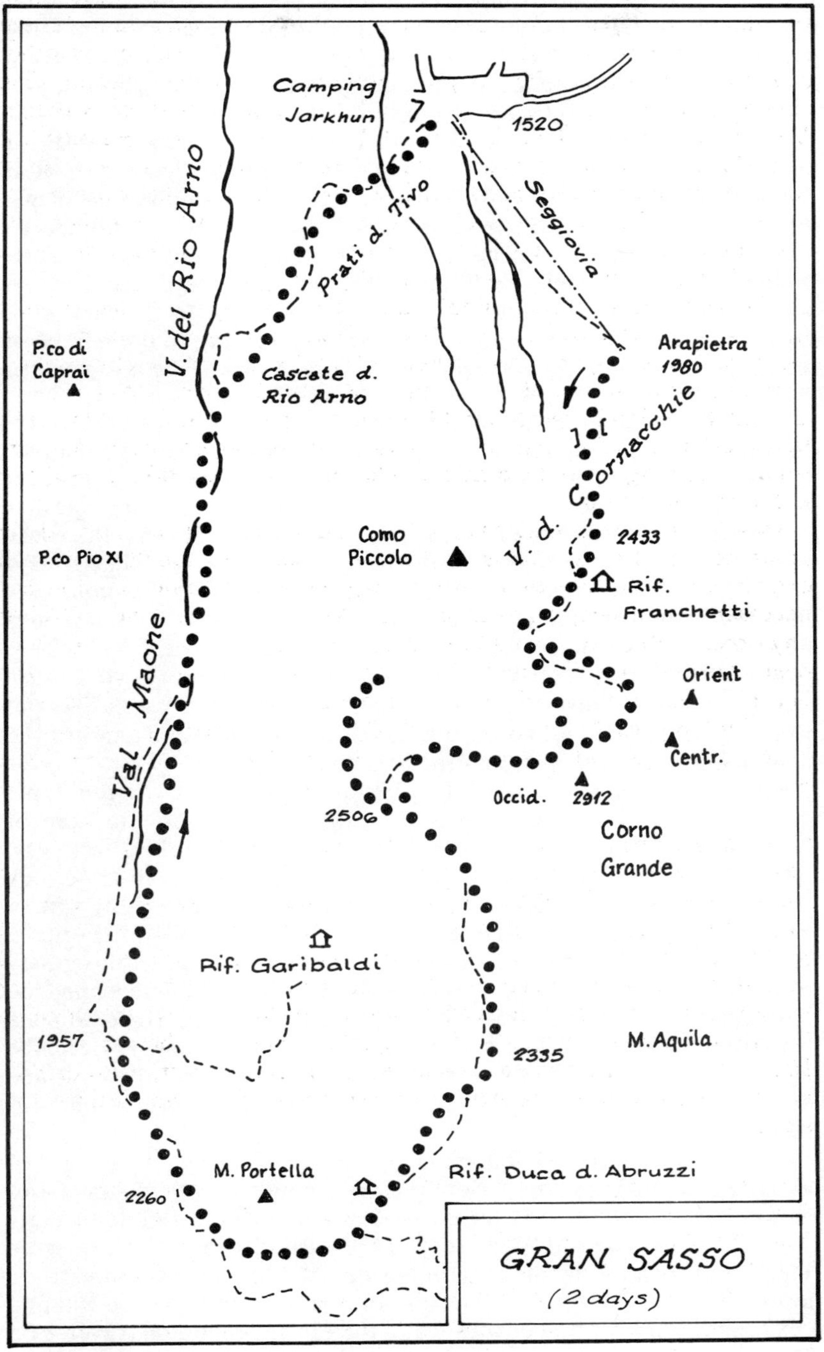
Camping
Jarkhun
1520
Seggiovia
Prati d. Tivo
V. del Rio Arno
P.co di
Caprai
Cascate d.
Rio Arno
Arapietra
1980
V. d. Cornacchie
Como
Piccolo
2433
P.co Pio XI
Rif.
Franchetti
Val Maone
Orient
Centr.
Occid.
2912
2506
Corno
Grande
Rif. Garibaldi
1957
2335
M. Aquila
M. Portella
Rif. Duca d. Abruzzi
2260
GRAN SASSO
(2 days)

You will not be alone on a weekend and you are supposed not to leave any litter. The most beautiful place to pitch a tent is right at the end of the road passing the campground, on a large grassy ridge, commanding magnificent views (especially at dawn) on Corno Grande's imposing east face, one hour's walk from the chairlift station. Camp where you want, but bring water from the Prati di Tivo.

On day one, start with an easy uphill climb on the chairlift, leaving it on the Arapietra ridge, at the foot of Corno Piccolo's faces. In front of you is Corno Grande, with the sea on the far left. Between the two mountains is Vallone delle Cornacchie, where your route starts. Should the chairlift be closed, the best path is the one following the skyline ridge left of the Prati, starting from the campsite suggested before. From the Arapietra, an impressive but perfectly easy path leads after an hour to the *rifugio* Franchetti (2,433 m), in the middle of the cirque (cwm), with a stunning view onto Corno Piccolo's eastern face.

From the *rifugio*, the path reaches the Sella dei due Corni (on the far side is Val Maone, where you will descend tomorrow), and then climbs an easy scree slope on the left, reaching the foot of the rocks. A short path branches to the left towards Calderone glacier, offering another magnificent sight not to be missed. The main path zigzags up the rocks (not more than 10 m of real scrambling but remember what I said before!), then goes right from Passo del Cannone (the *Cannone* is a black hole up on the left) reaching a large scree cwm. It then climbs directly along a strenuous scree slope to the top (2,912 m, 2 hours from Franchetti including a look at the glacier). If the weather is good, stop here for a while: close by are the other summits of Gran Sasso, and perhaps you can find a local mountaineer to pick out the names of the many mountains which stretch towards the horizon.

The easy way down follows the uphill steps down the last scree slope, and then traverses west towards the grassy terraces at the base of Corno Grande's west ridge. There are two more marked descents: both of them (the west ridge itself and the *direttissima*) have some rock scrambling, and are quicker than the normal one. From the grassy terraces, the trail turns left descending more scree into Campo Pericoli, right under Corno Grande's south face. It then crosses gentle grassy slopes leaving on the right a path to the Garibaldi hut, reaching the main dividing ridge of the massif, and going east (on the right) to Sella di Monte Aquila (2,336 m and 2 hours from the summit). Here the path divides: the left branch goes to Campo Imperatore, you continue along the ridge to the Duca degli Abruzzi hut (2,388 m, half an hour from the col).

On day two, start off following the same ridge, again facing east towards the imposing Pizzo Cefalone, reaching the little rocky col of Passo della Portella (2,261 m) crossed by the ancient trail connecting L'Aquila to Pietracamela. Here you turn right, descend more scree slopes, and then follow the path into green Val Maone, right under the impressive east face of Pizzo Intermesoli. At the end of it, you will find a dirt road: follow it first downhill and then in an ascending traverse on the right. When you cross the ridge, you are at the Prati di Tivo again, and will soon reach the hotel area (3 hours from the Duca degli Abruzzi). If you don't have a car to pick up here, follow the old path instead continuing down Val Maone to Pietracamela, through much nicer scenery. This will take half an hour. To make this day more complete, you can include the perfectly easy path climbing to Pizzo Cefalone's 2,533 m. It starts from Passo della Portella, continues up the ridge, then skirts left around the steep rocks of the Pizzo and climbs an easy gully to the top. The view is magnificent, similar but much more unimpaired than from Doca degli Abruzzi. From the Portella, add about 2 hours to your hike, including the descent.

THE MAIELLA CANYONS HIKE

Mighty Maiella, central Italy's second highest mountain, rises from the gently rolling lowlands of Chieti and Pescara just a few miles south of Gran Sasso, and reaches the highest point at Monte Amaro's 2,795 m. Apart from the height, Maiella is a completely different world from Gran Sasso, Velino, Sibillini and all the mountains of this area.

On the western side, Maiella's slopes are compact and barren and descend towards Sulmona's plain and the Sirente massif. On top, a four-mile long limestone plateau, Valle di Femmina Morta, offers a striking, wild atmosphere to the hiker emerging from the long slog up from the valley. To the north, the Blockhaus and Maielletta ridge declines slowly towards the Pescara river valley and the Rome to Pescara motorway. But the most impressive sight is on the eastern side of the massif.

From the summit plateau, stretching for a dozen miles at 2,400–2,600 m, a huge slope drops steeply towards the hills of Fara San Martino, Palena and Lama dei Peligni. Here, water and time have carved huge canyons within the mountain, as stark and beautiful as any other in Europe. Some of these offer serious adventures to the technical mountaineer: many others follow centuries-old paths which are extremely interesting for the hiker. Five natural reserves (and a sixth one on the way) make of Maiella a big, non-official National Park, and one which many nature-loving Italians have never heard of.

From the hiker's point of view, Maiella offers two completely different kinds of challenge. If you are interested in short, spectacular walks, the canyons of Orfento, Foro, la Valle, Selvaromana, Val Servierą, Santo Spirito and Taranta provide 1 hour to 1 day walks, that are better tackled out of the hottest part of summer: the height is between 400 and 1,000 m, and the sun can be powerful. In the higher part of the massif, walks are long, sometimes very long, but reward the hikers who choose them with a 'Mediterranean wilderness' atmosphere that, in Italy, is possible to enjoy only in the Sardinian mountains, on Etna or Pollino.

Two of these walks are along the traditional paths to the summit of Maiella. The less strenuous one starts from Maielletta, where a road coming from Chieti reaches an ugly skiing village and brings one to the top of Monte Amaro in about 4 hours. Another much-travelled way starts from Fonte Romana on the road between Pacentro and Campo di Giove, climbs steeply to the Femmina Morta plateau, and then turns north towards the top: it takes about 5 hours. But the 3 day hike I am suggesting here is much more interesting: I really feel it is one of the best hikes in the book!

There are not, around Maiella, technical mountaineering difficulties like those found on Gran Sasso. Vertical rock faces exist, but the normally-trodden paths are perfectly easy. Here, your main problems can be the length of the walks (you have to be fit!), the wind on the summit plateau and the lack of water after the last of the winter snow has melted in early July. Along the hike, you'll need a sleeping bag but not a tent, some cooking equipment and food for two days (you can eat but not purchase food at Maielletta's *rifugio*), and a large water bottle. The best period is between late June and the end of September; October is usually good, but then you'll have to be capable of withstanding serious cold and a fierce wind.

The relevant IGM maps are 147 III NO *Caramanico* and 147 III NE *Pennapiedimonte*. A 1:50,000 map published by Chieta's section of CAI is also available, and is sufficient even if not very accurate: many of the marked trails it suggests simply do not exist! More walks are in my *A Piedi in Abruzzo/2* guidebook or in Carlo Landi Vittorj's old (1955) *Appennino Centrale* (CAI-TCI) of which a new edition is expected soon.

How to get there One of the difficulties about Maiella is that the villages at its foot are a long way from each other. If you have two cars, dropping one at the far end of the hike will take a long time. By public transport your best bet is a bus to Caramanico (ARPA is the regional public bus line of Abruzzo) from Pescara, and another bus to Pescara from Fara San Martino. If you are rich and in a hurry, you could try finding a taxi to Caramanico from Pescara or Chieti.

The trail From the centre of Caramanico (the town is a popular spa resort so it is easy to find a cheap hotel or pension here) you start walking alongside the spa area, to reach the village of S. Croce, 10 minutes from Caramanico, where the path starts: the height is 631 m.

Turn left to register at the Guardia Forestale bureau (the valley is a Nature Reserve, and you will see it is worth it. There will be no problem in getting a permit), then cross Santa Croce, passing the church on the left and continue approaching the Orfento canyon's southern rim. The path climbs shortly along the rim, then traverses left entering the canyon, reaching its lowest point in about 1 hour from the start. The walk from here on is very beautiful, through a valley dominated by huge rock faces. The path is quite straightforward. Pass a smooth rocky canyon, climb steeply to the right, and reach a small bridge crossing a narrow gorge after 2 more hours. On the right, is a small road.

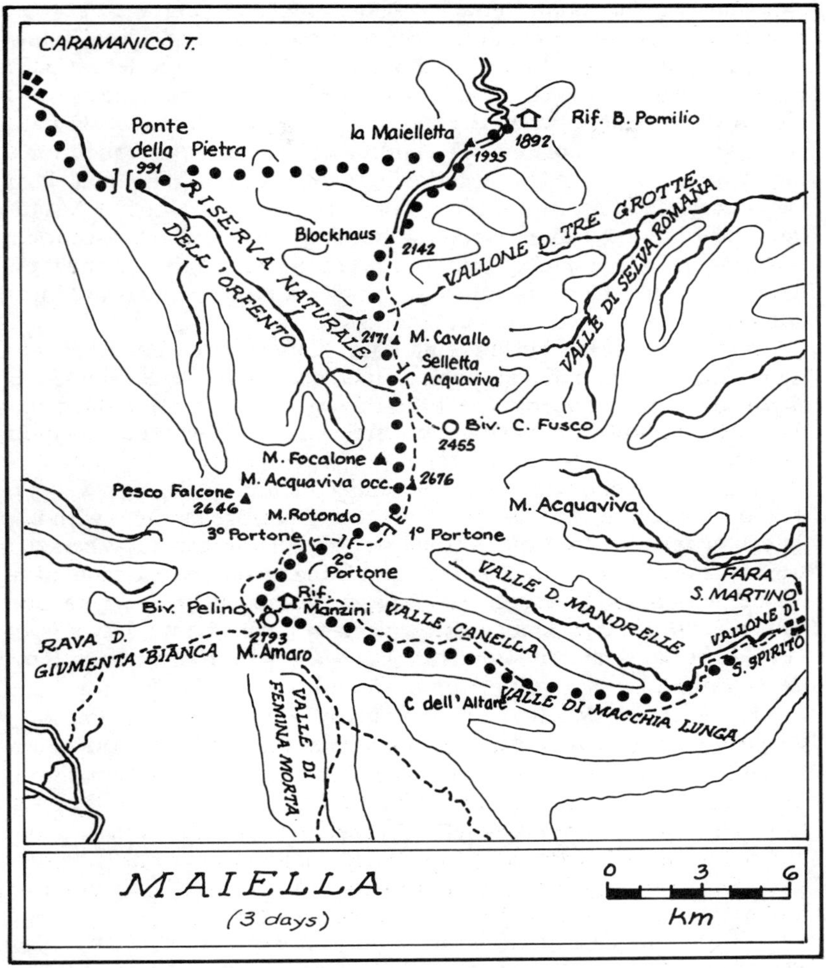

Cross the bridge, 991 m, and follow the path for the Pian Grande, passing nearby the small Sant'Onofrio hermitage. The views become increasingly good, but the going gets steep; a long series of switchbacks climbs the Orfento northern slopes, reaching the rim and the Pian Grande at about 1,750 m. The climb is on easy grassy slopes to reach the road and the Maielletta *rifugio*, at 1,892 m and 2½ hours from the bridge. The area is deceiving, and the *rifugio* itself pretty ugly, but the food is good, and the views over the eastern slopes of the mountain are breathtaking.

Next morning, start following the road going uphill and then, at the end of it, climb a short slope to the top of Blockhaus, where you see the Orfento again. On the top are the walls of an old barracks built in the eighteenth century by the Bourbon rulers of Naples to protect travellers against robberies and attacks. A beautiful path zigzags between the dense juniper bushes, and reaches the base of a steep ridge. Follow it to reach the top of Monte Focalone at 2,676 m; on the left, a path branches towards a small *bivacco*, useful in case of emergencies.

From the Focalone summit you can spot Monte Amaro; the path goes down to Primo Portone col, climbs steeply again, turns right for a long traverse, and then climbs to Pescofalcone plateau. The final ridge is very easy, an almost level scree slope at the end of which is Monte Amaro summit (2,795 m, about 4 hours from the start). Another *bivacco* will allow you to spend the night here comfortably enough: on the south, you'll have magnificent views over the Femmina Morta plateau.

You start day three by retracing your steps towards Pescofalcone. After a few minutes, a path branches right, and leads to the abandoned *rifugio* Manzini, in the middle of the impressive Valle Cannella cwm. From here follow the valley; you still have 2,000 m of downhill walking!

First, you descend Valle Cannella on scree and grass, then a steep slope brings you to the edge of the forest, in an area strewn with big white boulders, where you can have a very pleasant rest. When the forest becomes dense, descend Macchia Lunga valley to the beginning of the lower Santo Spirito canyon. This gets more and more impressive as far as you go, culminating at the end with a narrow rocky gorge, after which you 'emerge' from the mountain, 10 minutes from Fara San Martino. From the top, allow 5 hours of walking, stops not included. The San Martino area has many beautiful walks: the only hotel is quite expensive, but it is not impossible to find a room in a private house.

PARCO D'ABRUZZO: THE CHAMOIS' TRAIL

Parco Nazionale d'Abruzzo is Italy's third largest National Park, and lies in the southernmost part of the Abruzzo mountains. Its boundaries include the whole of the upper Sangro river valley, part of Giovenco and Sagittario river basins and despite the 'regional' name of the Park, continue to some extent well into nearby Lazio and Molise regions. There are many beautiful mountain villages, some of outstanding interest even after the extensive damages of the 1984 earthquake. But there is little doubt that its wildlife is the biggest asset of the Park.

The reserve was established in 1922, out of an older Royal game reserve, with the basic aim of helping the remaining bear population to survive. This is still the main reason for Abruzzo's Park to exist, even if the bears' numbers are not very high: they live in dense forest, are quite difficult to track, and actual estimates vary between 40 and 60 animals. Their habitat lies in some of central Italy's most outstanding forests, where deer, wild boars and wolves also live. In the higher, barren areas is a chamois population of about 450, very popular amongst the Park's many visitors because they are the easiest ones to spot.

The area has always been popular for vacations and weekends. But in the last few years the numbers of hikers, backpackers and cross-country skiers have dramatically increased, compelling the Park administration to introduce a controlled access system for some of its most affected spots. As a result, only three or four trails (Forca Resuni from Civitella Alfedena, Lago Vivo from Barrea, Prato Rosso from Pescasseroli and Val Fondillo from Opi) are heavily trodden by hikers. Still, the majority of the visitors to the area feel satisfied after a car tour and a visit to the Park's zoo and museum. Because of the dense forest, some paths require a fair amount of navigational skills.

Hikes of 3 to 4 days can include a complete north–south traverse of the area, from Villavallolonga or Passo del Diavolo to Barrea or Alfedena; or an east-to-west trek from Roccaraso to the Lazio lowlands and Sora. The Park offers a large number of well marked paths and hiking routes are a-plenty. Even if heavily trodden in some parts of the year, the Forca Resuni paths are too beautiful to be missed: the following description will be of interest to everybody, apart from those who seek total solitude in their hikes.

Basically, this is a 1 day hike, starting and ending in Civitella Alfedena, a village that has become almost a symbol of the Park. Two hostels, a big hotel and a camping area allow for a stopover for the night. Many more possibilities, including cheaper hotels and a couple of very good restaurants (the best known one is 'Il Pescatore', in Villetta Barrea) can be found in the villages nearby. At Forca Resuni col, an old *rifugio* allows you to divide the hike into 2 days, and to spend both sunset and sunrise, the best moments for spotting the wildlife, in the higher areas. However, it has been the Park's policy not to encourage people to sleep in the mountains: camping and bivouacking in the open are forbidden and for some years sleeping in the *rifugio* has been prohibited too. To be sure, you should enquire at the Park's headquarters in Pescasseroli. To sleep at Forca Resuni, you have to bring along a sleeping bag and a stove.

The hike described is included in IGM sheets 152 II NE *Villetta Barrea* and 152 II SE *Settefrati*, or in the 1:50,000 *Carta Turistica* published by the Park's administration.

How to get there By car, many good mountain roads will lead you into the Park. From Rome, drive along the A25 motorway to Pescina, and then cross Passo del Diavolo to Pescasseroli. Alternatively, you can drive south along the A2 motorway to Frosinone, drive on to Sora, and cross Forca d'Acero to Opi. From Naples, the best road is the A2 to Caianello, and then Vefro and Alfedena. From Pescara, leave the A25 motorway either at Cocullo (to Scanno) or Pescina (to the Sangro valley villages). Within the valley, a good road links Passo del Diavolo with Alfedena, crossing Pescasseroli, Opi, Villetta Barrea (Civitella Alfedena is nearby) and Barrea. The big artificial lake between Villetta Barrea and Barrea is a favourite spot for visitors.

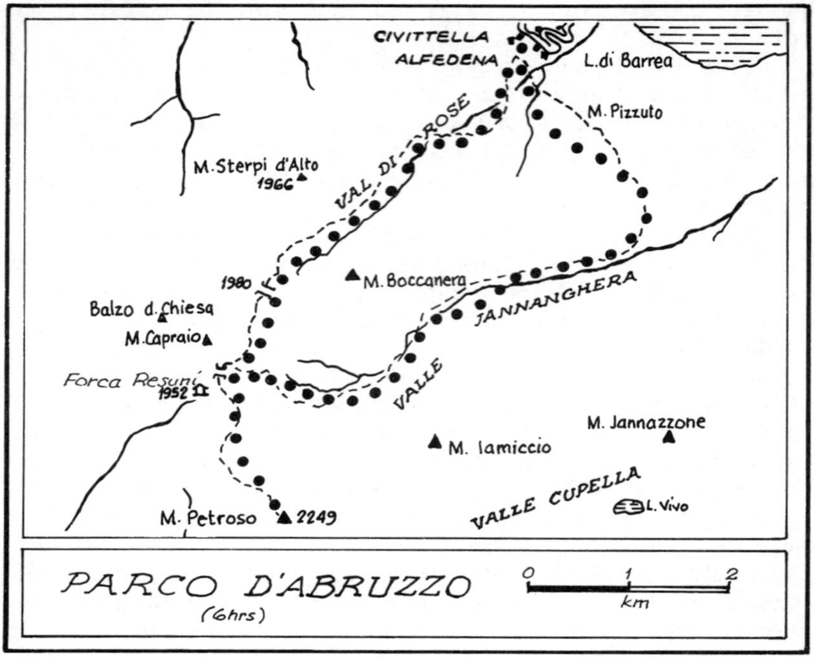

Travelling by public transport, the best place to catch a bus to Pescasseroli and Civitella is at Avezzano railway station, on the main line between Rome and Pescara. In summer, there are also direct buses (check at ARPA) from both cities.

The trail Entering Civitella Alfedena, pass between the Museo del Lupo and the entrance to the old part of the village. Start walking along the old paved street and then, before the well known Ostello la Torre, turn left on the old trail leading to Val di Rose and Forca Resuni. Climb a short staircase, and then start a steep ascent up a stony spur dominating the village, leading to Val di Rose. Once you get into the forest the going gets easier, and you continue on the northern side of the valley for a long while. When you get to the open again, you'll find yourself at the base of the big grassy slopes leading to Passo Cavuto, a tiny incut col on the rocky ridge above you. The path climbs with some zigzags: this is the best area to spot the chamois, usually grazing in the pastures nearby. Here, you are requested not to leave the established path.

When you get to Passo Cavuto, rocky Monte Petroso, the tallest of the Park, will appear in front of you; the path turns slightly right, traverses to the left again, and eventually leads to the col and the *rifugio* of Forca Resuni, at 1,952 m and 2½ hours from the base. A well-trodden path goes down the opposite side, towards Settefrati. If you are planning to stop, remember that the main part of the building is reserved for the Park's rangers: on the right is the entrance to the public part of the hut.

To climb to the summit of Monte Petroso, at 2,249 m the highest in the park, you have to follow the ridge starting immediately from the *rifugio*: climb to the foot of a rocky face, traverse right onto a path between large boulders, climb back to the ridge on grass and scree and then follow the crest to the summit. You'll need a couple of hours, including the descent.

From the *rifugio*, start your descent on a direct path on the east side, entering the impressive upper cwm of Valle Jannanghera, dominated by Monte Petroso's rocky north face. The path zigzags between isolated trees, and then enters a long, narrow and very interesting valley. This is Valle Jannanghera proper where you might meet a bear. Should this happen (and it's none too common), you should behave with the utmost respect: Abruzzo's brown bears are not grizzlies, have never harmed a single tourist, but are nevertheless big beasts of incredible strength. After a couple of hours' descent, you will meet a big spring on your right. This is the Sorgente Jannanghera, and after it you have to turn left onto a path starting with a short ascent, and then descending again. Zigzag between dense bushes before spotting the lake again, and Civitella Alfedena. At the end, you will arrive at the village exactly at your starting point; the descent from the hut takes almost 3 hours.

Chapter 11

The Adriatic Hills and Riviera

Pleasant hills, an unbroken coastline, popular and crowded beach resorts; from Rimini to Gargano, Italy's eastern coast is almost a continuous stretch of sand, 500 km of 'easy' coastline belonging to four different regions and very popular in summer. If the Tyrrhenian coast boasts rocky promontories, famous villages and high prices, its Adriatic counterpart is the popular, cheap seaside location, ideal for families with small children and little money to spend. In summer, Rimini's airport is one of Europe's busiest, with charter flights from everywhere.

Conero, a magnificent rocky promontory south of Ancona, is the exception: a true mountain in front of the sea, it has impressive white limestone cliffs, beautiful vegetation, and spectacular views in all directions. On clear days, the Apennines' Monti Sibillini, snowy in winter, can easily be spotted to the west.

Apart from Conero, the coast has very little interest for the hiker. Much more attractive are the inland hills, rich in interesting old towns and castles, much less frequented by foreigners than Tuscany or Umbria on the western side of the peninsula. The Montefeltro hills around Urbino and San Marino are the best known in a generally

The Gran Sasso

gentle and pleasant landscape. More to the south, the hills inland of Ancona and Macerata are wilder, rich in canyons and rocks.

Further to the south, again Abruzzo is well known as a mountain region: its summits are near the coast, and are described in another chapter of this book. Between these and the shore lies a pleasant land, rich in interesting geological formations. Harsh fighting in the Second World War destroyed many of the most interesting villages. Walking through valleys, passing old farms and villages, you never lose sight of the imposing eastern faces of Maiella and Gran Sasso.

THE LONG TRAILS

Like most places in the hills and lowlands of Italy, long distance trails do not exist yet, although they could appear soon. The *main divide's trail* reaches Bocca Trabaria, on the Tuscan border, and should be continued in a few years along the whole of the Umbria–Marche border, to Monti Sibillini. It will cross a series of small (1,200 to 1,600 m), interesting and quite wild mountains: Cucco, Catria, Pennino.

In 1984, I explored and suggested, together with Roberto Sigismondi, a *Sibillini to Conero* week-long trail, passing through Fiastra, San Severino Marche, Cingoli and Osimo. It was published in *Airone* magazine, but it does not seem to have become popular.

ACROSS CONERO

Mighty and isolated, Conero can be spotted from many of the Marche's hills, and from a long distance away on the Adriatic sea and coastline. Like Portofino or Circeo on the Tyrrhenian coast, it is another mountain in front of the sea, impressive if seen from the open Adriatic. On this side (north and east), Conero is rocky, steep and criss-crossed by impressive gullies and ravines. Its western and southern slopes are much more gentle, covered in dense vegetation, descending to the Ancona–Sirolo main road.

Conero itself is still an extremely wild area. Abandoned hermitages and buildings can be found engulfed in its thick undergrowth, while old paths have disappeared almost completely in many areas. Flora is still extremely interesting and varied, while wildlife has been almost destroyed by hunters. A park was proposed long ago for the area, but the hunters' opposition, and their influence on Marche's regional government, has stopped further progress. Villas are another serious problem. You will find far too many of them scattered along the sunny slopes, facing Sirolo beach.

I will describe (and suggest) a complete north to south traverse of Conero. This is an excellent expedition, but you must make an important choice first: the 'normal' trail is straightforward (if steep at the very beginning), whilst the 'Scoglio della Vela' path is tricky and exposed, with some route-finding problems. Competent hikers can also walk from and to Portonovo using both trails, reaching S. Pietro church and the nearby viewpoint over Due Sorelle rocks.

Francesco Burattini's excellent *Guida del Monte Conero*, a recent book with beautiful photographs, includes a large map of all the area's trails. It can be used also by those who do not speak Italian, and makes IGM maps wholly unnecessary.

How to get there Conero can be easily reached from nearby Ancona, or from the Ancona–Pescara motorway. By bus, you can travel by ATMA, from Piazza della Repubblica, Ancona: these lead to Sirolo and Numana, if you want to reach Portonovo you must get off at the junction and start walking half an hour along the paved road to reach it.

The trail The starting point, Portonovo, has one of the Marche's most interesting romanesque churches, Santa Maria di Portonovo. It lies at the end of the road, and a visit there is a must for everybody. Retracing your steps and walking a little further uphill, you will reach Hotel Internazionale, where the trail starts.

The beginning is hard. You walk up a staircase on the right of the hotel, pass the rooftop terrace and start following a very steep trail (first red and yellow, then yellow and blue paint marks) through a dense forest. Trees are helpful here. After a few minutes, walking becomes easier on a scree slope, at the end of which the trail turns sharply to the left. Pass a tiny but very evident rocky gully: the two trails separate 30 m later, just before a hairpin bend in the trail.

If following the *normal trail* continue along the main path, now wide and easy, to Pian Grande, a large meadow where you reach another trail starting from Poggio S. Antonio. Continue along the large ascending trail, reaching another meadow where there is a big ruined house (Casa Cipriani). Being now on the southern slopes of the mountain, on clear days there are magnificent views towards the faraway Apennine summits. From here onwards a series of trails branches out. Try to continue almost level, reaching the paved road very near to the old S. Pietro church, at a large saddle east of the summit.

To get here you need 2 hours. The old abbey has been turned into an hotel and the summit is not accessible as it is occupied by a military radar station. To find a good view, pass left of the church and hotel, reach a small brick pillar, and continue as far as a dirt road. A little to the left (10 minutes from the church) is Belvedere, Conero's best viewpoint, directly overlooks Due Sorelle twin rocks. The Yugoslav coast can be spotted on extremely clear days!

For the alternative *Scoglio della Vela* trail from that tiny rocky gully at the top of the steep slope from Portonova, turn left 30 m after the gully on the main trail. Descend a few metres into dense scrub, turn right onto a bigger trail, and find yourself at the beginning of a series of steep ravines and gullies, dominated by white rock and clay faces. First cross a ravine, leaving an ascending trail on your right, and descend left

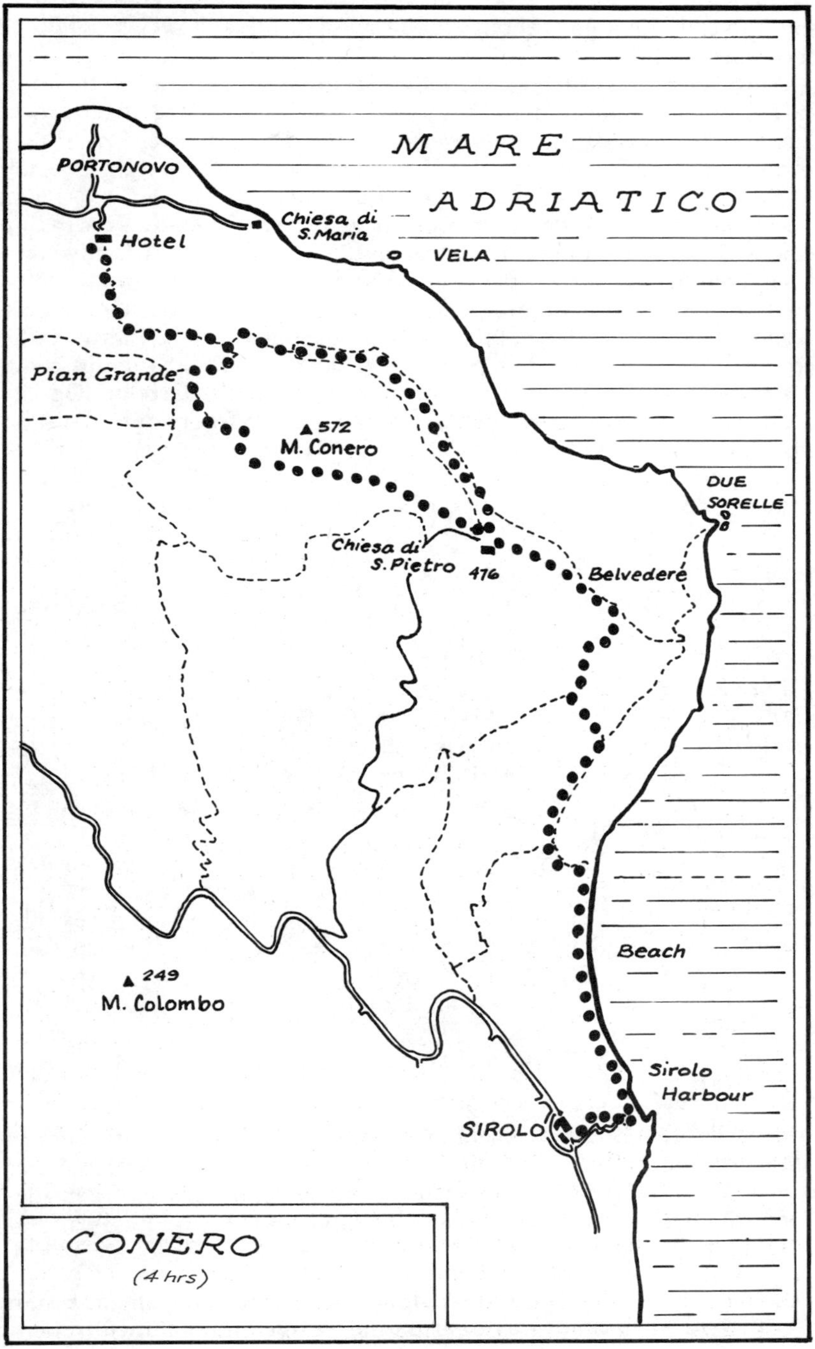
MARE
ADRIATICO
PORTONOVO
Chiesa di S. Maria
Hotel
VELA
Pian Grande
572
M. Conero
DUE SORELLE
Chiesa di S. Pietro
476
Belvedere
Beach
249
M. Colombo
Sirolo Harbour
SIROLO
CONERO
(4 hrs)

to a huge isolated boulder. Pass near this, continue amongst trees again, then traverse the larger ravine, where a trail has been partly cut into the clay. Though without real difficulties, this is a very steep area, requiring caution.

At the end of the ravine, you follow its rim to an abandoned building (a hermitage connected to S. Pietro in ancient times). Originally a large trail, now engulfed in vegetation, it continues ascending slowly through a beautiful forest. At the junction, you must turn right to reach S. Pietro again. Allow 2 hours from the start.

On the opposite side, from Belvedere, there are many descending routes. You can follow the zigzagging dirt road, or start following a small trail for a while on the slope's steep edge. Lower down, a lot of villas make a fixed route difficult to describe: just continue walking downhill, reaching the beach in about 1 hour from S. Pietro. Now continue walking the beach, passing a rocky spur where you must walk a few metres into the water, and reaching Sirolo's harbour. On the road, walk uphill to Sirolo,, where the walk ends: from your arrival on the beach, allow for another hour.

THE ATRI CALANQUES TRAIL

East of the imposing Gran Sasso massif, Atri is one of the most interesting small towns of Abruzzo. Easily accessible from the Adriatic coast, it has a magnificent medieval cathedral, more old buildings and a wonderful view, both towards the mountains and the Adriatic sea.

Perched on a hill, Atri is a good base to explore the interesting landscape, typical of the Abruzzo hills. The clay has been deeply eroded by water and calanques and gullies mark many hills in the region. The hills around Atri are the most famous and interesting in the area and a natural reserve is planned to stop further damage and excessive building in the area.

Once based in Atri, you have the choice between a car exploration of the area, a short walk south of the town to have a more 'natural' look at the calanques, or longer ventures. Whilst easy and accessible, the walk to Città Sant'Angelo (another interesting town, much damaged during the war) is 4 to 5 hours long, and pleasant enough to fill an enjoyable day. In summer, the Piomba river valley is normally too hot to make a walk agreeable. IGM's map is *Atri*, but it is not really necessary. More walks in the area can be found in my *A Piedi in Abruzzo/1*.

How to get there Both Atri and Citta Sant'Angelo are very near to the coastal motorway, and can be reached by frequent ARPA buses from Pescara. To walk the whole traverse, motorists can consider doing the whole trip from Pescara (or Silvi Marina), by buses and/or hitch-hiking.

The trail From the centre of Atri, after a visit to the cathedral, start on the road to Teramo, leaving from the western side of town. A little

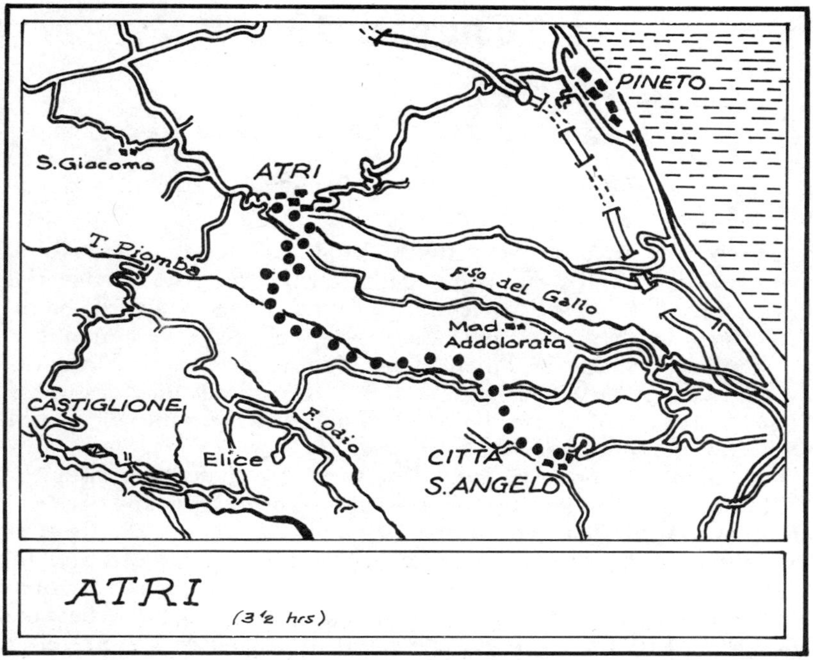

before the road junction to Città S. Angelo, turn left onto a dirt road to Fontana Vricciola, making a slightly descending route right in front of some of the most interesting *calanchi*. In half an hour, you reach the paved road to Città S. Angelo again, which you must cross to follow another dirt road descending with large zigzags into the Piomba river valley.

This part of the trail offers magnificent views on both Gran Sasso and Monti della Laga chains, and touches some interesting old buildings. When you reach the valley floor dirt road, you must follow it to the left, on a rather monotonous stretch of the walk. To the left, you have interesting views on more calanques and gullies. The road crosses the river three times; at the third bridge the valley gets larger, and Città S. Angelo can be seen on a hill in front of you. Pass a short uphill stretch, reach a crossroads and turn right onto a smaller track reaching the riverside.

Ford the Piomba, which is usually very low, to reach another large dirt road. This zigzags uphill, passing a series of farms and a horse-riding centre, and then reaches the paved road. Follow it left to Citta S. Angelo. Allow $1\frac{1}{2}$ hours from Atri to the Piomba valley floor, 2 hours to the ford, and $1\frac{1}{4}$ hours for the last uphill walk to Città S. Angelo.

Chapter 12

The Deep South

The best way to appreciate Italy's length is probably to take an overland trip towards the 'deep south', on the motorway connecting the capital and the rest of the country as far as Reggio Calabria, on the peninsula's southernmost tip. Pass Naples, then Salerno, continue to the south to Basilicata and then enter Calabria: here, on this border, is the mid-way point between Rome and Reggio. Travelling eastwards, Puglia is longer still; from the regional border to Otranto and Leuca, the distance approaches 400 km.

For somebody born in the USA, these are ridiculous distances. Within tiny Europe and the small Mediterranean basin they are not, and they mark important differences within the country. To the east, Puglia has always been a natural bridge towards Greece and the Middle East. From the seventh century BC Greek ships sailed around both peninsulas and around Sicily, building dozens of colonies between Naples and the Adriatic sea. Later on, these regions saw more settlements. In the hills of Calabria villages still exist inhabited by Greeks and Albanians who speak their original languages, although it is five centuries since they fled from the Turkish invaders.

Travelling and hiking this way, you will meet facets of Italy seldom known abroad; deep pine forests on the mountains, and limestone plateaux deeply eroded by canyons that rank amongst the most impressive in the Mediterranean. On the hills are strong medieval castles built to resist the Arab pirates' assaults. On the shores, *Magna Graecia*'s towns are still coming to light under the archaeologists hands, and new surprises emerge every year.

Pollino mountains and Morano Calabro

Today, the pattern is anything but equal. The whole of the South is by far the poorest part of the country. Nevertheless, Bari, Puglia's capital, is a thriving industrial and commercial area, and a turning point for business going east. The hills of Calabria are an area of poor farming and agriculture and the same applies to Basilicata. Again, on the Ionian Sea, Taranto boasts the most important – and polluting – industrial complexes in the whole country.

The physical differences are great. The main Apennine chain south of Matese runs deep into the Irpinia hills, flanked by grander mountains (Monti Alburni, Monti Picentini) towards the Tyrrhenian coast. More to the south, mountains become impressive again, well into Basilicata; on the border between this region and Calabria lies Pollino, one of Italy's most interesting and surprisingly wild areas. Southbound again, an uninterrupted chain rolls down to Reggio Calabria and the country's tip; the highlights are the Sila plateau (including huge pine forests and many lakes) and Aspromonte, the last summit of all. From its top, the smoke of Etna can easily be seen in the distance.

The eastern tip – eastern Basilicata and the whole of Puglia – is the only mountainless part of Italy. The former is a series of canyons descending towards the Ionian sea, the latter a long limestone plateau rich in caves, stretching the whole 200 km to Otranto, Italy's easternmost city.

Why put all this together in one chapter? The area is huge (almost a quarter of the country), and the landscape variable. But there is one particular point that puts it together. From the hiker's point of view, the whole of the 'deep south' is a world to explore. Marked trails are almost unheard of, guidebooks do not exist, maps are unreliable in many cases. You have to search and explore; in many areas hikers are almost unheard of, and you will arouse curiosity first of all. But this is a friendly country. Behave properly, and farmers and shepherds, away from the seaside resorts, will be helpful and friendly.

One last remark concerns the climate. Yes, it *is* hot, and the more so if you travel away from the seaside, which has at least a cooling effect. If you visit during summer, confine your explorations to the highest mountains, or walk during the cooler hours of the day.

Where and when to go This chapter includes a large part of Italy. It is difficult to give general information concerning the whole area. For the motorized traveller, access is by either the Naples–Salerno–Reggio–Calabria motorway (old, and with a lot of truck traffic), or the more pleasant Pescara–Bari–Taranto motorway in the east. The Napoli–Canosa motorway connects the two coasts, and is the only quick route across southern Italy. Elsewhere, roads are normally slow, apart from the brand new *superstrade* connecting some of the main towns.

Public transport is normally slower still and if travelling this way, it would be better to choose a small area to explore thoroughly, than try to travel long distances in one trip.

THE LONG DISTANCE TRAILS

Probably you will already understand from the previous pages that the 'deep south' of Italy has not, with one important exception, established and marked long trails. The situation is almost the same as in the central Apennines, but here long trails will probably not develop for a long time to come.

The only exception is *Alta via dei Monti Picentini*. It has a large network of trails (and not a single straight path), and it is interesting to note that its main axis, from Solofra to Senerchia, will be on the main chain's trail line, when (and sooner or later it will be!) it is continued south across all the country's mountains.

Another project is *Grande escursione pugliese*; the idea originated from two of Italy's easternmost regions' best known environmentalists and the trail should follow the whole length of the Murgia hills.

Although other areas lack marked trails, there are possibilities for the adventurous walker. You can walk an easy 4 day loop around Pollino, try a strenuous 8 to 10 days' Ionian–Tyrrhenian traverse across Pollino and nearby Orsomarso mountains, or have an easier (but very impressive) 4 to 5 days' walk along the dividing ridge between Amalfi and Sorrento, ending in front of Capri's *Faraglioni*.

HIGH ABOVE AMALFI'S RIVIERA

The sea is near at hand, and so is the volcanic shape of Vesuvio. Naples' traffic jams are a few minutes' drive away, but Sorrento and Amalfi's peninsula is a land of true mountains, directly overlooking an impressive, rocky coastline. This is one of Italy's most celebrated landscapes. Limestone summits such as Sant'Angelo a Tre Pizzi are a very important part of the area's natural heritage.

Sant'Angelo's 1,443 m are not a Himalayan height; but they are perched less than a mile as the crow flies from Positano's coastline; the slopes are rocky and steep, the valleys are impressive, and the scenery is unique. From the highest point, views are incredible. On clear winter days you have on one side the Apennines' snowy summits, and on the other, Capri's skyline, with the sun setting over nearby Faraglioni.

Walking the peninsula is not a very common sport, but the main trails are normally in good condition. At the start, you have to make a definite choice. To walk up from Positano or Amalfi is not for the faint-hearted, and it is not to be done on hot days. Amalfi's Vallone delle Ferriere is an impressive sight, and you can enjoy an easy walk (less than 1 hour from the town's square to an old abandoned industrial building amongst Dolomitic scenery), or a strenuous hike up to the summit of Monte Cervigliano, Sant'Angelo's eastern neighbour.

Much easier trails can be tried on the northern side, overlooking Vico Equense and Castellammare di Stabia. Because of the lack of sun, forests are deep, and the atmosphere in the higher mountains is like

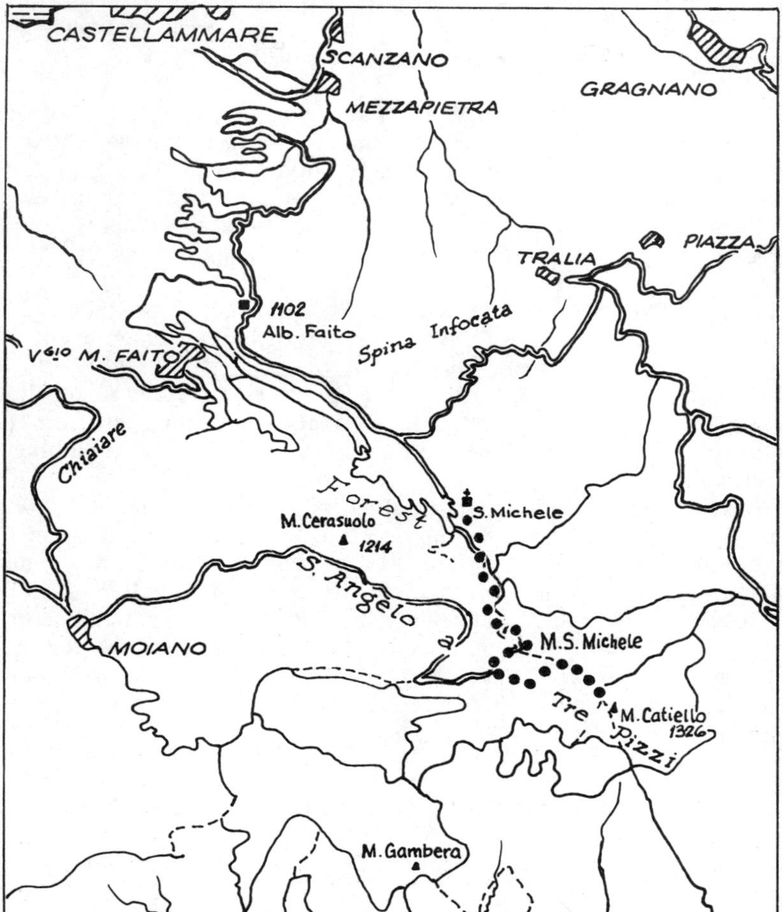

S. ANGELO a TRE PIZZI (Amalfi)
(2 hrs.)

BWI-J

the nearby Apennines. From where the road ends at Monte Faite, you can walk to Sant'Angelo in less than 1 hour. Other lovely walks can be had along the peninsula's westernmost tip, right in front of Capri. A walk to Punta Campanella (45 minutes from Termini village) is a magnificent place to enjoy a spectacular sunset.

How to get there To reach Monte Faito, you have the choice between a steep road from Vice Equense, a similar one from Positano, and the *funicolare* climbing up from Castellammare di Stabia. Vico Equense is easier to reach from the Napoli–Salerno motorway but take the cablecar if you're not driving a car. From the centre of Naples you can quickly reach Castellammare with Circumvesuviana trains.

The trail At the end of a steep climb, the road passes nearby the *funicolare* station, and continues climbing through a magnificent forest, very popular at weekends (and therefore, normally awfully dirty). From the *funicolare*'s 1,131 m, you again reach the ridge near a huge TV antenna. On foot, you will need about 45 minutes from the *funicolare*. Park here; a few red paint splashes mark the beginning of your walk.

Start traversing under a series of rocky gullies, passing near a large cave, and entering an interesting beech forest. At a junction follow the right hand trail, climbing in a series of zigzags towards the mountain's main ridge. When you reach this, you are above the tree line. Turn left to reach a grassy and rocky gully, and follow the path that climbs steeply to the top. This is an easy hour's walk from the antenna. Nearby summits are rocky, and can be reached only on exposed rock-and-grass climbs. The descent is very quick, and leaves time for a tour of the peninsula's main sights.

SHORT GARGANO HIKES

Unique along Italy's eastern coast, Gargano is more than a simple cape protruding into the Adriatic sea. Its loneliness, its shape, the differences between it and the surrounding lowlands of Puglia, make it seem like an island to the area's visitors. Steep on every side, Gargano is stopped by a huge plateau, at a height of 800 to 1,000 m above sea level.

The southern and eastern coast offers the most spectacular beaches; you can reach them while driving along the Manfredonia to Vieste coastal road, passing by the Baia delle Zagare's famous *faraglioni*. The northern coast is sand, popular amongst visitors with small children; near to Lakes Varano and Lesina are dozens of campgrounds, often full up during the peak summer months. To the wilderness lover, the plateau is the most interesting part of Gargano.

Its eastern end is occupied by Foresta Umbria, one of southern Italy's biggest forests, and a good example of the country's protected natural reserves. Small winding roads climb to the visitors' centre from

Vieste, Peschici, Vico del Gargano and Monte S. Angelo. Towards the west, the plateau gets barren and dry, impressive but not very interesting to the walker. The one notable exception is Castelpagano, an impressive fortress built on Gargano's westernmost outcrop, in the direction of S. Severo.

Gargano has many hikes that are normally not very long. Only in the depth of the Foresta Umbra can you try a longer expedition. The following short walks, very different in character from each other, give interesting looks at the different parts of the area. They are very good to complete a 'normal' visit to this surprising land.

How to get there Gargano is very easy to reach from the Pescara–Bari motorway, following Italy's eastern coast, which you leave at the Poggio Imperiale, S. Severo or Foggia exits. By public transport make use of two small railways connecting S. Severo to Rodi Garganico, and Foggia to Manfredonia. Foggia is the best place to catch buses to Gargano's towns, whilst in summer there are direct buses both from Naples and Rome.

The trails *Mergoli to Vignanotica* This is a short hike (less than 2 hours return), along the most spectacular part of the southeastern part of Gargano, offering magnificent views of sea cliffs, and a pleasant walk amongst very interesting flora. To reach it, follow the Mattinata to Vieste coastal road, as far as the first bend east of the hotel and village of Baia delle Zagare. The trail's beginning is very well marked and so is the rest of the path, descending gently along the coast's very steep slopes to reach Vignanotica bay, where you can stop for a swim. Returning uphill, the hike is slightly more tiring.

Monte Sacro abbey Not far from the Baia delle Zagare, there is another walk completely different from the first one. You must hike through a real 'jungle', steep and thick, to reach a magnificent abbey whose ruins are almost completely hidden by the forest, and which can only be seen when you reach them. This is a short walk, quite exciting, requiring some experience (and maybe, a map and a compass).

From Mattinata, follow the inland road to Vieste, as far as a small bend where a dirt road branches to the left: there is a small sign to Monte Sacro. Follow the road to its end, and then start walking towards the densely vegetated hill in front of you. The abbey is at the top, but to reach it is not as easy as it looks. Start on a good trail, which soon peters out; remember not to walk too far to the left, and keep instead to your right. When you reach the hill's ridge, you can spot the abbey; to reach it requires 1 to 1½ hours. The ruins are very impressive, and the return is back the same way: again, you could have some navigational problems.

Foresta Umbra trails The central, thickest part of the forest is truly magnificent, and offers a pleasant cool atmosphere if you come straight from the beach. During the peak season, the immediate surroundings

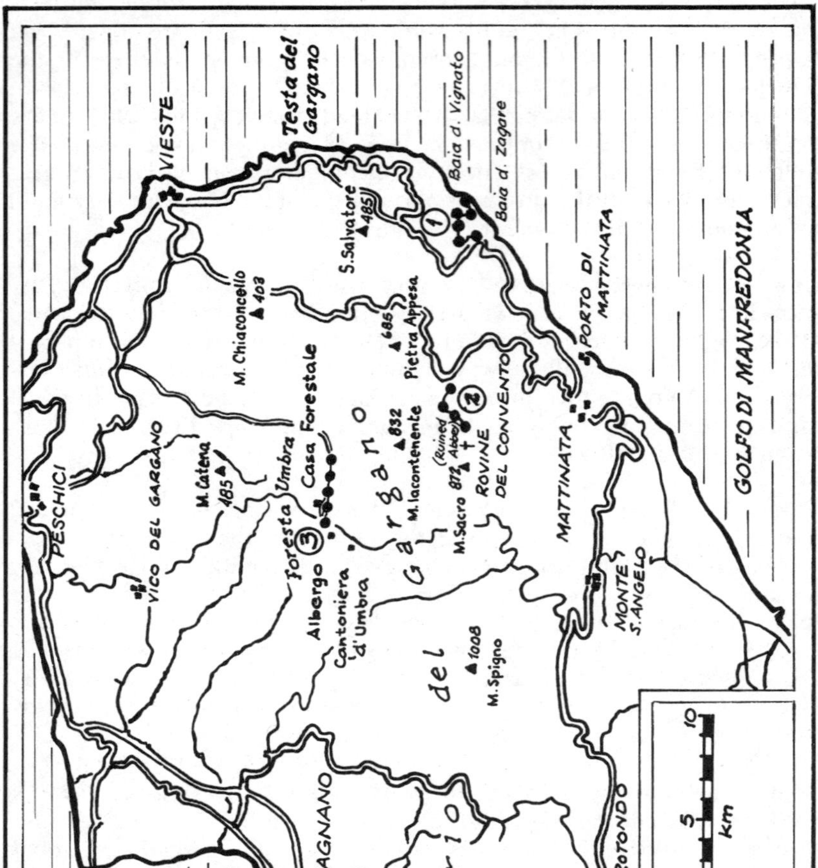
VIESTE
Testa del Gargano
Baia d. Vignato
Baia d. Zagore
S. Salvatore 485
PORTO DI MATTINATA
GOLFO DI MANFREDONIA
M. Chiaconcello 403
Pietra Appesa 685
Casa Forestale
Umbra
Foresta Umbra
PESCHICI
VICO DEL GARGANO
M. Catena 485
M. Iacontenente 832
(Ruined Abbey)
M. Sacro 872
ROVINE DEL CONVENTO
MATTINATA
MONTE S. ANGELO
Albergo
Cantoniera d'Umbra
M. Spigno 1008
Promontorio del Gargano
CAGNANO
LAGO DI VARANO
Coppa di Mezzo 902
1014 Montenero
S. GIOVANNI ROTONDO
S. MARCO IN LAMIS
SANNICANDRO GARGANICO
GARGANO
(① 1 hr; ② 3 hrs; ③ 2-4 hrs)
0 5 10
km

of the Visitors' Centre are quite crowded; but walk away for a short distance and you will find yourself on your own again. A simple map is available at the Centre, but trails are almost unmarked. A compass is not a bad idea!

The easiest walk starts a few hundred metres from *Centro di visita*, on the road to Vieste. On the right of the road, a dirt track leads to a small lake, and you must walk round to the right hand side. A good trail continues into the deep forest, passing by some dolines (sink holes), and reaching the fence marking the border of the Falascone natural reserve. Follow the fence to the left, and enter an area where the trail can be rather difficult to follow.

Leave by a small path on the left and then turn left onto a bigger trail leading to Caserma Murgia (45 minutes); this is an old building now used by WWF groups and schools. A bigger trail leads back to the Centre. When you reach a large dirt road, go left, reaching the starting point in about 45 minutes. If you want a longer walk, you can turn right onto this, towards the eastern part of the Forest. In a couple of hours you reach Monte Iacotenente's small outcrop, a good place to view the forest.

SURPRISING GRAVINA DI MATERA

Near to the Ionian coast, between the regions of Puglia and Basilicata is an area of deep, impressive canyons descending to the sea. The plateau's limestone has been eroded for hundreds of thousands of years: the result is a series of almost 30 canyons, deeply cut into the stone, which were used as shelters from the earliest times.

At the northwestern corner of the area, the town of Matera is a good example of how man and stone have co-existed. The *Sassi*, the oldest part of the town, is made up of houses cut directly into the stone: they were abandoned after the Second World War and are now slowly being occupied again, or turned into fancy cool houses for the summer. Matera is the best known area of all: but from here to Taranto, dozens of canyons have surprises for the visitor.

The local name for canyons is *gravine*: the one near Laterza is probably the most spectacular of all, while Massafra's boasts some of the most interesting houses and churches cut into the rock. At Petruscio, a short distance from Mottola, a large ancient village, completely carved into the limestone, can be seen. Matera's *gravina* has many more settlements carved into it. The Cristo la Selva church is situated in one of the most impressive areas of all.

There are two ways to reach it. The shorter one, a very simple walk, starts from the Matera–Montescaglioso road, crossing a small stream by an impressive bridge, and then passing by a water reservoir to a big cross marking the access to the monastery. From Matera itself, you can walk the whole eastern rim of the canyon, with many excellent views and a lot of surprises, including Grotta dei Pipistrelli, a large cave where prehistoric settlements have been discovered.

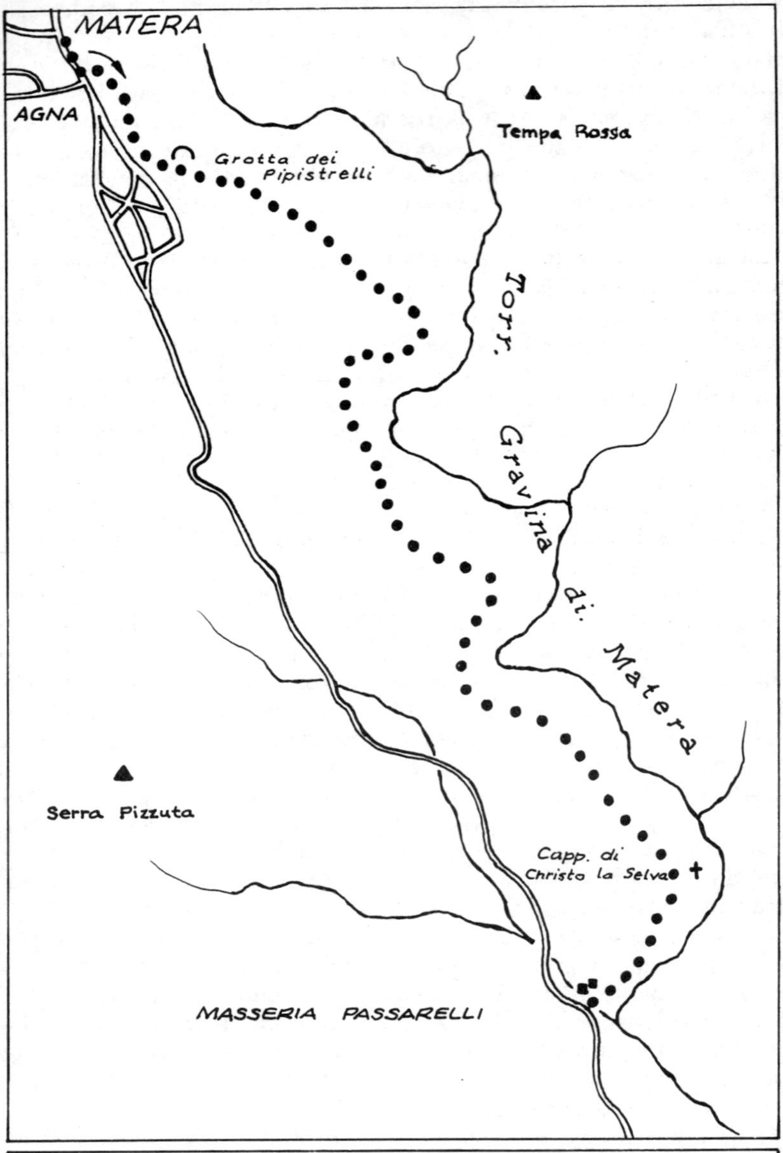

MATERA
(2 to 4 hrs)

How to get there Matera can be reached on good roads from Potenza, Bari (via Altamura) or the Ionian coast. There is a railway from Bari, while from Potenza, Naples or Rome it is much quicker to travel by bus. From the town centre, you can reach Agna suburb by bus. If you want to walk the whole length of the rim, you would be better off leaving your car in Matera, taking a bus to Agna, having your walk and then hitching a ride (or finding a bus) back to Matera.

The trail From Agna's entrance, you start walking along the road nearest to the canyon, with beautiful views onto the *gravina*. At a junction, you must take the central road, continuing through an agricultural area with old houses and villas; at the end of this, turn right to reach the surfaced road again. As this gets nearer to the rim it becomes dirt again: reach the very rim, and search about for a small path descending to Grotto dei Pipistrelli, about 1½ hours from the start. Take a flashlight to have a look at the inside of the cave.

Climb back to the road, follow it to the left, and leave it again, passing near a couple of high pylons, and continue near to the rim, now far from any human presence, with interesting views towards the deeply incut *gravina*. After a long while, you reach a big cross: a trail (white paint marks) descends along a series of staircases, to reach Cristo la Selva chapel (2 hours from the cave). Continuing along a series of ledges, you pass a long line of caves which were enlarged by man to become part of the monastery. At the very end, another incut staircase leads back to the rim: this access is very difficult to find when arriving from the Matera's side.

Walk back to the cross, and then descend to a reservoir and to a farm. The surfaced road is nearby (half an hour). Before it, on the left, another staircase leads to the very end of the canyon, a pleasant place for a stop.

UP TO THE SUMMIT OF POLLINO

High and impressive, Monte Pollino is southern Italy's highest peak, directly overlooking the Naples–Reggio Calabria motorway with steep rocky slopes. Even on a motorized tour, it is well worth getting the main road at Campotenese for a refreshing stop at Piano di Ruggio. From Frascineto, another short car trip leads to Civita, a village perched in front of the Raganello canyon, an impressive sight. When travelling north from Calabria, Pollino's skyline marks the way for a long while.

Again, this is a mountain of differences. On its southern side, nude slopes and gullies climb to remote ridges where *pini loricati*, the typical, dramatically shaped trees of the area are perched. On the northern side, large forests descend on the Basilicata side of the mountain, offering shelter to one or two dozen of the Apennines' last remaining wolves. Eagles still fly in the Pollino skies. On the eastern side of the mountain, a huge system of canyons – Barile, Scala di Barile, Raganello – are amongst the country's most impressive sights.

Right in the middle of Italy's south – Pollino's summit is the only one in Europe from which you can spy three different seas – this mountain has always been very important to man. Centuries ago, Albanians escaping from their country in the face of Turkish invaders came to live in the area; many of the inhabitants of the villages clustered around the mountain still speak Albanian and have Albanian traditions. A little more to the south, there are many Greek villages in the Calabrian highlands.

Pollino is also important in environmentalists' debates. Many years ago it was proposed as a National Park, and really it should become one. Flora is extraordinary, fauna is still important (but hunting, both legal and illegal, has massacred many species). The feelings of loneliness and remoteness that Pollino can inspire are really unique amongst Italian mountains. A look around Pollino can take a couple of hours: from the Campotenese exit on the motorway just drive to Piano di Ruggio, and then walk 15 minutes or so to Malevento's 'balcony', a surprisingly beautiful viewpoint.

To really know the area, you should stop for at least 2 or 3 days: *rifugio* De Gasperi, on Pian di Ruggio, can be an adequate base, or you can camp in many parts of the area. Amongst the villages, Terranova di Pollino, on the northeastern side of the mountain, is both the most interesting and the most remote. Rotonda and Viggianello are interesting bases, too. On the southern side (i.e. from Castrovillari, Morano Calabro, Civita) walks are always hard, and invariably hot in summer.

IGM 1:25,000 maps of the area are Frascineto and Morano Calabro. Mario Tommaselli's *il Massiccio del Pollino* (BMG, 1984) is the best guidebook to the area).

How to get there As I said before, Pollino is very easy to reach if you have a car. Leave the Salerno–Reggio–Calabria motorway at Campotenese (about 180 km south of Salerno, and 85 km north of

Cosenza). Briefly follow the road to Rotonda, and then turn right to Piano di Ruggio and *rifugio* De Gasperi at 1,650 m, and 10 km from the motorway. A short drive east, on the road to Viggianello, leads to a long level traverse, and then to a sharp bend to the left, where the road starts to descend. Park here: a short dirt track climbs to Colle dell' Impiso (1,573 m). *Impiso* means 'hanged man' in the local dialect, a good reminder of the bloody war that was fought in the area after 1860, when Italian troops fought against the outlawed followers of the King of Naples.

If you are not driving, this is a difficult area to reach. You can reach any one of the villages and try to find somebody willing to drive you to the mountain. Castrovillari and Rotonda are probably the best places to start from. On weekends, it should not be too difficult to hitch a ride on the Campotenese–*rifugio* De Gasperi road. For the really tough (and not on a sunny August day!) it is also possible to walk all the way up from Morano Calabro.

The trail From the surfaced road, you must reach Colle dell'Impiso, leave the road, and start walking uphill on your right, on a small trail with some red paint markers. You reach a small dirt road in Valloncello di Viggianello, and follow it to the right. On a sharp bend to

the right, turn to the left again, following another, smaller trail, not very easy to find. When you cross a small stream the path becomes more evident, climbing diagonally to the left. You walk round a large ridge to enter the magnificent Piano del Pollino (1,750 m, 1½ hours), a large plateau surrounded by the area's most important summits. On its opposite side, on Serra di Crispo's slopes, you can clearly spot *pini loricati*.

You continue crossing the plateau for a while, and then turn right to climb a grassy valley between Monte Pollino itself and Serra Dolcedorme: the latter is the area's highest summit. When you reach the summit ridge, you follow it to the left, with magnificent views to Serra Dolcedorme's summit (2,266 m, 1½ hours from Piano di Pollino).

From the summit, descend following more or less the northern ridge of the mountain, to a large saddle at Piano del Pollino's eastern end. A little east of this (right, as you descend) you reach Piano di Acquafredda, another large grassy plateau where the so called *alberi serpente* can be seen; these are incredibly twisted beech trees, unique to the area. This is also a good area to camp: if you're planning to do so, you should consider walking straight here from Piano del Pollino, dropping your load, and then reversing the described walk to the top of Serra Dolcedorme. From Piano di Acquafredda, you can also climb the area's other summits: Serra di Crispo is a very interesting balcony towards Terranova di Pollino's large forests, and the Raganello canyon.

On your return walk, once you reach the dirt road at Valloncello di Viggianello walk directly along this, reaching the grassy Piano del Vacquarro, which is crossed by a beautiful stream. With a gentle climb, the dirt road will lead you back to Colle dell'Impiso (allow 2 hours from Piano di Acquafredda, 3 hours from Serra Dolcedorme).

Chapter 13
Sardinia

Sardinia – Sardegna to Italians – is a strange, faraway place. Not because of sheer distance; flights from Rome to Olbia and Cagliari last little more than half an hour and the shortest ferry route to the island, Civitavecchia to Olbia or nearby Golfo Aranci, doesn't take more than 6 hours.

Nor is Sardinia remote because of political isolation. The region has given two presidents to the young Italian Republic (the last one, Francesco Cossiga, was elected in 1985), and one of its most important leaders, Enrico Berlinguer, was the leader of western Europe's largest Communist party, Italy's PCI. From Sardinia come politicians and football players, painters and writers, technicians and poets.

Anyway, the feeling of distance exists. Sardinia is the second major island in the Mediterranean (the first being Sicily), and in many ways it bears a distinct 'mediterranean' flavour, similar to nearby Corsica, and different from the rest of the country, or 'the continent' as true-born Sardinians still call the mainland. Sardinia has a different character, a different history, and is inhabited by a different people from the rest of Italy. A recent law (approved 1984) has guaranteed the islanders the right to use their own language (a true *language*, not a dialect) in public matters and in school. There are rare animals, and unique flowers and plants.

For the visiting tourist (and even for Italians) Sardinia has an image of wonderful beaches, stony *muraghes*, ancient fortresses perched on

hilltops and good food. Driving inland, the island boasts an incredibly wild nature and environment, and an atmosphere that can fascinate even the most expert nature lover. *Grifone* (a huge vulture), *Cervo sardo* (Sardinian deer), *muflone* (a large mountain goat) and *foca monaca* (a kind of seal) are the best known symbols of the island's wildlife. All of them are severely endangered, and *foca monaca* is really on the point of extinction.

Sardinia's coasts were remote just thirty years ago. During this time, the island's shoreline has been inundated by an incredible amount of concrete and villas. First on the spot was Karim Aga Khan's *Costa Smeralda*, a smart international resort on the northeastern corner of the island. Then others came, and nowadays, on Sardinia's coasts nature is largely non-existent. All the other parts are endangered.

Certainly, there were more complex reasons than the greed of big builders. For a long time, Sardinia has been poor, very poor. From Sardinia come many policemen and *carabinieri*, many FIAT workers in Turin, almost all the shepherds working in Tuscany and Lazio. Public intervention built huge isolated industrial plants in some parts of the island, but was not capable of assuring a decent and durable development for the locals. The massive building of houses and hotels at least brought jobs to the building industry, and temporary employment in restaurants and hotels. Hope exists that in the future new development will arise, together with the arrival of many more visitors interested in the island's unique environment and wildlife.

In the far north of the island, near to Garibaldi's Caprera and to the US Navy's Maddalena island, are the granite hills of Gallura, culminating in the south at Monte Limbara's 1,359 m. In the northwest is Nurra, a plain where Sassari (the island's second city) lies, and is bordered on the coast by limestone hills and the beautiful Capo Caccia area. Here Alghero is the main centre of Catalan influence and culture in Sardinia.

Towards the centre of the island, Nuoro is recognised as the shepherds' capital, and is the gateway to three magnificent areas. West to east, these are the Gennargentu massif (at 1,834 m by far the highest of the island) and the Supramonte limestone plateau and the rocky coast of Golfo di Orosei, without a road between the Cedrino river mouth and Arbatax harbour. Together, the three areas are being proposed as a national park, and offer the adventurous hiker a selection of magnificent hikes.

West and south of Gennargentu, Sardinia's hills get gentler and lower towards the Campidano lowlands stretching between Oristano and Cagliari. The Inglesiente hills, forming the southwestern corner, are rarely visited, wild and rich in minerals. On the west coast, the Sinis peninsula and San Pietro and Sant'Antioco islands are remarkable for their beautiful coastlines. East of Cagliari, the main city of Sardinia, the Sarrabus hills offer wild, little visited paths.

When and where to go Sardinia is an island so crossing to it is the first problem. Two state-owned companies, Ferrovie dello Stato and Tir-

Saffron Crocus

renia, link Genova, Livorno, Civitavecchia and Naples to Porto Torres, Olbia-Golfo Aranci, Arbatax and Cagliari. There are also ferries to Corsica and to Sicily. Being state-owned, ferries are quite cheap, and very cheap if you choose to cross without paying for a cabin. Your first taste of Sardinia will be a long night spent with Sardinian workers, soldiers and shepherds travelling back to their homes. Sleeping with a sleeping bag on the ship's deck is possible between April and early October. If you're driving a car, remember that securing a place on a ferry during the main tourist season can be a deadly job (ferries are booked up months in advance), and the same thing applies to the Easter and Christmas periods.

Alitalia flies to Alghero and Cagliari from most mainland airports, with reduced rates because this is supposed to be a 'social' service. The Agha Khan-owned Alisarda Airline flies instead to Olbia at higher rates. Within the island, apart from the railway connecting Cagliari to Sassari and Olbia, most transport is by bus. Hitch-hiking is good because people are friendly, but it is difficult on the less frequented roads because of the lack of cars.

For the hiker, Sardinia offers wonderful hikes and backpacking tours: but lack of water, navigational difficulties and the heat can cause serious problems. Having to travel in really remote places, you must not go alone. Good maps are essential, and knowledge of water sources a must in many areas. The only marked paths are being developed around Oliena, on Supramonte. The best periods are spring and autumn, the first being my favourite because of the abundance of wild flowers. In summer, you can hike but will probably suffer from the heat everywhere except on Gennargentu's main peaks. A tent will be useful in most tours.

THE LONG TRAILS

There are no 'organized' or long-distance marked paths in Sardinia. However, the Barbagia region in the island's centre and east is becoming an increasingly popular place for long-distance hikers. The *Cala Gonone to Baunei* hike is almost a long trail in itself, and can be continued crossing south to north nearby Supramonte, from Urzulei to Cologone and Oliena. On the whole, such a walk requires 7 to 9 days, and is one of the best in the whole Mediterranean basin. Navigational problems are very serious, however.

In 1 1982 issue of *Airone* magazine, Piero Pruneti proposed a coast-to-coast trail across Sardinia, from Cala Gonone to Sinis. The first two thirds of the hike is a very good proposal, the beginning of which you will find below, but the western part is flat and of little interest.

ON THE WILD EAST COAST OF SARDINIA: CALA GONONE TO BAUNEI

This is a magnificent tour, and one of the wildest that can be found in Italy. It crosses north to south one of the very last 'empty' stretches of the country's seashore. Because of the steepness of the coast itself, the path normally keeps inland, in bushy and rocky hill country. From Cala Sisine, a magnificent long canyon slowly rises to the San Pietro plateau, from which a dirt road slowly descends to Baunei.

Cala Gonone is one of the most popular beach resorts in the island: it was once a small village, completely isolated from the backcountry, reached only by boat until the beginning of the century. Now, in summer, it is a thriving resort, from which many tourists start the interesting boat trip to Grotta del Bue Marino. *Bue marino*, the 'sea ox', is the local nickname for a seal.

But when you leave Cala Gonone, you find yourself surrounded by nature; here and there you find small shepherds' huts, and in Cala Luna and Cala Sisine there are small restaurants reached only on foot or by boat. You need a tent (once it was possible to sleep in caves, but now most of them are far too dirty), a large water bottle, and supplies for the 4 day tour. In summer, when both restaurants are open, you will need 2 days for the Cala Sisine to Baunei stretch. In other periods (check at Cala Gonone!) you must carry food for the whole tour. This is hot country; you can wear shorts, but must have longer trousers for the worst bush areas. And beware of fires!

Alessandro Gogna's *Mezzogiorno di Pietra* (Zanichelli, 1982) has more information but it is an expensive book. IGM maps are *Dorgali*, *Grotta del Bue Marino*, *Punta s'Abradorgiu*, *Punta sa Poada*, *Capo Monte Santu*, *Baunei*).

How to get there Regular bus services to Cala Gonone exist from Dorgali, which can be reached from Nuoro or Olbia. Baunei is farther

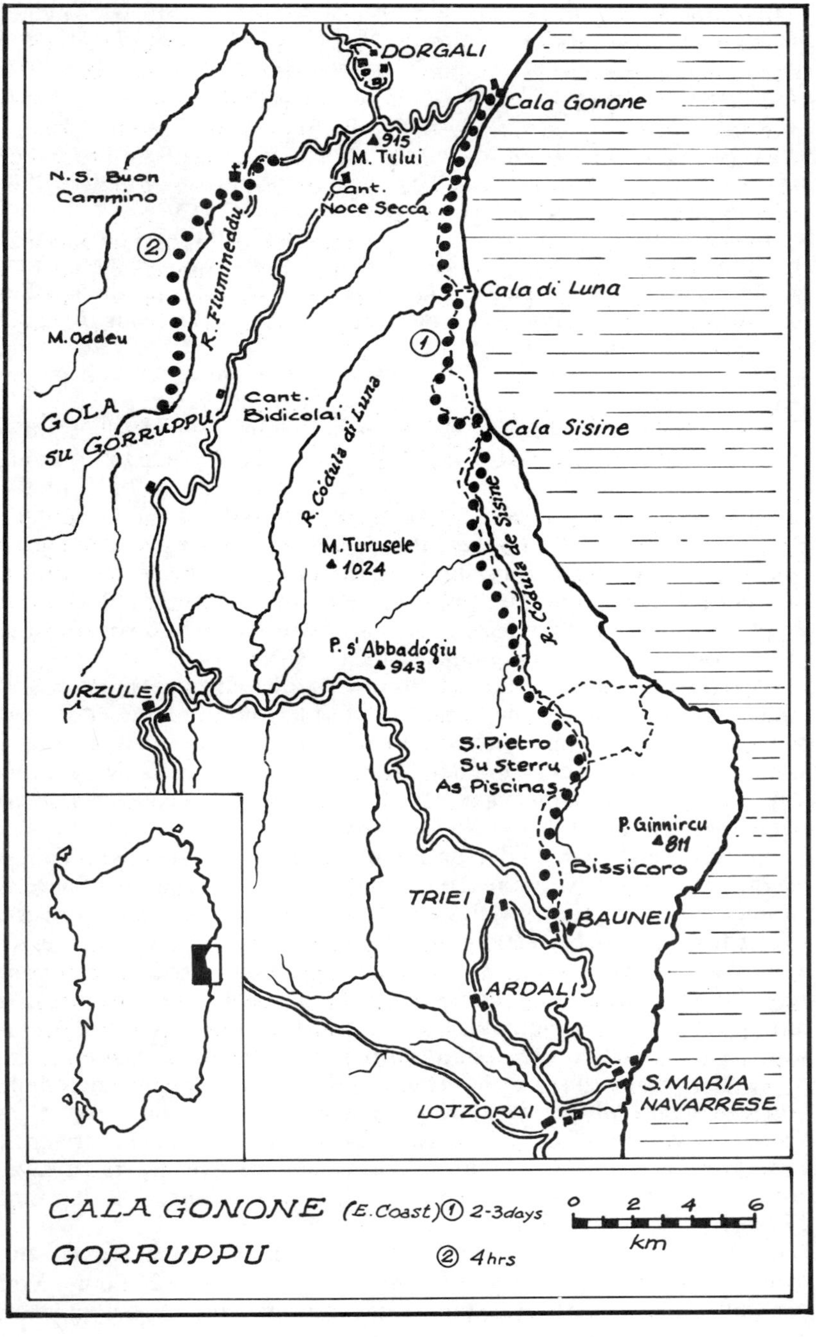
DORGALI
Cala Gonone
915
M. Tului
N.S. Buon Cammino
Cant. Noce Secca
2
R. Flumineddu
Cala di Luna
M. Oddeu
1
GOLA su GORRUPPU
Cant. Bidicolai
R. Códula di Luna
Cala Sisine
R. Códula de Sisine
M. Turusele
1024
P. s'Abbadógiu
943
URZULEI
S. Pietro
Su Sterru
As Piscinas
P. Ginnircu
811
Bissicoro
TRIEI
BAUNEI
ARDALI
S. MARIA NAVARRESE
LOTZORAI
CALA GONONE (E. Coast) 1 2-3 days
GORRUPPU 2 4 hrs
0 2 4 6
km

south on *statale* 125, and from there you can return north, or continue south to Cagliari. If you're driving a car, the best idea is to park it in Dorgali. If you have two, it is better still to leave one at Baunei, because the buses are not so frequent. From Cala Gonone, the best solution is to take a boat to Cala Luna, so reducing the trip to 3 days. Out of the tourist season, this is a 4 day hike.

The trail The first part of this applies only if you do not find a boat to Cala Luna. You start south from Cala Gonone on a dull, wide surfaced road ending abruptly after 3½ km in front of Cala Fuili cove. The path climbs up the far side, passes over Grotta del Bue Marino (there is no access to the cave from inland), and continues along faint tracks to another cove, Cala di Oddoana. Follow its rim on the right to find a path descending into the canyon; after traversing a small forested area, you turn left on the main path descending to Cala Luna, where you find an amazing drinkable water lake a few metres from the sea. This part of the hike takes 4 hours.

On the second day, you have the most serious route-finding problems. You must not follow Codula di Luna, the big canyon starting from the cove; instead, climb a steep path right at the back of the restaurant, get to the plateau, and cross it to enter another canyon, Badde de Lupiru. Walk up the entire length of this canyon, leaving on your left an imposing natural limestone arch. At the end of the canyon, the path brings you to Cuile Saccederano, a large abandoned shepherds' hut, on an amazing plateau overlooking the sea. To the south, you have your first glimpse of Cala Sisine.

Here the difficult part starts. Follow the path, which gets fainter and fainter, for some 20 minutes, then turn left to follow a large vegetated gully. A few years ago this was almost impassable and required a long, tough walk to get through it. More and more hikers now walk this way, and this probably makes the path easier to recognize and to follow. At the end of the gully, you descend some scree slopes towards Cala Sisine, and then find a path which zigzags to the cove. This is maybe less impressive than Cala Luna, but is more remote. There is another restaurant and a well nearby. From Cala Luna, allow 6 hours.

The third day is perfectly easy, and leaves the sea for the plateau. Simply follow the canyon, without any possibility of missing the right way. After a couple of kilometres, at a junction, keep on walking through the left canyon, which is the largest. Further on you find a stony road, which you follow to the rim of the plateau. Again on the road, you cross this to the church of San Pietro, an incredible Mexican-style building flanked by a good water fountain. From Cala Sisine, allow 4 to 5 hours. You can buy cheese from local shepherds, and have a glance – with caution! – at the impressive Su Sterru cave, not far from the church. It is an open air well, falling to a depth of 270 m.

On the fourth day, you follow the dirt road which crosses the plateau's rim, and descends to Baunei, a walk of about 2½ hours. You can walk from Sisine to Baunei in 1 day, but the San Pietro area is too beautiful to be crossed in such a hurry.

GORROPU CANYON

Impressive and huge, the Gorropu canyon amazes the motorized traveller on his way between Dorgali and Baunei. Its faces are 400 m and offer the rock climber many difficult ascents: to the visitor, they are a beautiful sight. But they are not the only surprise in the Gorropu!

Behind and out of sight of the road, the Gorropu stretches for about 25 km, crossing all the Supramonte plateau. To begin with the canyon seems a normal valley, then becomes steeper and rocky, with sheer vertical walls. After a while, the valley opens up again: at a beautiful junction, marked by a series of small lakes, Codula Orbisi drops steeply into the main canyon, which is crossed nearby by a path joining Orgosolo and Oliena to Urzulei.

At the end, the canyon gets high and wild again, a series of vertical drops halting the visitor. The final gorge, which can be seen from the road, starts here. All along the canyon, the Flumineddu river appears and disappears. At the end, amongst the lower rocks, it makes a final, impressive appearance, before flowing north towards Dorgali.

The complete descent of the canyon, although increasingly popular, is a serious undertaking reserved for expert climbers and cavers: though not too difficult, it involves a series of rappels (the longest one being 30 m) and some lakes where you need an inflatable dinghy. On foot, you can either walk from the Urzulei road to Codula Orbisi junction (4 to 5 hour round trip, once you find the *exact* starting point of the path), or walk the very lowest part of the gorge, which is the most impressive one. This is what I suggest here.

Again, Gogna's *Mezzogiorno di Pietra* is the only book around. *Monte Oddeu* is the IGM relevant map.

How to get there Again, your starting point is Dorgali. From the town, a complicated network of dirt roads zigzags southwards along the fertile plain crossed by the Flumineddu river, bordered on the west side by Supramonte's rock faces, and on the east by the road to Baunei and Arbatax. There are several ways to start: in the end all the roads merge into one, which reaches a large concrete bridge at 199 m and 10 km from town. If you're not driving a car, your best option is to find somebody willing to drive there. Around the bridge, there are many nice spots to camp.

The trail Start following the smaller dirt road southwards on the west side of Flumineddu, crossing a small riverside forest, and then starting to climb on the steep slopes dominated by Monte Oddeu's cliffs. The scenery is wild and richly scented, and the trail is very easy to follow. After a little more than 1 hour, you reach the last of the many grassy spurs of Monte Oddeu, from which Gorropu canyon can finally be seen. On the left a smaller path descends to the heavily vegetated riverside: a few metres from here, the Flumineddu river comes to light again forming a beautiful pool, which is a welcome sight in summer.

The path climbs towards the right, passes a few caves and reaches the impressive entrance of the Gorropu itself. Here, the walls on both sides reach an impressive height, and the canyon seems to close like a tunnel, 2–300 m above the ground. The first part is a large zig zag, after which you must scramble over very easy slabs barring the way; paint marks show the best route. However the most impressive part of it all is the very first one, that can be reached without having to scramble at all.

Going further up, you start to get out of the most impressive part of the canyon. Then you meet a couple of blocks that require more serious scrambling. In the end, you reach the foot of a 20 m vertical step where the exploration has to stop anyway. To get back to the bridge, follow the same route; allow 1½ hours to the entrance of Gorropu, a little less for the way back, and 1–2 hours for exploration inside the canyon.

TO THE TOP OF GENNARGENTU

Here is the top of Sardinia, and a completely different area from the ones we have encountered before. The environment is similar to the highest mountains in the peninsular Apennines, or to those in Sicily. There are limestone ridges, deep valleys and large scree slopes: the atmosphere is beautiful, even if far less majestic than in the limestone deserts of Supramonte and the island's east coast.

Gennargentu is an interesting mountain, and a good destination for hikers in summer, when it is too hot to walk around coast and lowland Sardinia. The hike described here is by far the easiest to the main summet of the massif, 1,834 m, Punta la Marmora. Views are interesting, and the deep valleys around suggest many more hikes in the deep canyons plunging towards Flumendosa river in the south, and Tirso in the north.

Around Gennagentu, you will find interesting villages like Sorgono, Fonni and Tonata, and old fashioned shepherds' huts. Right at the beginning of the trail there is also a sign of a different kind: an almost abandoned skilift, built right in one of the least likely places in Europe for skiing. The northernmost part of Gennargentu's summit ridge is also spoiled. The rest is beautiful and wild, right up to the top. To plan longer tours, you need IGM maps of *Desulo* and *Punta la Marmora*.

How to get there This is a hike for motorized tourists. First reach Fonni from Nuoro, and head south to Desulo. A large dirt road branches off to the left, climbing 10 km to the base of Bruncu Spina skilift. Travelling by bus, start from Desulo, following the ancient path which climbs to Bruncu Spina from the western summit of s'Arcu de Tascussi.

The trail Start by following the skilift to the summit of Bruncu Spina (1,825 m), the northernmost summit of Gennargentu. Then you follow the ridge: it goes south-east to Punta Paulinu, then veers south to the large col of Arcu Gennargentu, at 1,659 m and 2 hours from the car

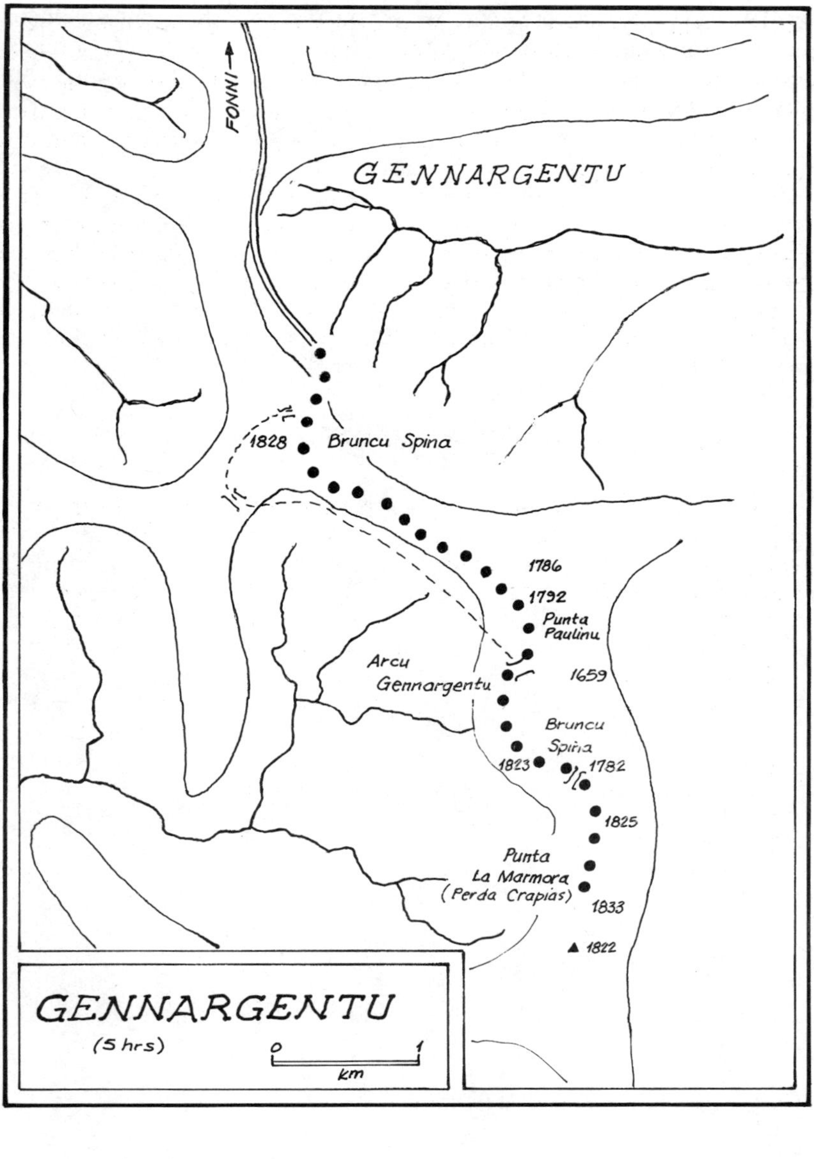

park. A little to the west of the col is an abandoned and ruined hut, in an area full of small springs. Start climbing again, to another Bruncu Spina summit (1,823 m, but it could be an error on the map!), then across smaller outcrops, and arrive in the end at Punta la Marmora, at 1,833 m (1 hour from Arcu Gennargentu). On the way back you must retrace your steps to Arcu Gennargentu, then turn left, and follow a horizontal path with some red paint marks to a second col, Arcu

Artilai, west of Bruncu Spina. Here you traverse the right again, to reach the main north-to-south ridge of the massif, after which a quick descent brings you to your starting point. It takes about 2 hours this way from Punta la Marmora.

Chapter 14
Sicily

Gently rolling hills, a blue sea and the huge pyramid of Etna, Europe's largest active volcano, looming in the distance. This is the background for many Sicilian hikes, both on the mountains that form the island's backbone and in the nearby hills. Heavily populated but still very remote in many areas (it's the biggest island in the Mediterranean!), Sicily is not an obvious place for the hiker to go, but it can be an extremely interesting one for any kind of traveller.

Around the world, Sicily's image is not a good one. On one side you have the posh resorts like Taormina, with international festivals going on in a seemingly endless stream. And on the other side you have the Mafia; shootings, heroin, stories of corrupt officials and murdered *carabinieri*. I would not deny this as it is one of the country's biggest tragedies. Many books and newspapers or magazine stories can easily tell you more about that.

From the tourist's (and the hiker's) point of view, it does not create any difficulties. Downtown Palermo, its poorest area as in any big Italian town, is not a good place in which to walk around carrying a large camera bag, or with a big roll of banknotes protruding from your pocket. In the smaller towns and countryside, travelling is perfectly safe, if long and tiring because of old twisting roads and a scorching summer heat. Summer is not the best time of the year to choose for a Sicilian hike.

There are exceptions, however, Mount Etna being the biggest and

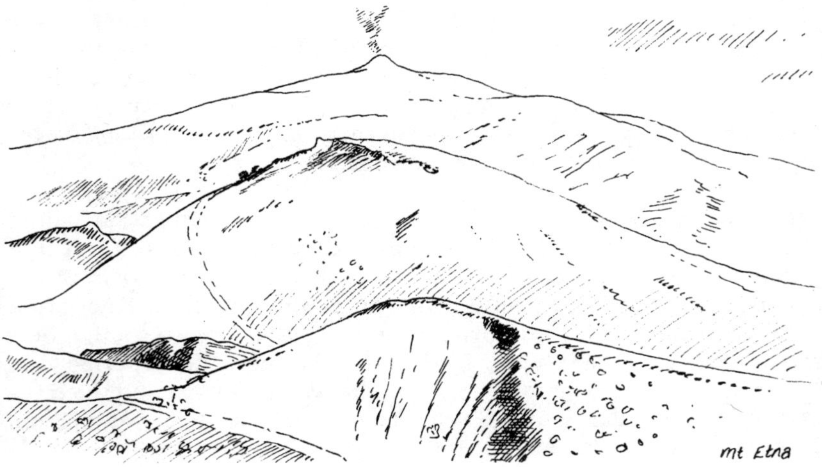

best-known one. The volcano reaches a respectable 3,342 m, and is snowcapped from November to May. During the winter months it provides downhill ski slopes around *rifugio* Sapienza and Linguaglossa and then ski-mountaineering tours, cross-country ski tracks, and even some ice climbing routes. Because of its isolation, it can be the windiest place in the Mediterranean all the year round.

North of Etna, a long chain of mountains forms the backbone of the island. The Monti Peloritani chain start at Messina (continuing the line of the mainland's Apennines), culminate in Montagna Grande's 1,374 m, and usually comprise barren, arid slopes and ridges. West of them, the Monti Nebrodi chain is a completely different world: huge forests, impressive isolation, a respectable height (Monte Soro is the loftiest at 1,820 m) make it an interesting idea for any kind of hiker, and for cross-country skiers in winter.

More to the west, almost directly south of Palermo, the Madonie massif is the island's second highest area, culminating in Pizzo Carbonara's 1,979 m. These are limestone mountains again, with large rock faces, deep incut canyons and the typical *quarare*, the Sicilian word for the very large *dolina* that are found between the massif's summits. Being close to Palermo (and suitable for downhill skiing), the Madonie are far easier to reach than Nebrodi or Peloritani, and offer an Alpine-style network of mountain huts.

Still, Sicily is not only made of mountains. Between Palermo and Trapani (and within Palermo itself!) huge limestone cliffs offer magnificent opportunities for the rock climber, and some interesting short walks. South of the mountains, an impressive plateau slowly drops towards the Mediterranean coast of the island, directly facing Africa. The southernmost part of the island, between Siracuse and Ragusa, offers some hikes of interest through the big canyons – here they are called *caves* – that crisscross the country.

Sicily is not a single island. Many smaller islands are to be found around it. The Eolie (or Lipari) islands are to the north, on a straight line between Milazzo and Naples; Stromboli and Lipari itself are active volcanoes, and offer extremely interesting hikes (apart from superb swimming and sea diving). Ustica, isolated, lies north of Palermo and west of the other Eoli. The Egadi islands lie west of the westernmost tip of Sicily: they can be reached from Trapani and have a steep limestone coastline and isolated beaches. Marettimo is one of the wildest places to hike around in all Italy.

When and where to go Being very near to the tip of Italy, Sicily does not offer the traveller the 'traffic jam' niceties that can turn a trip to Sardinia into an ordeal. If you come from the northern part of the country, Tirrenia offers you a night ferry from Naples to Palermo: a highly recommended 7 hour trip, instead of 12 hours on a train or on a motorway. There are even ferries from Genova to Palermo and Catania, while the 20 minute ferry trip between Messina and the coast of Calabria operates every few minutes in peak season. Catania and Palermo airports are amongst the country's busiest.

Like many other areas in the south, Sicily is a difficult place to travel around in if you are without a car: Etna and the smaller islands are your best destinations in this case, because trying to travel around the Nebrodi chain can be an almost impossible task.

As Sicily is the southernmost part of the country, it is not a recommended place for the hiker in summer. Mid-seasons, as usual, are the best times of the year, while some hikes can be very interesting in winter too. The altitude, the forests and the sea nearby provide a variety of trails in July and August. Bring a water bottle and a hat, anyway!

LONG DISTANCE TRAILS

How can long distance trails exist, in an island where short marked trails are almost unheard of? Well, the Sicilian landscape and wildlife are superb, mountain scenery is wild, and long distance walks are beginning to grow. Many years will probably pass before proper trails are established; but in 1986, two long, interesting and unmarked trails have been proposed.

The first one was suggested by Franco Barbagallo in *Atlante* magazine. It involves a long tour around Etna, sleeping in the existing huts, visiting lava caves, and crossing the crater area on the return trip; a 4 day, very exciting hike, which is not very strenuous apart from the climb from Linguaglossa to the main crater.

I had the pleasure of searching out the other trail, together with Simonetta Lombardo and Toti Seminara. The description has been published in *Airone* magazine. The suggested walk is a 11–12 day trip from Madonie to Etna, crossing the different facets of the island's landscapes. You start from Collesano, cross Pizzo Carbonara, enter the Nebrodi forests at Mistretta, descend to Nelson's palace at Maniace, and start climbing up the volcano's slopes; the last stage is again the classic north to south traverse of Etna. It is a strenuous tour, you have to carry a tent and, while crossing Nebrodi, a 3-day reserve of food.

UP TO THE MADONIE PLATEAU

Very different from Etna and Stromboli's volcanic rocks, Madonie are limestone mountains, barren and dry, impressive when seen from the Palermo to Catania motorway, or spotted from the northern coast of Sicily between Termini Imerese and Cefalu. In winter, their snowy summits offer an impressive sight even from the sea.

Close to Palermo, the Madonie are popular both in summer and in winter. Piano Battaglia, the area's tourist centre, has a few skilifts, a couple of cheap *rifugios*, a lot of small villas and cottages and plenty of room to camp. Petralia Sottana and Polizzi Generosa are very interesting small towns, and give a very good idea of Sicilian mountains only a short distance from the main roads.

The summit plateau can be reached in less than one hour's walk from Piano Battaglia. It is a complicated series of rocky outcrops, small stony valleys and *quarare*, the large and impressive sink holes that have both a special name and a fascinating atmosphere. Palermo is close-by, and the area has a series of huts reminding one of the best-known alpine areas. From the plateau's northern rim, on clear days, there is a unique view over the Tyrrhenian sea. On excellent days, Stromboli, Ustica and Filicudi islands can be spotted far away out to sea.

A big city nearby obviously creates serious problems for any wildlife area; this is especially true when the latter is Palermo, a town where the building industry is very active, and whose builders have savagely destroyed one of the Mediterranean's best landscapes. In the Madonie you will still find beautiful scenery, interesting flora, eagles and vultures nesting in the impressive rocky cliffs. But you will also find unnecessary roads, ugly buildings, and plans are afoot to destroy all the nature which is left.

There are no guidebooks to the area: IGM's 1:25,000 *Pizzo Carbonara* map is the relevant one.

How to get there Many (too many!) roads lead to Piano Battaglia, the best place to start walking in the area. From Palermo, you have to drive south on the motorway to Catania. You can leave it at the Tre Monzelli exit and drive through Petralia Sottana, or exit at Scillato and travel through Collesano and Piano Zucchi instead. The first road is a bit longer but smoother, the latter is somewhat wilder and more isolated. A third possibility is to pass Polizzi Generosa, which you can reach from both exits. Driving from Catania, the Petralia road is by far the best. Apart from occasional ski buses on winter wekends there is no public transport from Palermo. The best bet for a small group is to share a taxi from Termini Imerese or Cefalu.

The trail From Piano Battaglia *rifugio* Merlino (*rifugio del CAS*) start on a steep trail directly from the door of the hut to exit on the road's upper loop. Follow it left to a bend (obviously you can drive here, but you will save only a few minutes), and immediately after it start climbing on a steepish trail, traversing north across the mountainside. The trail climbs with a few zigzags: where these end there is a junction, and here turn right onto a smaller path (a few red paint marks), climbing directly towards the high plateau. When you emerge from the forest, you are very near to a small *rifugio*, again owned by *CAS*, which is normally closed; keys can only be obtained in Palermo. Hiking north, you pass a small col; keep left to avoid a large stony valley, and continue along an awkward stony ridge to Pizzo Carbonara's highest summit, marked by a large cairn. You are at 1,979 m (Sicily's second highest point) and this walk takes about $1\frac{1}{4}$ hours.

From here, there are many choices open. A map is useful, but you will have no problems in finding your route back if there is no fog. From Pizzo Carbonara, walk straight east, passing a little to the left of Antenna della Principessa (the area's second highest summit, only 2 m

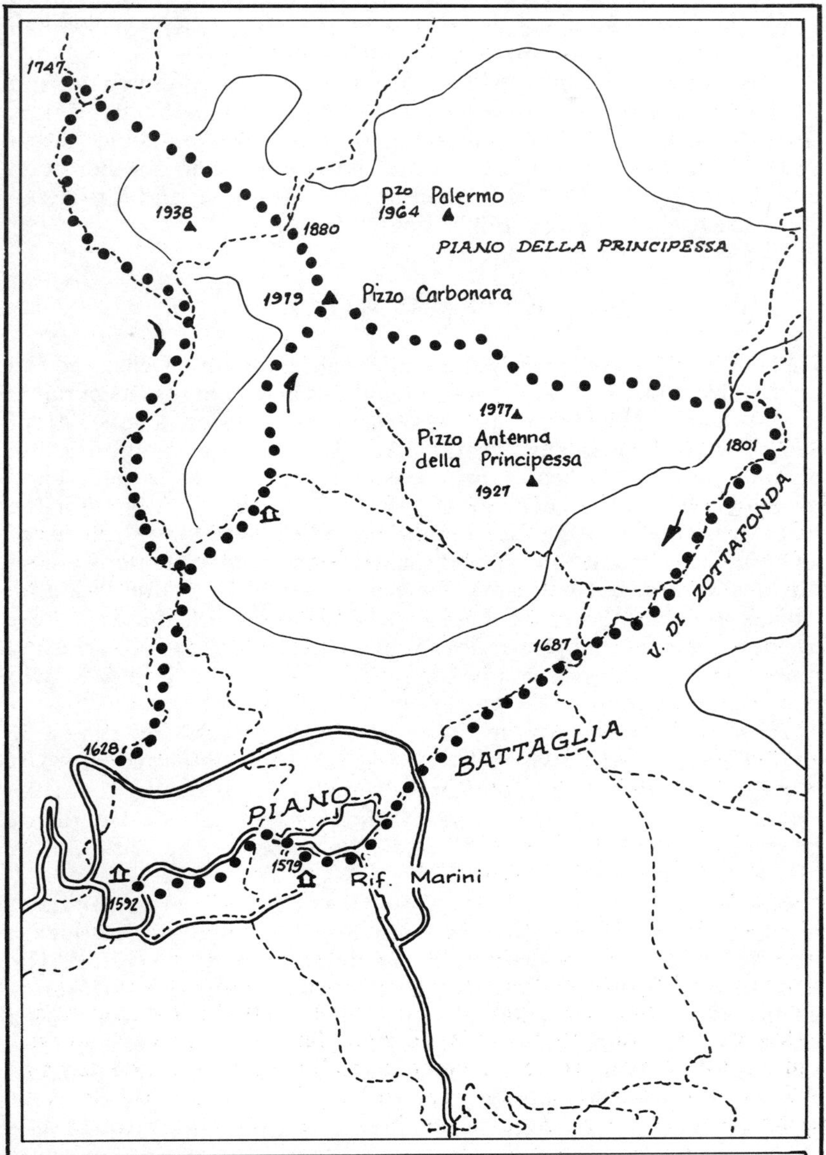

MADONIE

(4 hrs)

lower than Pizzo Carbonara), and then descend into Zottafonda Valley. Here you find a larger trail, with some red paint marks, leading you right to Piano Battaglia (allow 2 hours to reach *rifugio* Merlino again).

More interesting still is to head northwest, first on the plateau, and then on a steeper slope, towards the rocky rim of the plateau. This is clearly seen as you descend, and offers a striking view on Piano Zucchi and the coastline. A little before the rim you will find another good trail. Follow it to the left; it is the one you started on, and it will lead you back to *rifugio* Merlino in 2 hours.

ETNA WALKS

High and impressive, Etna is the major sight in eastern Sicily, and can be seen from many of the island's mountains and summits. Its pyramid can be clearly spotted from the Calabrian coast and from a large part of Sicily's southern plateaux. For the hiker, Etna requires a bit of careful planning: during the peak tourist season the crater area is spoiled and over-used by guided jeep tours. On the other side, away from the jeeps' tracks, the volcano is isolated and harsh, with long stretches of awkward lava grounds, hard and tiring to negotiate. Eruptions are an obvious hazard, but not a real danger to hikers. Get information on what is going on where, avoid going as far as the crater's rim if smoke is too dense, keep a damp scarf near at hand and press it to your nose and mouth and run down if you get engulfed in a cloud. It is very easy to descend the volcanic scree quickly in case of danger.

There are two gateways to Etna's upper wilderness. *Etna sud* is the *rifugio* Sapienza area, which can be reached from Zafferana Etnea or Nirolosi. A chairlift to Montagnola was destroyed during the 1983 eruptions, and this is the start of one of the jeep tracks to the craters. Like its northern counterpart, this is reserved for authorized (i.e. official guided tours') vehicles.

Etna nord can be reached from Linguaglossa, a more pleasant area far away from Catania's concrete horrors. A road climbs through a magnificent pine forest to the start of another track to the craters. The first part crosses the downhill ski tracks. Another dirt track traverses all the western side of the volcano, crossing interesting forests and impressive lava beds. This is about 40 km long, there are regularly-spaced huts: it would be an extremely appealing idea, if only it could be closed to private jeeps.

If you travel by public transport, you can organize a 2 day complete traverse of Etna: north to south is the best direction. If you are driving a car, the best hike is the one that is described later on, from *rifugio* Sapienza to the summit and back. In 3 to 4 days you can include both an ascent to the craters and a level walk on the western lava fields. Maps are IGM's 1:50,000 *Randazzo* and *Acireale*, or 1:25,000 *Etna nord* and *Etna sud* sheets. For information about guided tours (you could consider joining one, and then leaving it to walk down alone) phone Linguaglossa's STAR company at (095) 643180.

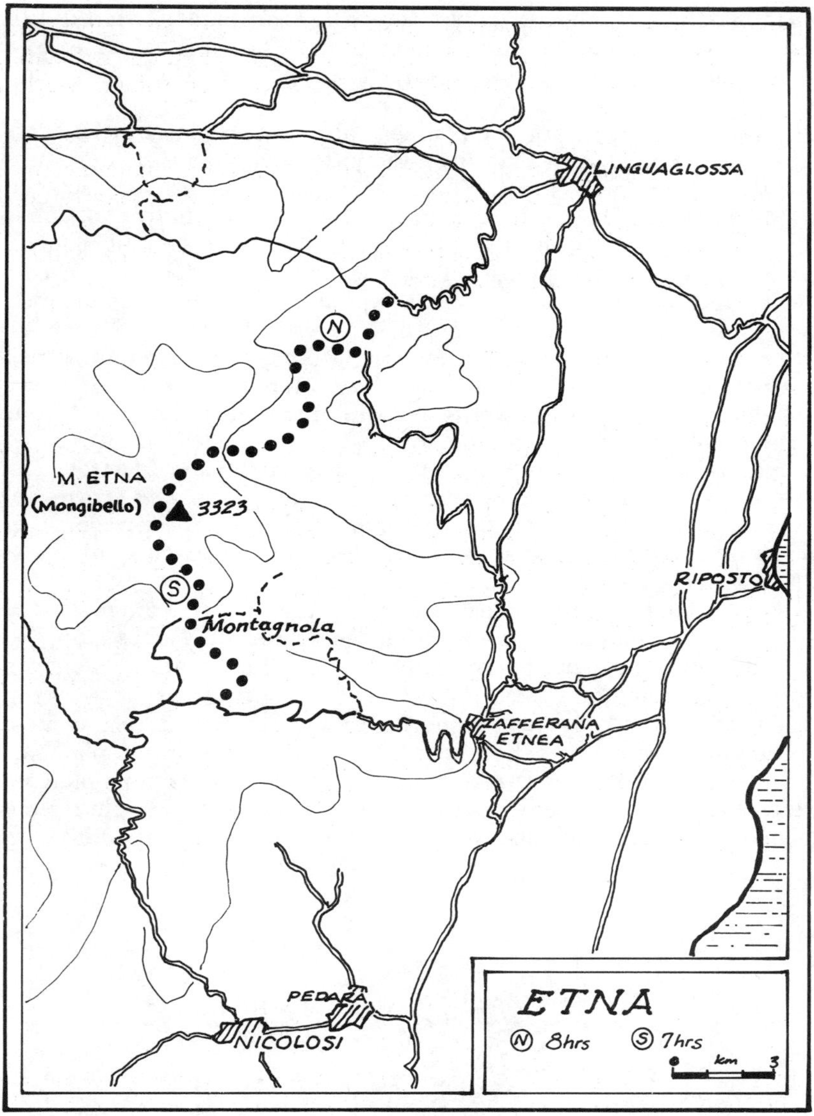

How to get there There are many (too many) roads around Etna, and some of the upper ones are often closed by eruptions. At the time of writing, for instance, the *Mareneve sud* road from Nicolosi to *rifugio* Sapienza was closed, but they hope to re-open soon. With a road map, you can easily find your way to Linguaglossa and Zafferana Etnea, and from there to the starting points of the walks. Both are near the Messina–Catania motorway.

Public transport is slow, and information cannot be got very easily. Catania's EPT English-speaking staff (095/ 317720) will tell you about bus timetables. There are daily buses to *Rifugio* Sapienza but not to Etna nord: to reach the latter you can hire a taxi in Linguaglossa; a group could consider hiring one directly from Catania or Taormina.

Etna sud trail A very interesting walk, this begins at the Zafferana–Sapienza road (2 km from the latter) where a dirt track runs across a sparse pine forest. You start walking on this, to reach the southeast ridge of la Montagnola in about 45 minutes. In front of you is a steep rocky face (Cisternazza) above which is the summit plateau, while the huge valley almost directly below is Valle del Bove, Etna's most interesting lava valley. This viewpoint is a highly recommended short walk for the motorized tourist.

Turn left, and start walking towards Montagnola's summit, which can be reached or passed on the right side. Here there is a huge rocky plateau. Follow it north towards the core of the main craters. On your right is Valle del Bove's rim, on your left an old chairlift destroyed by eruptions: lower still you can spot the cablecar station (destroyed in 1983). Head left past a clearly visible building (*rifugio* Torre del Filosofo, a scientific observatory with an emergency shelter room), to reach a beautiful plateau at the foot of the final cone. This point is at 2,900 m, and 2½–3 hours from the road.

A dirt track climbs to the left in the last stage. You reach the Linguaglossa track, near a small hut where tourists' jeeps stop. No definite indications can be given for the very top: conditions change very quickly, and you must follow the existing trails to the very top (3,342 m) and to the nearby northeast crater, nowadays the most continuously active one. You need about 1½ hours from the plateau.

In descent, you must retrace your steps to the Montagnola plateau. Here you have a choice: if you want a shorter walk, head right for the ruined cablecar station, and then descend to *rifugio* Sapienza either on

the long jeep road, or on more direct trails. Or reach the Valle del Bove rim, and then find the distinct scree gully (many are good but one is the best) for an exhilarating descent to Valle del Bove's floor, where you will find another ruined hut: *rifugio* Menza. If you have enough water (or if there is still snow around) you can camp here. If not, you must walk another hour on an obvious trail to a spring (Acqua della Rocoa). A short walk will lead you to the Zafferana–Sapienza road, about 4 km from the starting point. Allow 4 hours for this descent, $2\frac{1}{2}$ for the direct one to *rifugio* Sapienza.

Etna nord This is an easier walk to find: you just have to follow the jeeps track starting from Linguaglossa forest, from a large parking area. Obviously, this is not the way to climb Etna on foot when lots of tourist jeeps travel along the same road. This is a good route to the craters if out of the tourist season, and it is by far the best way up Etna for ski-mountaineers. If you have to walk this way when the jeeps travel, start very early in the morning, or bring a tent, start in the afternoon and bivouac in the summit area. You can also travel uphill in a jeep, then walk down: obviously you will have to pay for the full return trip.

The trail starts with a lot of zigzags on the bare slopes dominating the end of the road, reaching the higher plateau at a large scientific observatory which can be easily seen from the start. Here turn left off the track and continue traversing to Piano della Conca, and up again to the crater's foot, where the *rifugio* Sapienza track joins up from the southern side. Directions for the craters' area are the same as for the previous itinerary. From the Linguaglossa forest, allow 5 hours.

In descent, you can consider walking straight north to the plateau's rim near Punta Lucia, and then descending northwest on long lava fields to the level dirt track, crossing all the western side of the mountain. Keeping to the right side of a clearly defined ridge, and descending northwest to Bronte, you will reach Monte Scavo *rifugio* in 3 hours from the summit. Not marked on the map, the *rifugio* can be found on 1:50,000 Monte Etna map, at the junction between the lower dirt road and a path to Monte Egitto.

Spend the night in the *rifugio* because from here to the Linguaglossa forest, you will need about 6 hours. The Monte Spagnolo hut is on the way, while Monte Maletto's lies on a side road to the right. Vegetation is the trail's most fascinating feature; you end up on the road coming from Linguaglossa, less than 1 hour's walk from the starting point.

MARETTIMO WILDERNESS

Off the west coast of Sicily, Marettimo is one of the Mediterranean's wildest islands. A limestone ridge lying in a northwest to southeast line, it lies about 30 km from Sicily, double the distance of more popular Levanzo and Favignana. Ferry trips are short and make it a possible destination for a short tour of the island.

Marettimo, the island's harbour and village, lies in the middle of the sheltered eastern coast. North of it, Punta Troia is a spectacular rocky cape, where the ruins of an old castle are perched. On the opposite coast, the big lighthouse is another interesting destination. On the northwestern corner of Marettimo, around Punta Mugnone, is a series of magnificent, rocky inlets and coves; these can be approached by boat, or by following the very difficult marked 'trail' making the complete tour of the island. This is a magnificent 3 day hike involving rock pitches up to grade III.

For the non-climbing wildlife enthusiast, a stop in Marettimo can be a very rewarding experience. Marettimo village is the only one offering accommodation and food, and makes an excellent base. All the trails described are half day outings. As the island's geography and structure are quite simple, IGM's *'Isola Marettimo* map, though useful, is by no means necessary. Don't forget a hat and water!

How to get there Trapani is western Sicily's most important city, and can be reached from Palermo by train, bus or motorway. There are also direct flights from Rome. Ferries to Marettimo depart daily for the 2 hour trip, including a stop in Levanzo and/or Favignana.

The Faro hike This is entirely on a dirt road, starting from Marettimo harbour and heading south along the coast. After a mile or so the roads start climbing, to cross the island's main ridge at about 200 m above sea level. On the far side, you continue with a spectacular traverse, leading to a deeply incut valley, and to the final descent to the lighthouse, about 1¼ hours from Marettimo, overlooking spectacular cliffs. The return trip takes the same time, while you can spend another interesting hour walking down towards Punta Libeccio, a promontory clearly visible from the lighthouse.

Punta Troia hike This leads to the northeastern cape of Marettimo, an isolated rocky outcrop where an old castle is perched. Start from the village on a good trail heading north along the shore, and then climb up, crossing a series of gullies. The slopes get steeper and steeper; in the end a series of zigzags descends to the isthmus between Marettimo's mainland and Punta Troia, which is reached by another uphill climb. Allow 1¼ hours from the village, and the same for the return trip.

Semaforo and Monte Falcone hikes Like many small islands in the Mediterranean, Marettimo was used as a jail. Here, the jail's ruins are perched in a magnificent position, almost at the southeastern end of the island's main ridge. A good trail starts west from the village, climbing to a big spring and continuing with a few large zigzags to the main ridge, which is reached at 453 m. Heading left, the trail skirts an elevation on the ridge and leads to the ruins, which were used later as a lighthouse (Semaforo on the map). You need about 1½ hours, and from here there are two choices.

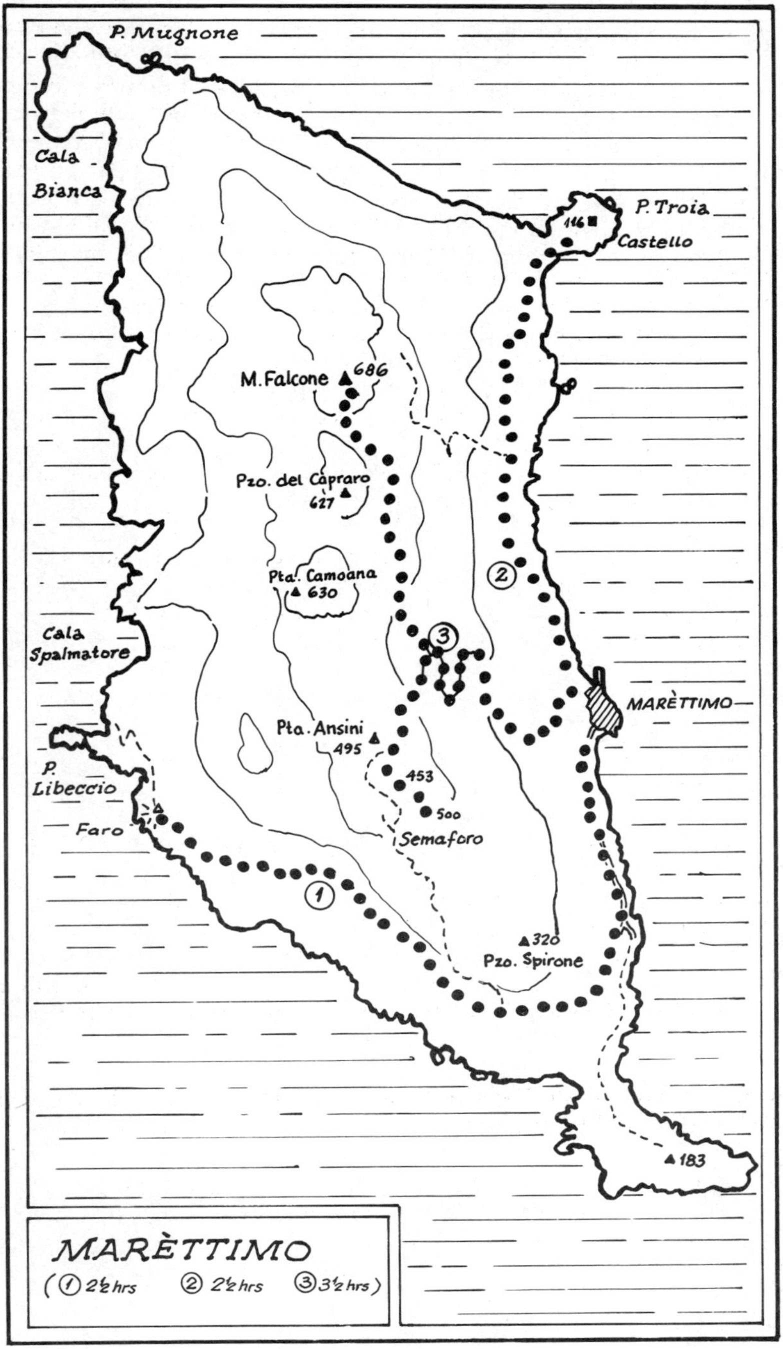
P. Mugnone
Cala Bianca
P. Troia
116
Castello
M. Falcone
686
Pzo. del Capraro
627
Pta. Camoana
630
2
3
Cala Spalmatore
MARÈTTIMO
Pta. Ansini
495
453
500
P. Libeccio
Faro
Semaforo
1
320
Pzo. Spirone
183
MARÈTTIMO
(1 2½ hrs 2 2½ hrs 3 3½ hrs)

To return by the same way is quick, or you can descend west from the 453 m col to the Faro (small trails not very easy to follow, but the general direction is obvious), and then walk back on the dirt road leading to Marettimo. Another possibility is to walk north on the island's ridge to Monte Falcone, at 686 m the highest point of Marettimo. From the 453 m col, turn to the right (Marettimo) side between the first two summits (Punta Campana and Pizzo del Capraio), to reach the ridge again before the last ascent. Or descend the first part of your ascent's trail, leave it at a hairpin bend, and continue down the mountain's eastern slopes. From the lighthouse to Monte Falcone allow 2 hours, Marettimo to Monte Falcone, without getting to the ridge is $2\frac{1}{2}$ to 3 hours.